westermann

W0342753

CAMDEN TOWN

Oberstufe

Qualifikationsphase

Erarbeitet von

Martin Beling
Hans Georg Henkel
Daniel Schönbauer
Tina Türk
Alexander Woltin

Druck A^{5} / Jahr 2023
Alle Drucke der Serie A sind im Unterricht parallel verwendbar.

Redaktion: Dr. Philippa Söldenwagner-Koch (www.lektoratbilingual.de) und Scarlett Milner-Stopps
Umschlaggestaltung: Gingco.Net Werbeagentur GmbH & Co. KG, Braunschweig
Layout: PER Medien & Marketing GmbH, Braunschweig
Druck und Bindung: Westermann Druck Zwickau GmbH, Crimmitschauer Straße 43, 08058 Zwickau

ISBN 978-3-425-**73646**-4

Inhaltsverzeichnis

ISBN 978-3-425-73646-4

Inhaltsverzeichnis

Einleitung

Das vorliegende Heft enthält Klausurvorschläge für die Qualifikationsphase der Oberstufe sowie die dazugehörigen Lösungen und Erwartungshorizonte.
Die Klausuren sind thematisch auf das Schülerbuch *Camden Town Oberstufe* Qualifikationsphase zugeschnitten und enthalten authentisches Textmaterial und Prüfungsaufgaben zu den Kapiteln:

1. The individual and society
2. Science and technology
3. The media
4. Globalization
5. Britishness
6. The American experience
7. Postcolonial experiences
8. Shakespeare

Pro Kapitel werden zwei Klausuren angeboten – eine auf **grundlegendem** und eine auf **erhöhtem Anforderungsniveau**. Jede Klausur beinhaltet die Prüfungsteile **Hörverstehen**, **Sprachmittlung** und **Schreiben**. Während *Writing* und *Mediation* in offenen Aufgabenformaten geprüft werden, gibt es für *Listening* geschlossene bzw. halboffene Aufgaben in den gängigen Prüfungsformaten *multiple choice, table completion/short answers, sentence completion, multiple matching* und *gap-fill*. Wird bei *table completion/short answers* mehr als eine Antwort erwartet, so ist dies angegeben (z. B. *name two aspects*). Ansonsten wird **eine** von ggfs. mehreren möglichen Antworten erwartet.

Die Klausuren liegen als direkt im Unterricht einsetzbare Kopiervorlagen vor. Sie sind aber auch als einzelne, editierbare Word-Dokumente auf der CD-ROM enthalten.

Der Zugang zu den Audioaufnahmen für die Hörverstehensaufgaben erfolgt über **Webcodes**, (z. B. WES-73646-01). Die Webcodes stehen im Lösungsteil (ab S. 79) direkt neben den Aufgaben. Für den Zugriff auf das Audio-Material geben Sie bitte den jeweiligen Webcode auf www.westermann.de ins Suchfeld ein. Wird für eine *Listening*-Aufgabe nur ein Ausschnitt aus einem längeren Hörbeitrag benötigt, so ist dies mit der genauen Minutenangabe vermerkt.

Listening 1: First woman on Canadian bank notes

Listen to an interview by radio hosts Audie Cornish and Ari Shapiro with professor Barbara Crow of York University in Toronto on choosing to put a woman on one of Canada's banknotes. (2:32)

You will hear the recording twice. First you will have time to read the task. After each listening, you will have time to complete your answers.

While listening, fill in the missing information. You do not need to write complete sentences.

1.	What the US Treasury has added or will add on American bank notes	
2.	What all Canadians were asked to do in March	
3.	Number of suggestions by the Canadian people	
4.	How long the selection process lasted	
5.	What the five final candidates have in common (name two aspects)	a) b)
6.	Who Viola Desmond was	
7.	Who Pauline Johnson was	
8.	Who Elsie Gregory Macgill was	
9.	Who Bobbie Rosenfeld was	
10.	Who Idola Saint-Jean was	
11.	The woman already on Canadian money	

ISBN 978-3-425-73646-4

Listening 2: Border crossings into Canada

Listen to a report about Haitians who illegally crossed the US-Canadian border. (3:34)

You will hear the recording twice. First you will have time to read the task. After each listening, you will have time to complete your answers.

While listening, tick (✓) the correct answer (a, b, c or d). There is only one correct answer.

1. Several thousand Haitians who illegally crossed from the US into Canada were
- ☐ a) asking for asylum.
- ☐ b) afraid of US President Trump.
- ☐ c) fleeing from an earthquake in Haiti.
- ☐ d) afraid they were deported from Canada.

2. The Canadian government
- ☐ a) accepted only 300 Haitians.
- ☐ b) had enough space for Haitians in Montreal.
- ☐ c) found temporary housing in Montreal for 300.
- ☐ d) put 300 in a conference centre in Cornwall, Ontario.

3. Francois Bonhur
- ☐ a) is originally from Miami.
- ☐ b) had also felt welcome in the US.
- ☐ c) took a taxi to get to the Canadian border.
- ☐ d) was hired to play with refugee boys and girls.

4. Francois Bonhur says that
- ☐ a) he didn't feel safe in the US.
- ☐ b) Trump didn't care about them.
- ☐ c) the US government is the best.
- ☐ d) he didn't even have three meals a day.

5. Cornwall City Councilor Elaine MacDonald says
- ☐ a) the smiles for Canada weren't real.
- ☐ b) the Haitians have a positive attitude.
- ☐ c) the Haitians were auditioning for jobs.
- ☐ d) there was some hidden desperation in the people.

6. MacDonald wants the Haitians to stay because
- ☐ a) they would have their own schools.
- ☐ b) they would make Canadians feel younger.
- ☐ c) they could help against the aging population.
- ☐ d) they can help prevent factories in the town from closing.

7. The 7,000 mostly Haitian migrants
- ☐ a) were welcomed by all Canadians.
- ☐ b) were welcomed by Prime Minister Trudeau.
- ☐ c) entered Canada after the previous summer.
- ☐ d) thought Prime Minister Trudeau was a sort of anti-Trump.

8. Prime Minister Justin Trudeau
- ☐ a) is hoping for more migrants to come.
- ☐ b) likes tolerance and diversity in refugees.
- ☐ c) is confident that migrants love Canadian laws.
- ☐ d) tries to dissuade more Haitians from coming north.

9. Sophie Bezinet
- ☐ a) fears for her new bike to be stolen.
- ☐ b) says that refugees should apply properly.
- ☐ c) thinks that migrants can count on Canada's help.
- ☐ d) has no problem with migrants crossing the border.

10. Beverly Wright
- ☐ a) demands bus tickets for refugees.
- ☐ b) thinks Canada is big enough for people in need.
- ☐ c) is concerned that the migration wave is too much.
- ☐ d) believes Canada's improvement depends on migrants.

ISBN 978-3-425-73646-4

Listening 3: Apology to Canada's LGBTQ community

Listen to an interview by radio host Kelly McEvers with reporter Brian Mann about Prime Minister Justin Trudeau's apology to the Canadian LGTBQ community. (3:55)

You will hear the recording twice. First you will have time to read the task. After each listening, you will have time to complete your answers.

While listening, fill in the gaps.

Today the prime minister of Canada, Justin Trudeau, made a formal apology to the country's LGBTQ community.

Trudeau (1) ____________________ Canada's so-called "gay purge", the name given to the decades of injustice suffered by this community.

Similar injustices were felt in the US, where gays and lesbians also faced (2) ____________________ and were purged from the military and government service. Canada's attempts to identify members of the LGBTQ community were very aggressive, and included (3) ____,

(4) _________________________, and (5) _____________. This policy (6) _____________ many people's lives and careers. One victim of this policy was Martine Roy. The Canadian government made Roy leave her military service and instead sent her to (7) ____________________________________.

By claiming that people like Martine Roy were vulnerable to (8) ____________________________________, the government used the Cold War to justify these practices.

Today, Canada hopes its compensation of a (9) _________________________________ will help rectify the injustices suffered by the victims. It also has plans to invest in (10) _______________________________ to help prevent further suffering by the LGBTQ community.

Many within the Canadian LGBTQ community have said that their country's

(11) _________________________________ is an important step which the rest of the world has yet to take.

This shows a particular contrast with the USA, where President Donald Trump wants to

(12) ______________________________ which would prevent (13) ________________ people from serving in the American military.

Meanwhile, Trudeau has also offered apologies to other persecuted parts of Canadian society, in particular,

(14) ____.

ISBN 978-3-425-73646-4

Mediation: Emigrating to Canada

A friend of yours from Ireland is planning to live and work in Canada after finishing school. You are thinking of joining them and searched the Internet for reports by people who have left Germany for Canada. You have come across this blog post on the downsides of living and working abroad. Write an email to your friend about the challenges of emigrating to Canada based on what Irene, the blogger, has written.

◂◂ / ▸▸ https://www

© istock/vikialis

Kanada: Die 5 Schattenseiten über das Auswandern

Kennst du noch die Goodbye Deutschland Serie, die auf Vox lief (oder läuft die noch?)? Mit den Menschen, die immer total gut gläubig bloß weg vom ach so schlechten Deutschland wollen? So ähnlich muss es sich wohl für meine Freunde und Familie angehört haben, als ich gesagt habe, "Ich will nach Kanada!" Dabei ging es mir nie darum, dass es in Deutschland "scheiße" ist. Ganz und gar nicht. Ich mag Deutschland, das soziale Auffangnetz, die Mindestanzahl an Urlaubstagen (in Kanada sind es nur 10 Tage (!!!)), das Bildungssystem. Ich hab es geschätzt. Aber ich hatte schon immer den Traum in einem englischsprachigen Land zu arbeiten. [...]

Und auch nach fast 7 Monaten Kanada bereue ich es nicht weggegangen zu sein. Nichts desto trotz möchte ich dir nicht nur davon erzählen wie toll und leicht das Auswandern ist – ist es nämlich nicht. Es sieht immer total schön aus, wenn ich hier so von meinen Abenteuern und den Erlebnissen in der Natur Kanadas berichte, aber es gibt auch die Schattenseiten über das Auswandern von denen ich dir heute erzählen will. [...]

1. Die Arbeitswelt wartet hier nicht auf dich

Bevor ich hier große Töne spucke muss ich dir gestehen, dass ich recht schnell einen Job gefunden habe. Aber (!) man muss, wie eigentlich bei jeder Jobsuche, Kompromisse eingehen können. Sprich vielleicht musst du auch einen Job machen, der dir nicht zu 100% gefällt oder nicht unbedingt deinem Lebenslauf entspricht. Du musst flexibel sein, denn die finanziellen Ressourcen werden in Kanada schnell aufgebraucht (das Leben ist teuer hier!). Kleiner Tipp am Rande, bevor du auswanderst stelle sicher, dass du genug Arbeitserfahrung gesammelt hast – denn das ist das A und O hier drüben. Die meisten wollen mindestens 2–3 Jahre Berufserfahrung in dem jeweiligen Job sehen.

2. Soziale Kontakte knüpfen ist hart

Da bin ich ganz ehrlich. Wenn man als Paar auswandert, hat man sich, was natürlich gut ist, aber man ist fauler, geht weniger raus und lernt wenig neue Leute kennen. Die einzigen Menschen, mit denen man regelmäßigen Kontakt haben wird, ist der Partner und die Arbeitskollegen. Wenn man Pech hat, haben die alle schon Familie und sind verheiratet und dementsprechend gibt es weniger Berührungspunkte, weniger gemeinsame Gesprächsthemen [...].

3. Die Familie wird dir unendlich fehlen

Das betrifft vor allem die Familienmenschen unter uns – von daher auch mich. Gerade jetzt wo Weihnachten immer näher rückt, fehlt mir meine Familie umso mehr. Manchmal ist es wirklich hart, wenn man am Wochenende mit der Family skyped und alle sind zum Kaffee und Kuchen da – nur du nicht. Du siehst die Gesichter, bist aber dennoch zu weit entfernt, um sie zu umarmen. Das ist für mich persönlich das härteste.

4. Man fühlt sich einsam

Das ist eine logische Konsequenz, die sich aus den eben erwähnten Punkten ergibt – man fühlt sich einsam. Ich bin eigentlich ein offener Mensch und lerne schnell neue Menschen kennen. Als ich neulich im Café saß, habe ich ein total nettes Mädel kennengelernt, Nummern ausgetauscht und auch hin und wieder getroffen. Aber es ist dennoch nicht immer mit einer langjährigen Freundschaft zu vergleichen. Und auch wenn man selten alleine ist, da ständig jemand da ist (ob Partner, Arbeitskollegen oder Bekannte) wird es Momente geben, in denen man sich einsam fühlen wird. Alles ist anders und an manchen Tagen fühlt es sich noch befremdlicher an.

5. Man fühlt sich schuldig

Vor kurzem hatte meine Oma einen Schlaganfall und ich konnte nicht für sie da sein. Ich habe sie im Krankenhaus angerufen und ihre fragenden Worte: "Wann kommst du denn wieder nach Hause?" versetzten mir Stiche in der Brust. Die Familie zurücklassen ist nicht nur hart für dich, sondern natürlich auch für sie! Und auch wenn es meine eigene Entscheidung war nach Kanada auszuwandern, bedeutet es nicht gleich, dass sie mir leichtgefallen ist. Es tut weh und das Schuldgefühl ist ein ständiger Begleiter, gerade jetzt zu Weihnachten. Ich erzähle das hier nicht, um dich vor der Entscheidung auszuwandern abzuhalten. Viel mehr sage ich das so offen, um dir ein möglichst objektives Bild zu geben. Nur immer davon zu berichten wie schön es ist auszuwandern wäre falsch, denn so aufregend und bereichernd es sein kann, es ist auch mit viel Schmerz und Kompromissen verbunden. Also bitte keine naiven, aber dafür bewusste Entscheidungen treffen.

ISBN 978-3-425-73646-4

Writing: Multicultural Canada

Read the following extract from a speech given by Canadian writer Erna Paris at the University of Toronto, as published on the website of the Canadian newspaper *The Globe and Mail*. Then complete the tasks below.

1. **Comprehension:** Point out what defines Canadian identity today and describe how that view has developed over the years.
2. **Analysis:** Analyse Paris' use of rhetorical devices in order to get her message across.
3. **Creative writing:** Imagine you were a Canadian with an immigrant background visiting your relative in Germany. Your relative is complaining about his difficult situation in Germany becoming really and fully integrated. You tell him about your experiences in Canada, what would have to change in Germany and what your relative could do. Write their dialogue.

Opinion

Canada's multiculturalism is our identity

By Erna Paris, 27 August 2018, The Globe and Mail online

Multiculturalism with a capital M was born of smart crisis management – of political agility[1] and the characteristic Canadian willingness to compromise in the service of national unity and nation building. The trigger, as you may know, was the Quebec crisis of the 1960s and early 1970s, when the so-called "Quiet Revolution" exploded into nationalism and violence. In 1963, the government of Lester B. Pearson created the Royal Commission on Bilingualism and Biculturalism to recommend means of defusing the issue.

But something unexpected happened. Paul Yuzyk, a new senator from Saskatchewan, spoke up. Canada, he said, was not "bicultural," but "multicultural." The commissioners were shrewd[2] enough to understand what Mr. Yuzyk meant: He was saying that a solution for Quebec had to include the rest of Canada, or it wasn't going to fly. So, they agreed to take into account the contribution made by other ethnic groups to the cultural enrichment of Canada – and how to safeguard that contribution.

In response, then-prime minister Pierre Trudeau did something exceptionally audacious[3]. On Oct. 8, 1971, he introduced capital-M Multiculturalism to the House of Commons. In addition to becoming an officially bilingual land, Canada would formally respect the diversity of its citizens' languages, religions and cultures. The goal was integration; it was also about appeasing[4] opposition to bilingualism. Mr. Trudeau faced no opposition in the House.

Who knew then how that policy would play out? To many, and I admit to being one of them, the proposal felt a bit cringeworthy[5]. The 1970s were not the 1930s when immigrants from outside Britain were rejected as "unassimilable." Didn't we already respect the diversity of language, religion and culture unofficially? And were we really supposed to don[6] national garb[7] and sing and dance for one another? The political strategy was transparent.

But quietly over the next decades, official multiculturalism lost its hokey[8] qualities, as well as its capital letter, and evolved into an ingrained collective value. Canadians began to define themselves as citizens of a multi-ethnic, multireligious society, not unlike the citizens of medieval Hispania, who appear to have understood their environment as a diverse community. In 1985, when asked what made them proudest of their country, Canadians placed multiculturalism way down the list – at No. 10. By 2006, it was in second place – above hockey. Somehow multiculturalism had evolved into a shared identity – a loose identity – Canadian style.

The reasons are down home and practical: increased mutual interaction. In a 2015 Environics poll, 95 per cent of respondents said that immigrants are as likely to be good citizens as the native-born. Poll results can vary according to the questions asked, but as recently as March 2017, the Canadian Studies Association reported that Canadians were increasingly comfortable with diversity. Today, almost half of newcomers to Canada have a college degree, compared with 29 per cent in the United States; and the second generation is more likely to attend a university than those whose parents are native-born. Citizenship rates are high. Immigrants express approximately the same level of satisfaction with life in Canada as other Canadians. Intermarriage rates are growing – a strong index of racial and cultural integration.

One of the most important reasons for Canada's success is the fact that we have eschewed[9] demands for total assimilation to a defined identity in favour of integration. Integration is the foundation of the support we offer newcomers. Its most salient[10] feature is that no one attempts to alter the core identity of an individual or group.

What we have historically promoted is citizenship. Citizens obey the law, pay their taxes and, in this country, are generally tolerant of difference (not always – we, too, have outbreaks of xenophobia) in high enough numbers to make this pluralist society work not perfectly, but reasonably well. Ideally, we live under an umbrella of Canada, not unlike the ways of multicultural Andalusia. When tensions and misunderstandings arise, as they inevitably do, the challenge of leadership is to balance competing rights and interests. We succeed – and I always add "for now" – because Canadian policy making has historically tended towards accommodation[11], as does our common-law legal system, which is based on cases, or precedents, and is often called upon to settle disputes related to multicultural cohabitation.

→

ISBN 978-3-425-73646-4

In retrospect, Pierre Trudeau's single most important statement as he introduced his new policy in 1971 may have been that no singular culture could, or would, define Canada. Canadian leaders of both major parties had historically promoted both immigration and citizenship, but the idea that no singular culture would define this country – in other words, that there would be no overriding cultural identity to assimilate to – would become the root of our contemporary success in the world. As populism and intolerance increase elsewhere, it is this deliberate looseness when it comes to identity, this unique approach to pluralism, that will help to protect us – if we remain vigilant[12].

And that, in my view, is why multiculturalism matters.

(818 words)

[1] **agility** = intelligence, quick thinking
[2] **shrewd** = intelligent
[3] **audacious** = brave
[4] to **appease** = to quieten
[5] **cringeworthy** = embarrassing, painful
[6] to **don** = to put on
[7] **garb** = a special type of clothing
[8] **hokey** = overly sentimental
[9] to **eschew** = to avoid doing sth
[10] **salient** = relevant, meaningful
[11] **accommodation** = *here:* mutual understanding
[12] **vigilant** = watchful, observant

ISBN 978-3-425-73646-4

Listening 1: Ireland's historic vote on abortion

Listen to a radio interview with Fintan O'Toole from *The Irish Times* about Ireland's vote to repeal the 8th amendment to their constitution, which bans abortion. (3:52)

You will hear the recording twice. First you will have time to read the task. After each listening, you will have time to complete your answers.

While listening, answer the questions. You do not need to write complete sentences.

1.	What have the Irish decided on with their vote?	
2.	Which sentence did Fintan O'Toole write in *The Irish Times* after this vote?	
3.	Why did Ireland, according to O'Toole, have such strict abortion laws? (name two aspects)	a) b)
4.	Why does O'Toole think that this is not necessary anymore?	
5.	How could people who want to keep the abortion laws feel after a change?	
6.	What kind of people are those who want to keep the laws as they are?	
7.	What did such votes cause in the USA in the past?	
8.	What kind of a society is Ireland to O'Toole?	
9.	What would be a tragic development for Ireland?	
10.	Will the people who voted to keep the amendment give up?	
11.	What makes the vote still powerful?	

ISBN 978-3-425-73646-4

Listening 2: The Scots-Irish

Listen to part of a podcast on Irish culture and politics. The hosts are answering a question by one of their listeners about the Scots-Irish in Northern Ireland and Scotland. (3:12)

You will hear the recording twice. First you will have time to read the task. After each listening, you will have time to complete your answers.

While listening, fill in the missing information. You do not need to write complete sentences.

1.	Where the listener with the question is from	
2.	What kind of party the DUP is	
3.	What many Protestants in Northern Ireland describe themselves as, apart from Scots-Irish	
4.	Scots-Irish is a … identity	
5.	Two reasons why there are such close ties between Northern Ireland and Scotland	a) b)
6.	Irish nationalists have historically seen the Protestants in Ireland as …	
7.	What happened in the 19th century	
8.	Why Catholic Irish went to Scotland	
9.	Where many Catholic Irish ended up	
10.	What the two football teams stand for	Celtics: Rangers:

 ISBN 978-3-425-73646-4

Mediation: Discussions on abortions

Ireland is known for its Catholic conservatism in many private issues such as sex, partnership or abortion. Recently, Ireland has voted in a referendum to reform the country's strict abortion laws, which had effectively banned all pregnancy terminations. Your Irish friend Sarah is preparing a panel discussion at school about how other countries are dealing with the topic of abortion. She has asked you for a contribution telling her how Germans think about that issue. You have found the following article on *Spiegel Online*. Send Sarah an email, telling her which aspects of the topic are being discussed in Germany, according to Valerie Höhne's article.

Paragraf 218: Eine Abtreibung muss legal möglich sein

Die Debatte über das Werbeverbot für Schwangerschaftsabbrüche wird von Gegnern und Befürwortern mit höchster Empörung geführt. Doch in Wirklichkeit geht es nicht um die Werbung, sondern um das Recht auf Abtreibung.

Ein Kommentar von Valerie Höhne, 13. Dezember 2018, Spiegel Online

„Das Private ist politisch!" riefen die Aktivistinnen der Frauenbewegung der Siebziger. Frauen wollten über ihren Körper selbst bestimmen dürfen. Eine ihrer Forderungen: Abtreibung sollte legalisiert werden. Schon damals demonstrierten Aktivistinnen für die Abschaffung des Paragrafen 218.

Den Streit gibt es bis heute. Doch statt über diese grundsätzliche Frage zu sprechen, debattieren die Minister der Großen Koalition über das Werbeverbot für Schwangerschaftsabbrüche, geregelt im Paragrafen 219a des Strafgesetzbuchs. Das aber ist ein Stellvertreterkonflikt. Wir – als Gesellschaft – müssen über Abtreibungen reden. Denn eigentlich geht es darum.

Kaum jemand redet über Abtreibungen

Bislang findet diese Diskussion aber nur bei Aktivisten statt. Entweder bei den selbst ernannten Lebensschützern, die ausnahmslos jede Abtreibung ablehnen [...]. Oder bei radikalen Feministinnen, die eine Abtreibung im Zweifelsfall selbst im Endstadium der Schwangerschaft noch befürworten. Manchmal wirkt es, als würden nur die lautesten Stimmen in dieser Diskussion gehört.

Das macht sich auch an den Reaktionen auf die Debatte um den Paragrafen 219a bemerkbar. Die Bundesregierung hat hier mittlerweile einen Kompromiss vorgelegt, und der ist nicht einmal schlecht. Sofort aber liest man auf Twitter und anderswo empörte Kommentare [...].

Kritik gibt es vor allem an zwei Punkten

Es gibt zwei konkrete Kritikpunkte an dem Paragrafen: Es gibt keine offiziellen Listen, auf denen Ärzte und Krankenhäuser stehen, die Abtreibungen vornehmen. [...]

Das führt zu der kuriosen Situation, dass eine der umfassendsten Listen auf einer Internetseite zu finden ist, die von einem bekannten Abtreibungsgegner betrieben wird. [...] Der zweite Punkt ist ebenso schwerwiegend: Ärzte, die auf ihrer Website darüber informieren, dass sie Schwangerschaftsabbrüche durchführen, können auf Grundlage des Paragrafen 219a angeklagt und verurteilt werden, wie jüngst bei der Ärztin Kristina Hänel geschehen.

Auf beide Punkte geht das Kompromisspapier ein. Es sei geboten, dass neutrale, medizinisch und rechtlich qualitätsgesicherte Informationen auch von Seiten staatlicher oder staatlich beauftragter Stellen zur Verfügung stünden. [...] Außerdem solle Rechtssicherheit für Ärztinnen und Ärzte sowie Krankenhäuser geschaffen werden. Deshalb werde rechtlich ausformuliert, dass und wie Ärzte darüber informieren könnten, dass sie Schwangerschaftsabbrüche durchführten. Der Paragraf 219a ist damit nicht abgeschafft.

Aber eine Abschaffung kann man von einer Großen Koalition, zumal unter Führung einer Union, die sich gerade wieder verstärkt ihren konservativen Werten widmen will, nicht erwarten. Das bedeutet aber nicht, dass die Diskussion um Abtreibungen nicht geführt werden sollte.

Einige Kommentatoren stören sich daran, dass in dem Kompromiss vom „Schutz des ungeborenen Lebens" die Rede ist. Das sei ein Kampfbegriff im Stil der Abtreibungsgegner, finden sie. Doch der Kompromiss basiert unter anderem auf der letzten Grundsatzentscheidung des Bundesverfassungsgerichts aus dem Jahr 1993. Darin heißt es: „Das Grundgesetz verpflichtet den Staat, menschliches Leben, auch das ungeborene, zu schützen." [...]

Aus dieser Entscheidung wurde schließlich das Gesetz, das bis heute gültig ist: Abtreibung ist rechtswidrig, aber in den ersten drei Monaten der Schwangerschaft straffrei, wenn sich die Frau vor dem Eingriff beraten lässt. [...]

Das echte Problem ist Paragraf 218

Die fortgesetzte Rechtswidrigkeit der Abtreibung ist ein Problem. Frauen, die eine Schwangerschaft abbrechen, handeln also rechtswidrig. [...]

Gleichzeitig ist der Paragraf 218 aber nicht einfach ein weiteres Gesetz, das Frauen diskriminiert. Denn selbstverständlich kann ein Fötus von einem bestimmten Entwicklungsstadium an etwas spüren, und es ist ethisch nicht verantwortbar, den Fötus dann nicht zu schützen. [...]

Schon von der 24. Schwangerschaftswoche an gelten Föten als außerhalb des Mutterleibs lebensfähig, vom sechsten Schwangerschaftsmonat an. Eine Fristenregelung ist also notwendig, und sie sollte selbstverständlich schon vor dem sechsten Monat greifen. [...]

ISBN 978-3-425-73646-4

Writing: Irish youth and Catholicism

1. **Comprehension:** Summarize the article below.
2. **Analysis:** Explain the changing attitudes of the Irish young towards Catholicism.
3. **Writing a discussion:** Should religions change with their societies or should they remain institutions of tradition in an ever faster changing world? Discuss by giving examples from the text and materials studied in class.

'Young people of Ireland' have mixed views on church

By Jackie Fox, 23 August 2018, RTE News

In 1979, Pope John Paul II's declared at a youth mass[1] in Ballybritt: "Young people of Ireland, I love you."

Almost 40 years later, Ireland, the Catholic Church and young people have all changed.

Abuse[2] scandals continue to be revealed, church attendance has fallen rapidly, and many parishes[3] are now run by a single priest.

The young people of Ireland know the recent history and controversies, but only have their parents' memories of that time in Ballybritt in 1979.

"You're more able to express what your religious belief is and you're allowed to be different from your family" said 16-year-old Victoria Borsuk at Youth Work Ireland in Navan, Co[4] Meath.

Victoria, originally from Poland but living in Ireland for 12 years, was raised Catholic. However, she's interested in science and doesn't have faith.

Her peers at the local young people organisation are on a similar wavelength. The group of six young people were all baptised and raised Catholic.

17-year-old Ciara Purvis said she considers herself agnostic. She said: "As you get older you start to question it. You're like 'Well, how does this logically work and scientifically work?'"

Ciara said that when she started to learn about what the Catholic Church had done in the past, she wanted to disconnect from it.

For 16-year-old Michael Folan, he said he is in the "minority". He said he would consider himself Catholic but struggles with the church's relationship with the LGBT+ community, particularly after they were dropped from promotional material produced by the World Meeting of Families earlier this year.

Irrespective of faith, the Catholic Church's relationship with the LGBT+ community is a concern echoed throughout the Navan youth group.

Ciara said she thinks as society changes and leans towards equality, "the church needs to say 'OK maybe our ideals and ideas weren't exactly 100% correct, maybe we need to move forward as society does as well'."

The group members don't understand or don't know the church's stance[5] when it comes to the LGBT+ community, and that bothers them.

Not too far from the teenagers is the Columban Missionaries in Dalgan Park.

It was here where Archbishop of Dublin Diarmuid Martin, at the beginning of July, warned of a "growing alienation[6] between young people and the church".

Fr[7] Donal Hogan, Columban Deputy Designated for Safeguarding Children, said he thinks it is more than alienation; he thinks young people see the church as irrelevant.

When told that some young people's concerns lie with the church's stance on the LGBT+ community, he said: "I think there is more openness coming in the official church... I mean in [Pope] Francis."

"I would hope that there is some signs of encouragement given to people to show that we are the church. It's not just the bishops and those with collars. We are the church," Fr Hogan said.

A report in March of this year found that Irish people between the ages of 16 and 29 rank among the most religious in Europe. A young people's Catholic group in south Dublin says it's challenging having faith and there can be a certain stigma attached to it.

Pauline Fogerty says she feels like she can be on the defence and admits that the church could be more open when it comes to different communities. Other members though, are not on the same page, further blurring the message of inclusivity. Some in the group say homosexuality is a sin and others say sexual relations outside of marriage are wrong.

One member who is gay said those comments in the group used to hurt him but not anymore.

He said that he knows God loves him and LGBT people, and hopes the Catholic Church can become more open to people.

Fr Chris O'Donnell in Dublin is trying to make that happen. He came to the nation's attention last year, when hundreds of young people in his home diocese in Limerick appealed to Pope Francis not to move him to Dublin.

Now almost a year in the capital, the Adare native[8] says after hearing young people's concerns about church scandals and its relationship with the LGBT community, he hopes the church's teaching will evolve.

"We are learning more about people. We are learning more about sexuality.

"If I can't change teaching of the church, well I just have to put my energy into making sure that no LGBT community member ever feels alienated by me. I always say that to people who feel disempowered."

(743 words)

[1] **mass** = *Messe*
[2] **abuse** = *Missbrauch*
[3] **parish** = *Gemeinde*
[4] **Co** = short for County
[5] **stance** = way of thinking
[6] **alienation** = the process of growing apart
[7] **Fr** = short for Father; Catholic priests are commonly addressed as "Father"
[8] coming from Adare, a village near Limerick

ISBN 978-3-425-73646-4

Listening 1: Delivery robots

Listen to a report about self-delivery robot “6D57” in Washington D.C. (3:48)

You will hear the recording twice. First you will have time to read the tasks. After each listening, you will have time to complete your answers.

While listening, match the speakers **1** to **4** with the sentences **A** to **D**.

1	Kat Lonsdorf
2	Maria Garcia
3	Russell Cook
4	Nick Handrick

A	The speaker fears that people might lose their jobs because of delivery robots.
B	The speaker believes that robots will be used to deliver fairly cheap items.
C	The speaker is confident that 6D57 knows how to cross a road.
D	The speaker compares the robot to a remote control car.

1	2	3	4

ISBN 978-3-425-73646-4

Listening 2: Real-life cyborgs

Listen to a report about the artist Neil Harbisson and what makes him special. (4:13)

You will hear the recording twice. First you will have time to read the tasks. After each listening, you will have time to complete your answers.

While listening, fill in the missing information. You do not need to write complete sentences.

1.	Who Neil Harbisson is	
2.	Neil's feeling towards technology	
3.	Neil's disability	
4.	Function of the "eyeborg"	
5.	How the antenna is attached to Neil	
6.	How Neil feels about the antenna	
7.	What else Neil can perceive through the antenna (name three aspects)	a) b) c)
8.	How Amal Graafstra enhances his human capabilities	
9.	What Amal can do with this enhancement (name two aspects)	a) b)
10.	How gamers get superhuman focus	
11.	Which possibilities researcher Michael McAlpine sees in bionic technologies (name two aspects)	a) b)
12.	What people thought Neil's antenna was throughout the years (name three aspects)	a) b) c)
13.	What Neil predicts for the future	

 ISBN 978-3-425-73646-4

Mediation: Artificial intelligence

You have dealt with artificial intelligence as an important force of the digital revolution. While browsing the Internet you have come across a German article that indicates that artificial intelligence is becoming increasingly creative. You decide to share your new insight with an international science community for high school students on their website. Write a blog post which informs the community about advances in AI, its market value and the critical concern that is associated with its development.

Künstliche Kunst

Künstliche Intelligenz malt, dichtet und macht ihre eigene Musik. Christie's hat jetzt für mehr als 400 000 Dollar das Gemälde eines Computers versteigert und auch unsere Hörgewohnheiten verändert KI täglich.

Von Michael Moorstedt, 28. Oktober 2018, Süddeutsche Zeitung online

Das Auktionshaus Christie's hatte soeben eine Veranstaltung zu bieten, die es beinahe mit dem Banksy-Stunt des Konkurrenten Sotheby's aufnehmen konnte. Zum ersten Mal wurde ein von einer künstlichen Intelligenz gemaltes Bild versteigert. Das Motiv erinnerte an einen derangierten Rembrandt'schen Patrizier, die Bieter scheint das Bild jedoch beeindruckt zu haben. Für 432 500 Dollar ging es schließlich weg. In der kleinen, aber feinen Szene, die sich schon seit Jahren mit künstlicher Intelligenz und Kreativität beschäftigt, sorgte die PR-Aktion aber für ziemlichen Ärger. Nicht nur, weil es nicht das erste derartige Bild war, nicht nur wegen der Zweifel an der handwerklichen Qualität, sondern auch, weil das französische Kunstkollektiv Obvious, aus dessen Rechner das Bild kam, einen fremden Code benutzte, um es zu malen – oder besser: malen zu lassen. Die Frage, wer hier eigentlich der wahre Künstler ist, dürfte so manchem Urheberrechtler Kopfzerbrechen bereiten.

In den aufgeregten Meldungen der Kunstmagazine gingen Fragen nach dem Alleinstellungsmerkmal von menschlicher Kreativität und den üblichen Verdrängungsängsten angesichts zunehmender Automatisierung unter. Dabei ist es ja nicht nur die Malerei, die inzwischen von Robotern betrieben wird. Auch Gedichte, ja ganze Bücher werden von Computern geschrieben. Und überhaupt: Würde sich die Musik mit ihren klar definierten Regeln, Tonleitern und Rhythmen nicht sogar noch viel besser als Kunstform eignen, die von einer KI berechnet werden kann?

Hörgewohnheiten verändert

Schon heute verändert künstliche Intelligenz unsere Hörgewohnheiten bereits täglich. Wenn sie etwa die Spotify-Playlists und personalisierten Empfehlungen anhand der aktuellen Vorlieben von Millionen Nutzern neu sortiert. Labels wie Sony Music und Warner Music Group investieren ebenso in KI-Start-ups wie die legendären Abbey Road Studios. IT-Riesen wie IBM und Google haben eigene Programme zur automatischen Komposition im Produktportfolio. Und Amazon verpasste seinem smarten Assistenten Alexa kürzlich eine App namens Deep Music, die je nach Stimmung selbständig Samples zu Easy-Listening-Beschallung zusammenstellt.

Computerprogramme liefern Lieder im Stil der *Beatles* oder der *Strokes*, der sogenannte Lyric AI Assistant hilft Künstlern beim Schreiben von vermeintlich originellen Songzeilen. Das Unternehmen AI Music dagegen verspricht, bereits existierende Musik dem Kontext anzupassen, in dem sie gespielt wird. Etwa die Schlagzahl zu erhöhen, wenn man mit dem Auto unterwegs ist, oder die Bässe hochzudrehen, wenn der Hörer gerade seinen Sonntags-Dauerlauf unternimmt.

Kommt jetzt der total individualisierte Soundtrack des eigenen Lebens, der schon so oft besungen wurde? Auf der Homepage des KI-Start-ups Amper Music reicht es jedenfalls schon, Stimmung und Genre – Wohlfühl-Pop, moderne Klassiker – einzugeben. Nach einer knappen Minute Rechenzeit spuckt das Programm dann ein komplett neues 30-sekündiges Sample aus. Die Tonproben können beinahe schon überzeugen. Sie sind sicherlich nicht Grammy-würdig, und selbst im Formatradio hätten die Computerkompositionen wohl noch ein paar Schwierigkeiten. Aber zur Einbettung eines Werbespots oder als Fahrstuhlmusik ginge die Computermusik schon durch.

ISBN 978-3-425-73646-4

Writing: Machines taking over

Imagine you are taking part in an international school project on the chances and risks of new technologies. You have come across an article about an automated vending machine (A) and a cartoon about robots taking over human jobs (B). You decide to write an article for the project's website entitled "Machines taking over business: a blessing or a curse?"

1. **Comprehension:** State what the "Clifton Speedy Shop" is and also name its advantages.
2. **Analysis:** Analyse the most striking pictorial elements in the cartoon with reference to the given topic.
3. **Writing an article:** Write an article in which you discuss the automatic vending machine and the robot in the office within the context of "Machines taking over business: a blessing or a curse?" with concrete references to materials A and B. You may also refer to materials dealt with in class.

(A)

Can the UK's first 'automated shop' vending machine keep customers satisfied?

Chris Green visits the unexpected item in Clifton's car park – a giant vending machine[1]

By Chris Green, 21 March 2014, The Independent

[...] [At] the car park at the back [of Mrs Garside's pub] sits [...] UK's first "automated shop" – a bus shelter-sized giant vending machine selling everything from fresh milk and eggs to umbrellas and cat food. Designed to look like a quaint[2] village shop, yet with the advantage of more reliable opening hours, it is intended to lead a quiet, mechanised revolution in rural areas across Britain, filling the gap left by widespread closure of traditional stores.

The Clifton SpeedyShop [...] has been gratefully welcomed by residents [...]. "We haven't had a village shop for about 13, 14 years and there are no bus services through the village any more, so if you want a pint of milk you have to walk into town if you don't drive. [...] I think it's marvellous."

The machine is the brainchild[3] of Peter Fox, [an] electrical engineer who used to live in a small village and became frustrated at coming home late from work to find nothing in the fridge. [...] He now hopes that similar machines can be rolled out nationally, but says he doesn't have the resources to expand as quickly as he would like [...]. [...] Accepting cash or credit cards, the machine emails Mr Fox whenever it dispenses[4] an item, so he can keep track of stock levels. Although he is reluctant[5] to reveal just how good business has been so far, [...] he says there has been a "steady stream" of villagers buying [nearly] everything [...].

[...] The machine carries another benefit for Mrs Garside: relieving the pressure on her pub to act as an informal grocer[6] for naive tourists who rent self-catered cottages[7], only to be baffled at the village's lack of a Tesco[8] Express. [...]

(298 words)

[1] **vending machine** = a machine that you can get items from by putting money in, [2] **quaint** = unusual and attractive, especially in an old-fashioned way, [3] **brainchild** = idea, [4] **to dispense** = to give sth out, [5] **reluctant** = rather unwilling, [6] **grocer** = *Lebensmittelhändler,* [7] **self-catered cottage** = *kleines Ferienhaus mit Selbstverpflegung,* [8] **Tesco** = a British supermarket chain

(B)

© cartoonstock/Harley Schwadron

ISBN 978-3-425-73646-4

Listening 1: Dystopian novel *The Water Cure*

Listen to part of an interview with writer Sophie Mackintosh about her debut novel *The Water Cure*. (4:22)

You will hear the recording twice. First you will have time to read the tasks. After each listening, you will have time to complete your answers.

While listening, tick (✓) the correct answer (a, b, c, or d). There is only one correct answer.

1. The setting of *The Water Cure* is …
- ☐ a) our world.
- ☐ b) an island in the future.
- ☐ c) an island without men.
- ☐ d) a future without other humans.

2. According to radio host Leila Fadel, the genre of "feminist dystopian novel" deals with …
- ☐ a) mainly violence.
- ☐ b) positive aspects of female life.
- ☐ c) women wanting to give birth to children.
- ☐ d) unpleasant and touching aspects of female life.

3. Sophie Mackintosh's original idea for her book was about …
- ☐ a) a family living on their own.
- ☐ b) a family living in a science lab.
- ☐ c) a family living in a world of tragedy.
- ☐ d) a family living in quarantine after a disaster took place.

4. In the story, men are presented as …
- ☐ a) forbidden for women
- ☐ b) very damaging to women.
- ☐ c) only being there for reproduction.
- ☐ d) something women can live without.

5. Mackintosh's choice for changing her original idea was due to …
- ☐ a) an illness she suffered in 2016.
- ☐ b) what her friends posted on social media.
- ☐ c) positive actions towards women in 2016.
- ☐ d) changes in the way women were treated.

6. In her novel, water cures are …
- ☐ a) castigation.
- ☐ b) medication.
- ☐ c) punishment.
- ☐ d) immunization.

7. Water cures originally were …
- ☐ a) a form of therapy.
- ☐ b) cleansing methods.
- ☐ c) invented for women.
- ☐ d) rituals to stay healthy.

8. According to Mackintosh, water is …
- ☐ a) feminine and modern.
- ☐ b) primal and interesting.
- ☐ c) life-saving and feminine.
- ☐ d) life-creating and destructive.

9. When two men and a boy appear …
- ☐ a) the story starts to evolve.
- ☐ b) the sisters are welcoming.
- ☐ c) the sisters' reactions are contrary.
- ☐ d) one of the sisters starts a relationship with the boy.

10. For Mackintosh the process of writing was influenced by …
- ☐ a) her love for water and emotions.
- ☐ b) her desire for a beautiful language.
- ☐ c) her willingness to describe ugliness.
- ☐ d) the need to give it a futuristic quality.

ISBN 978-3-425-73646-4

Listening 2: Facial recognition technology

Listen to a conversation between Rick Smith, CEO of Axon, and Scott Simon, host of a radio show, about the use of facial recognition technology for police officers. (4:35)

You will hear the recording twice. First you will have time to read the tasks. After each listening, you will have time to complete your answers.

While listening, fill in the missing information. You do not need to write complete sentences.

1.	Two aspects the newly created ethics board of Axon has to consider	a) b)
2.	Risks of real-time facial recognition according to various civil rights and tech groups (name two aspects)	a) b)
3.	The benefit of facial recognition according to Rick Smith	
4.	What facial recognition software is still not good at	
5.	Smith's suggestion concerning a misuse of modern technologies	
6.	Benefits of modern technologies like DNA technology (name one aspect) and facial recognition (name two aspects), according to Smith	DNA technology: facial recognition: a) b)
7.	What Smith thinks about all-encompassing surveillance (name two aspects)	a) b)

ISBN 978-3-425-73646-4

Mediation: "Designer babies"

Your former American exchange partner is currently working on an essay for his social studies class on "designer babies" and is wondering how this issue is treated in Germany. Having read an interesting article about this subject, you decide to write him an email in which you outline He Jiankui's alleged scientific achievement and corresponding responses by politics, churches, and experts in the field of ethics.

Genmanipulierte Babys in China: Empörung über „Designerbabys"

Nach der Geburt der mutmaßlich ersten genmanipulierten Babys in China hält die Kritik an. Bundesgesundheitsminister Jens Spahn (CDU) sagte: „Der Mensch soll nicht Gott spielen." Auch der EKD[1]-Ratsvorsitzende Heinrich Bedford-Strohm kritisierte das Vorgehen des chinesischen Forschers He Jiankui scharf.

Von Stephan Cezanne, 29. November 2018, Sonntagsblatt online

Die Berichte über die Geburt der ersten genmanipulierten Babys in China haben eine neue Wertedebatte ausgelöst. Das Bundesforschungsministerium bezeichnete den Vorgang als „eindeutige Grenzüberschreitung". Sollten die aktuell diskutierten Experimente tatsächlich wie behauptet stattgefunden haben, „widersprechen diese den etablierten ethischen Maßstäben für die medizinische Forschung", sagte eine Sprecherin auf Anfrage dem Evangelischen Pressedienst (epd) in Berlin. „Sie werden auch von zahlreichen chinesischen Wissenschaftlern sowie der Universität, der der verantwortliche Wissenschaftler angehört, verurteilt", betonte das Ministerium.

Bundesgesundheitsminister Jens Spahn (CDU) erklärte zu den Vorgängen: „Der Mensch soll nicht Gott spielen. So etwas ist mit unseren Werten nicht vereinbar." Dieses „Experiment am menschlichen Erbgut" sei ein Weckruf für Europa, sagte Spahn der „Neuen Osnabrücker Zeitung" (Online). Spahn forderte die Europäer dazu auf, massiv in Forschung und Entwicklung zu investieren. „Nur, wenn Europa selbst Spitze ist, kann es Maßstäbe für die Welt setzen, die unseren Werten entsprechen", erklärte der Minister.

Forscher He verteidigt Experimente mit „Designerbabys"

Medienberichten zufolge hat der chinesische Forscher He Jiankui seine Arbeit auf einem Genomforscher-Kongress in Hongkong inzwischen verteidigt. Wie die Zeitung „South China Morning Post" berichtete, sagte He, eine weitere Frau könne möglicherweise mit einem genmanipulierten Baby schwanger sein. Zugleich habe er sich dafür entschuldigt, mit seiner Forschung eine weltweite Kontroverse ausgelöst zu haben.

Der Forscher hatte erklärt, mit Hilfe der sogenannten Gen-Schere das Erbgut von Embryonen so verändert zu haben, dass sie nicht an Aids erkranken könnten. Die Zwillinge sollen vor einigen Wochen auf die Welt gekommen sein. Bislang galten solche Experimente auf dem Weg zum „Designerbaby" als Tabu. Die betroffene Southern University im chinesischen Shenzhen reagierte mit Unverständnis auf die Versuche und kündigte eine genaue Untersuchung an. He sei seit Februar freigestellt, teilte die Universität mit.

Forscherin Amunts warnt vor Folgen der Genom-Editierung

Die Hirnforscherin Katrin Amunts, stellvertretende Vorsitzende des Deutschen Ethikrats und Direktorin des Instituts für Neurowissenschaften und Medizin am Forschungszentrum Jülich, erklärte: „Das Genom der beiden Mädchen, die nach Angaben der Forscher mit CRISPR[2] behandelt wurden, wurde durch einen Eingriff in die Keimbahn unter Anwendung einer noch sehr neuen, experimentellen Technik verändert. Offenbar war die Genom-Editierung nur bei einer von ihnen vollständig." Mögliche Folgen dieses Eingriffs für ihre weitere Entwicklung seien schwer absehbar und würden sich möglicherweise erst in vielen Jahren zeigen, sagte Amunts.

Der Wiener evangelische Sozialethiker [und Theologieprofessor] Ulrich H. J. Körtner stellte grundsätzlich die Frage, „wie die Gesellschaft insgesamt in die komplexe biopolitische und bioethische Debatte eingebunden werden kann". Die gesellschaftlichen und kulturellen Folgen, wenn das Leben immer mehr als technisches Produkt statt als Gabe verstanden werde, „seien gravierend", erklärte [er] in Wien. Wissenschaftsfreiheit sei ein hohes Gut, aber „sie hat ethische Grenzen".

EKD-Chef Bedford-Strohm warnt vor „Menschenzüchtung"

Der Ratsvorsitzende der Evangelischen Kirche in Deutschland (EKD), Heinrich Bedford-Strohm, warnte vor einem „Einstieg in die Menschenzüchtung". So „drastisch muss man es sagen", erläuterte er am Rande der Herbsttagung der bayerischen Landessynode in Garmisch-Partenkirchen. Es brauche nun dringend eine Debatte um die Grenzen solcher Forschung, sagte der bayerische Landesbischof. Der Ethikexperte der katholischen Deutschen Bischofskonferenz, Weihbischof Anton Losinger, forderte in der „Neuen Osnabrücker Zeitung" für die Biogenetik „ähnliche Schutzstandards wie bei den Menschenrechten".

[1] **EKD** = *Evangelische Kirche Deutschland*
[2] **CRISPR (clustered regularly interspaced short palindromic repeats)** = *„Genschere", die das Erbgutmolekül DNA präzise an einer bestimmten Stelle durchtrennen kann. Forscher können so Gene ausschalten oder an der Schnittstelle neue Abschnitte einfügen. Auf diese Weise lässt sich das Erbgut sehr viel einfacher und schneller verändern als bisher.*

ISBN 978-3-425-73646-4

Writing: *The forever kitten*

Read the following extract from the short story *The forever kitten*[1] (2005) by Peter F. Hamilton and complete the tasks. The story is about Joe Gordon, a wealthy venture capitalist who lives with his wife Fiona and their two daughters in a mansion. While their younger daughter, Heloise, is an adorably cute, innocent and well-behaved child, their older teenaged daughter, Saskia, has gone completely astray. She has quit school, consumes drugs, steals from her parents, shoplifts and, thus, has often been arrested by the police. Consequently, she causes her parents great trouble, which leads to frustration and even health issues for Fiona.

1. **Comprehension:** Summarize the extract.
2. **Analysis:** Analyse the narrative perspective and the atmosphere it creates.
3. **You choose:**
   a) Writing an article: You are taking part in the international school project "How far should scientific research go?" You have decided to write an article for the project website. In your article, discuss whether there should be limits to scientific research and if so, who should define them. Refer to Hamilton's short story and to materials dealt with in class.
   OR
   b) Creative writing: The short story has an open end. Continue the story, finding a suitable ending.

The mansion's garden was screened by lush[2] trees. I never thought I'd be so entranced by anything as simple as horse chestnuts[3], but that's what 18 months in jail on remand[4] will do for your appreciation of the simple things.

Joe Gordon was waiting for me; the venture capitalist[5] and his wife Fiona were sitting on ornate metal chairs in a sunken patio[6] area. Their five-year-old daughter, Heloise, was sprawled on a pile of cushions, playing with a ginger[7] kitten.

"Thanks for paying my bail[8]," I said.

"Sorry it took so long, Doctor," he said. "The preparations weren't easy, but we have a private plane waiting to take you to the Caribbean – an island the EU has no extradition treaty[9] with."

"I see. Do you think it's necessary?"

"For the moment, yes. The Brussels Bioethics Commission is looking to make an example of you. They didn't appreciate how many regulations you violated."

"They wouldn't have minded if the treatment had worked properly."

"Of course not, but that day isn't here yet, is it? We can set you up with another lab out there."

[...]

I looked at Heloise again. She was a beautiful child, and the smile on her face as she played with the kitten was angelic[10]. The ball of ginger fluff was full of rascally high spirits, just like every two-month-old kitten. I kept staring, shocked by the familiar pattern of marbling[11] in its fluffy light fur.

"Yes," Joe said with quiet pride. "I managed to save one before the court had the litter[12] destroyed. A simple substitution[13]; the police never knew."

"It's three years old now," I whispered.

"Indeed. Heloise is very fond of it."

"Do you understand what this means? The initial stasis[14]-regeneration procedure is valid. If the kitten is still alive and maintaining itself at the same biological age

© shutterstock/Nadezhda Sarkisian

after this long, then in theory it can live for ever, just as it is. The procedure stabilized its cellular structure."

"I understand perfectly, thank you, Doctor. Which is why we intend to keep on funding your research. We believe that human rejuvenation[15] is possible."

I recognized the greed in his eyes: it wasn't pleasant. "It's still a long way off. This procedure was just the first of a great many. It has no real practical application, we can't use it on an adult. Once a mammal reaches sexual maturity its cells can't accept such a radical modification."

"We have every confidence that in the end you'll produce the result we all want."

I turned back to the child with her pet, feeling more optimistic than I had in three years. "I can do it," I said through clenched teeth. "I can." Revenge, it is said, is best served cold. I could see myself looking down on the gravestones of those fools in the Bioethics Commission in, say...oh, about 500 years' time. They'd be very cold indeed by then.

[...]

I smiled over at Heloise, who had started playing with the kitten again. [...]

Joe seemed to make some kind of decision. "Before you leave, I'd like you to perform the cellular stasis-regeneration procedure for me."

"I don't understand. I explained before, it's simply the first stage of verifying the overwrite sequence we developed."

→

ISBN 978-3-425-73646-4

His attitude changed. "Nevertheless, you will do it again. Without my help you will be going back to prison for a long time."

"It's of no use to adults," I said helplessly. "You won't become young, or even maintain your current age."

"It's not for me," he said.

"Then who..." I followed his gaze to Heloise. "Oh."

"She's perfect just the way she is," he said quietly. "And that, Doctor, is the way she's going to stay."

(620 words)

[1] **kitten** = a young cat
[2] **lush** = trees that are lush grow many leaves and look healthy and strong
[3] **horse chestnuts** = *Rosskastanien(-bäume)*
[4] **on remand** = in custody or on bail awaiting trial or completion of one's trial
[5] **venture capitalist** = *Risikokapitalanleger*
[6] **patio** = a place similar to a veranda
[7] **ginger** = with red hair or fur
[8] **bail** = *Kaution*
[9] **extradition treaty** = *Auslieferungsabkommen*
[10] **angelic** = like an angel
[11] **marbling** = *Marmorierung*
[12] **litter** = a group of baby cats or dogs born at the same time
[13] **substitution** = replacement
[14] **stasis** = a state or period in which there is no change or development
[15] **rejuvenation** = *Verjüngung*

ISBN 978-3-425-73646-4

Listening 1: Fake news

Listen to a radio interview about fake news on the Internet. (4:02)

You will hear the recording twice. First you will have time to read the tasks. After each listening, you will have time to complete your answers.

While listening, tick (✓) the correct answer (a, b, c, or d). There is only one correct answer.

1. Customer ratings of apps can be faked by
- ☐ a) click farms.
- ☐ b) fake user accounts.
- ☐ c) viruses and malware.
- ☐ d) illegal financial transactions.

2. With the increase of fake information, people
- ☐ a) lose their trust in media.
- ☐ b) mistake real news as fake.
- ☐ c) are less likely to read information online.
- ☐ d) deepen their sense of what is right and what is wrong.

3. 2018 was a record year in terms of
- ☐ a) software innovations.
- ☐ b) criminal online activity.
- ☐ c) fake stories that were published.
- ☐ d) economic success of ad blocking.

4. Deepfakes is a technology that enables users to
- ☐ a) produce fake media.
- ☐ b) spread fake information.
- ☐ c) identify fake information.
- ☐ d) share warnings about fake videos.

5. Websites try to make sure that real people, not robots, are trying to log into their accounts by asking
- ☐ a) for the date of birth.
- ☐ b) for a secure password.
- ☐ c) for fingerprint identification.
- ☐ d) for identification of real world images.

6. The interviewer raises the question if
- ☐ a) Instagram tries to identify fake accounts.
- ☐ b) Instagram is the platform that has most fake followers.
- ☐ c) a follower of Instagram can be influenced by the pictures.
- ☐ d) it makes a difference whether the number of Instagram followers is faked.

7. Fake information makes people
- ☐ a) refer to reliable platforms such as Netflix.
- ☐ b) wonder all the time what they can believe.
- ☐ c) refer to Twitter to check if the information is correct.
- ☐ d) angry at Twitter because it massively spreads false information.

8. Private online comments and jokes are suddenly seen as
- ☐ a) intruding privacy.
- ☐ b) contradicting online politeness.
- ☐ c) being initiated by large companies.
- ☐ d) being motivated by personal economic interests.

9. One solution to the problem is to
- ☐ a) break up networks.
- ☐ b) find the truth in media again.
- ☐ c) implement detection software.
- ☐ d) build up trust in institutions and other people.

10. Companies have to regain trust by
- ☐ a) improving their technology.
- ☐ b) cooperating with politicians.
- ☐ c) helping discover fake news.
- ☐ d) changing their business methods.

ISBN 978-3-425-73646-4

Listening 2: Teenagers and their phones

Listen to a US radio programme about smartphone addiction. (3:50)

You will hear the recording twice. First you will have time to read the tasks. After each listening, you will have time to complete your answers.

While listening, fill in the missing information. You do not need to write complete sentences.

0.	What fear people had in 2018	fear of using technology too much
1.	What Apple was demanded to do	
2.	How the World Health Organization sees the problem	
3.	A study found that parents …	
4.	Three examples of how intense screen time can affect people	a) b) c)
5.	Apple and Android have programmed tools to …	
6.	Why Facebook and Snapchat don't help people reduce online time	
7.	What the first girl says about her smartphone	
8.	What kind of anxiety the girl has experienced	
9.	Why the second girl experiences lack of sleep	
10.	Why the mother doesn't stop smartphone use at night	
11.	Number of teenagers who have tried to cut down their smartphone use	
12.	Two reasons why it is difficult to reduce screen time	a) b)

ISBN 978-3-425-73646-4

Mediation: A scandal in journalism

Together with your American partner school, your English class is working on a project about journalism today. You have come across the following article about a journalistic scandal in Germany's famous news magazine *Der Spiegel*. Write an article for the project website about this scandal, focusing on criteria of journalistic quality that were ignored.

Ein Fall für die Lehrbücher

Claas Relotius wurde auf der Jagd nach der perfekten Geschichte zum Betrüger. Zweifel wurden weggewischt. Doch der Schock könnte heilsam für den Journalismus sein.

Von Holger Stark, 21. Dezember 2018, Zeit Online

Ein junger Reporter, ein Shootingstar einer ganzen Branche, einer, der in das Räderwerk der Geschichte einzugreifen versuchte, hat sich als Hochstapler und Fälscher erwiesen. Claas Relotius, so heißt der Reporter, ist vor ein paar Tagen aufgeflogen, er hat eingeräumt, in seinen Reportagen Dialoge manipuliert, Protagonisten erfunden und Fakten fabriziert zu haben. Er hat vergangene Woche gekündigt. Der Spiegel, so heißt sein bisheriger Arbeitgeber, bezeichnet dies als „Tiefpunkt in der 70-jährigen Geschichte" des Nachrichtenmagazins. Das ist nicht übertrieben. Der deutsche Journalismus durchläuft in diesen Tagen eine Wahrhaftigkeitskrise [...].

Für den Spiegel, der für sich selbst mit dem Slogan wirbt, „keine Angst vor der Wahrheit" zu haben, ist dies ein Fiasko, weil es die Werte infrage stellt, die das Nachrichtenmagazin verkörpert: harte Recherche, gute Schreibe, Fakten, die im besten Fall so unverrückbar wie ein Felsblock sind. Was für eine Ironie: Angst muss der Spiegel nicht vor der Wahrheit da draußen haben, wie er es in seinem Werbespruch versichert, sondern vor der Unwahrheit, die im eigenen Haus geboren wurde.

Zugleich berührt die Relotius-Affäre aber auch den Journalismus an sich, der in Zeiten von Fake-News und Medienkritik ohnehin im Blitzgewitter steht. Ein Fälscher unter vielen Tausend sauber arbeitenden Journalistinnen und Journalisten ist hinreichend, um ein ganzes Gewerbe unter Generalverdacht zu stellen. In jeder Branche passieren Fehler. Aber der Journalismus ist keine Branche wie jede andere. Ihm kommt eine Wächterfunktion zu und damit eine besondere Verantwortung. Wer andere kritisiert, oft auch beißend und unerbittlich, der steht selbst unter Beobachtung und daran ist nichts Falsches.

Das Publikum mag sich daran gewöhnt haben, dass manche Politiker ein taktisches Verhältnis zur Wahrheit haben, dass sie mitunter lügen wie gedruckt. Journalisten aber sollen drucken, wie Politiker lügen, sie haben in einer Demokratie die Kontrollfunktion eben jener Mächtigen inne, sie sollen enthüllen, wenn die Mächtigen ihre Macht missbrauchen. Wie glaubhaft kann man andere kritisieren, wenn man selbst nicht der Wahrheit verpflichtet ist? Das ist die eine große Frage, die zuvorderst, aber nicht nur den Spiegel betrifft. [...]

„Ich versuche, meine Geschichten so zu schreiben, wie ich sie gerne lesen würde", sagte Relotius einmal 2015, als er schon für den Spiegel schrieb, aber auch noch für andere Redaktionen. Daraus entstand seine ganz eigene Art der Dekonstruktion der Wirklichkeit: Er versuchte dort, wo er mit journalistischen Mitteln nicht weiterkam, die Realität nach der eigenen Fantasie zu formen. [...]

Der Versuch, in einer Livewelt konkurrieren zu können, in der wir uns daran gewöhnt haben, dass die Realität in Echtzeit gestreamt wird, ist nicht nur ein Irrtum, er trägt bereits den Kern des Problems in sich. Der geschriebene Journalismus kann das nicht simulieren. Er kann den Wettlauf nicht gewinnen. Geschriebener Journalismus muss nachdenklicher, reflektierter, tiefer recherchiert und ja, langsamer daherkommen. [...] Relotius' Texte waren großes Kino. Mit der Suche nach der Wahrheit oder zumindest den Tatsachen hatten sie wenig bis nichts zu tun. Dass er dafür mit dem Deutschen Reporterpreis überhäuft wurde, sagt viel über die Sehnsucht der Branche nach der ultimativen Geschichte. [...]

Relotius' preisgekrönter Text [...] werde es in die Schulbücher schaffen, schwärmte die Chefredakteurin der Deutschen Welle, Ines Pohl, Anfang Dezember, als sie beim Reporterpreis die Laudatio auf Relotius hielt.

Hoffentlich. Nur müssen es die Lehrbücher der Journalistenschulen sein – als ein Beispiel dafür, was im Journalismus niemals passieren darf.

ISBN 978-3-425-73646-4

Writing: Too much information

Read the following excerpt from the non-fiction book *The Organized Mind* (2014) by American-Canadian author Daniel Levitin and complete the tasks.

1. **Comprehension:** Outline the challenges of the information age as they are presented in the text.
2. **Analysis:** Analyse how the author tries to convince the readers of his opinion. Consider his choice of words and stylistic devices.
3. **Writing a discussion:** On his website, Daniel Levitin says that he would enjoy hearing from his readers. Write an email to him in which you discuss the benefits and problems of digital media from your own point of view.

Our brains are busier than ever before. [...]

Today, we are confronted with an unprecedented amount of information, and each of us generates more information than ever before in human history. As former Boeing scientist and New York Times writer Dennis Overbye notes, this information stream contains "more and more information about our lives – where we shop and what we buy, indeed, where we are right now – the economy, the genomes of countless organisms we can't even name yet, galaxies full of stars we haven't counted, traffic jams in Singapore and the weather on Mars." That information "tumbles faster and faster through bigger and bigger computers down to everybody's fingertips, which are holding devices with more processing power than the Apollo mission control." Information scientists have quantified all this: In 2011, Americans took in five times as much information every day as they did in 1986 – the equivalent of 175 newspapers. During our leisure time, not counting work, each of us processes 34 gigabytes or 100,000 words every day. The world's 21,274 television stations produce 85,000 hours of original programming every day as we watch an average of 5 hours of television each day, the equivalent of 20 gigabytes of audio-video images. That's not counting YouTube, which uploads 6,000 hours of video every hour. And computer gaming? It consumes more bytes than all other media put together, including DVDs, TV, books, magazines, and the Internet. [...] Our brains do have the ability to process the information we take in, but at a cost: We can have trouble separating the trivial from the important, and all this information processing makes us tired. [...]

This information explosion is taxing all of us, every day, as we struggle to come to grips with what we really need to know and what we don't. We take notes, make To Do lists, leave reminders for ourselves in e-mail and on cell phones, and we still end up feeling overwhelmed. [...]

Why is information overload such a serious problem now? For one thing, we're doing more work than ever before. The promise of a computerized society, we were told, was that it would relegate[1] to machines all of the repetitive drudgery[2] of work, allowing us humans to pursue loftier[3] purposes and to have more leisure time. It didn't work out this way. Instead of more time, most of us have less.

[...] Beyond doing more work, we are dealing with more changes in information technology than our parents did, and more as adults than we did as children. The average American replaces her cell phone every two years, and that often means learning new software, new buttons, new menus. We change our computer operating systems every three years, and that requires learning new icons and procedures, and learning new locations for old menu items. But overall [...] we are just getting so much more information shot at us. The global economy means we are exposed to large amounts of information that our grandparents weren't. We hear about revolutions and economic problems in countries halfway around the world right as they're happening; we see images of places we've never visited and hear languages spoken that we've never heard before. Our brains are hungrily soaking all this in because that is what they're designed to do, but at the same time, all this stuff is competing [...] with the things we need to know to live our lives.

Information has always been the key resource in our lives. It has allowed us to improve society, medical care, and decision-making, to enjoy personal and economic growth, and to better choose our elected officials. It is also a fairly costly resource to acquire[4] and handle. As knowledge becomes more available – and decentralized through the Internet – the notions[5] of accuracy and authoritativeness[6] have become clouded. [...] Many of us find we don't know whom to believe, what is true, what has been modified, and what has been vetted[7]. We don't have the time or expertise to do research on every little decision. Instead, we rely on trusted authorities, newspapers, radio, TV, books, sometimes your brother-in-law, the neighbor with the perfect lawn, the cab driver who dropped you at the airport, your memory of a similar experience. – Sometimes these authorities are worthy of our trust, sometimes not.

(715 words)

[1] to **relegate** = to hand over, [2] **repetitive drudgery** = hard and boring work, [3] **lofty** = grand, noble, [4] to **acquire** = *erwerben*, [5] **notion** = idea, [6] **authoritativeness** = *hier: Zuverlässigkeit der Quelle*, [7] to **vet** = to check thoroughly

ISBN 978-3-425-73646-4

Listening 1: Losing your accent

Listen to an extract from a podcast about a language school in New York City where people learn to lose their accents. (4:58)

You will hear the recording twice. First you will have time to read the tasks. After each listening, you will have time to complete your answers.

While listening, tick (✓) the correct answer (a, b, c, or d). There is only one correct answer.

1. Some immigrants who come to New York try to
- ☐ a) write a protocol.
- ☐ b) change their accent.
- ☐ c) become a business coach.
- ☐ d) find a job in a New York business.

2. Survival words are those that
- ☐ a) are needed every day.
- ☐ b) are difficult to pronounce.
- ☐ c) have more than three syllables.
- ☐ d) can be used in dangerous situations.

3. The banker's accent was irrelevant in his first job, because
- ☐ a) all colleagues were Estonian.
- ☐ b) his bank was located in Estonia.
- ☐ c) his bank was located in Australia.
- ☐ d) all colleagues had the same accent.

4. He wants to lose his foreign accent because customers have often
- ☐ a) reported him to the management.
- ☐ b) had difficulties understanding him.
- ☐ c) asked him to repeat what he had said.
- ☐ d) asked him to translate into their language.

5. Most people see losing their accent as a way to
- ☐ a) increase their income.
- ☐ b) feel more confident.
- ☐ c) have better employment opportunities.
- ☐ d) reduce prejudices against ethnic minorities.

6. Before teaching at a language school, the accent coach was
- ☐ a) a musician.
- ☐ b) a cab driver.
- ☐ c) a news anchor.
- ☐ d) a speech pathologist.

7. A lot of clients now are
- ☐ a) actors.
- ☐ b) professors.
- ☐ c) cab drivers.
- ☐ d) office workers.

8. The students do NOT worry about
- ☐ a) discrimination.
- ☐ b) unemployment.
- ☐ c) costs of the course.
- ☐ d) lack of career opportunities.

9. A survey showed that
- ☐ a) white speakers spoke better English than Asian speakers.
- ☐ b) Asian speakers spoke better English than white speakers.
- ☐ c) the listeners' expectations have an impact on their understanding.
- ☐ d) the listeners could identify if the speaker of a recording was white or Asian.

10. Criticizing people for their accents
- ☐ a) has become a taboo.
- ☐ b) has become as common as gender discrimination.
- ☐ c) is less accepted than making jokes about other ethnicities.
- ☐ d) is more accepted than making jokes about other ethnicities.

11. The linguist states that
- ☐ a) some people have no accent at all.
- ☐ b) accents are part of the speaker's identity.
- ☐ c) teachers are very critical towards accents.
- ☐ d) people can improve their accents with the help of a grammar book.

ISBN 978-3-425-73646-4

Listening 2: Technology and the future of English

Listen to an extract from a podcast about computer innovations in the language sector. (4:18)

You will hear the recording twice. First you will have time to read the tasks. After each listening, you will have time to complete your answers.

While listening, fill in the missing information. You do not need to write complete sentences.

0.	The focus of the podcast's first programme	technology
1.	What computers will be able to do in the future	
2.	What might be a threat to English as a global language	
3.	Where the programme was recorded	
4.	Two innovations that are studied there	a) b)
5.	What is said about Netflix and Google	
6.	Next innovation planned	
7.	Evan Macmillan's job profile	
8.	What the company has developed	
9.	What the company's focus of research was	
10.	Where this innovation can be used	
11.	Why humans are still needed there	
12.	How well the company's software handles English variations	
13.	How the software will be improved	

ISBN 978-3-425-73646-4

Mediation: Language learning

Your American host brother, who is going to college, is planning to spend a semester in Japan. He sent you an email, asking for your opinion. Using the information from the following interview, write an email to him, focusing on how to make most of the semester in terms of language learning.

Auslandsstudium

Was will ich im Ausland

Es gibt viele Gründe, während des Studiums ins Ausland zu gehen: Die einen wollen Vorlesungen bei Nobelpreisträgern besuchen oder ein Praktikum in London oder New York machen, die anderen ein Semester lang Tequila-Shots aus Bauchnabeln schlürfen. Für 70 Prozent der Studenten ist es wichtig, dass sie im Ausland die Landessprache lernen.

Von Marie Gamillscheg, 5. April 2016, Zeit Campus

[...]

ZEIT Campus: Frau Hufeisen, Ihre Abwesenheits-Mail ist in sieben Sprachen formuliert. Es gibt Menschen, die sind eben sprachbegabt – und andere sind es nicht. Oder?

Britta Hufeisen: Viele Studierende nehmen dies gerne als Ausrede, wenn sie im Ausland kaum ein Wort gelernt haben. Wissenschaftlich ist nicht bewiesen, dass jemand untalentiert für das Sprachenlernen sein kann. Wir haben es alle geschafft, unsere Muttersprache zu lernen, warum also nicht eine weitere?

ZEIT Campus: Wem fällt es besonders leicht?

Hufeisen: Leuten, die motiviert sind. So klischeehaft es klingt: Die Liebe kann zum Beispiel ein Motor sein. Ich habe oft erlebt, dass jemand erst meinte, er sei furchtbar untalentiert – aber als er verliebt aus dem Ausland zurückkam, brannte er für die neue Sprache.

ZEIT Campus: Lohnt es sich, schon vor der Abreise mit dem Lernen zu beginnen?

Hufeisen: Auf jeden Fall! Ein Sprachkurs ist gut oder ein Tandempartner. Schon im Laufe eines Semesters kann man große Sprünge machen!

ZEIT Campus: Was, wenn ich keine Zeit habe?

Hufeisen: Dann können Sie einen Intensivkurs belegen, in den Ferien oder am Wochenende. Oder Sie können mit Sprachsoftware zumindest ein paar erste Vokabeln lernen. Gerade bei seltenen Sprachen stößt man bei den Einheimischen schon auf große Begeisterung, wenn man bei der Ankunft ein paar Worte spricht.

ZEIT Campus: Auslandssemester dauern wenige Monate. Wie kann man in so kurzer Zeit ein gutes Sprachlevel erreichen?

Hufeisen: Reden, reden, reden. Dazu sollte man gerade am Anfang hartnäckig sein: Wenn der Gegenüber auf Englisch antwortet, obwohl man in der Landessprache gefragt hat, kann man darum bitten, bei der Landessprache zu bleiben – auch wenn es länger dauert und man viele Fehler macht. Nur nicht von Augenrollen einschüchtern lassen. Wird jemand ungeduldig, einfach weitersprechen.

ZEIT Campus: Für schüchterne und unsichere Menschen ist das eine schwierige Sache.

Hufeisen: Ja. Aber nur so kann man es lernen.

ZEIT Campus: Welche Hindernisse gibt es noch?

Hufeisen: Oft bleiben Erasmus-Studierende unter sich und sprechen nur Englisch miteinander. Wenn man in England oder den USA studiert, ist das kein Problem. Um aber auch anderswo die Landessprache zu lernen, muss man mit einheimischen Studierenden in Kontakt kommen: Man kann zur Erstsemester-Party des Studienfachs gehen oder sich im gleichen Labor wie sie eintragen. Oder man lässt sich von den Einheimischen in ihre Lieblingsbar mitnehmen. Sehr viel bringt es, sich eine WG mit Muttersprachlern zu suchen.

ZEIT Campus: Wie macht man Fortschritte, wenn man die Sprache im Alltag bereits gut kann?

Hufeisen: An den Unis werden meist weiterführende Sprachkurse angeboten. Man kann sich auch spezifisch für sein Studium vorbereiten, zum Beispiel Fachvokabular lernen. Eine Sprache hat man nie ausgelernt.

[...]

Britta Hufeisen
Die 55-Jährige ist Professorin für Linguistik an der TU Darmstadt.
Sie leitet dort auch das Sprachenzentrum.

ISBN 978-3-425-73646-4

Writing: Global English

1. **Comprehension:** Outline the dominance of the English language as it is presented in the article.
2. **Analysis:** Analyse the stylistic devices the author uses and the effect they have on the reader.
3. **Writing a comment:** Readers are invited to post a comment on the *Guardian* website. Write a text in which you comment on the author's critical remark that English "is now seen as the access code to the global elite. If you want your children to get ahead, then they better have English in their toolkit." Refer to your own experiences and materials studied in class.

Behemoth[1], bully, thief: how the English language is taking over the planet

No language in history has dominated the world quite like English does today. Is there any point in resisting?

By Jacob Mikanowski, 27 July 2018, The Guardian online

[...] [T]he world [...] is threatened by English.

Behemoth, bully, loudmouth, thief: English is everywhere, and everywhere, English dominates. [...] [It] has grown to vast size and astonishing influence. Almost 400m people speak it as their first language; a billion more know it as a secondary tongue. It is an official language in at least 59 countries, the unofficial lingua franca of dozens more. No language in history has been used by so many people or spanned a greater portion of the globe. It is aspirational[2]: the golden ticket to the worlds of education and international commerce, a parent's dream and a student's misery, winnower[3] of the haves from the have-nots. It is inescapable: the language of global business, the internet, science, diplomacy, stellar navigation, avian pathology[4]. And everywhere it goes, it leaves behind a trail of dead: dialects crushed, languages forgotten, literatures mangled[5].

One straightforward way to trace the growing influence of English is in the way its vocabulary has infiltrated so many other languages. For a millennium or more, English was a great importer of words, absorbing vocabulary from Latin, Greek, French, Hindi, Nahuatl and many others. During the 20th century, though, as the US became the dominant superpower and the world grew more connected, English became a net exporter of words. [...] A few of the most prevalent include "last-minute", "fitness", "group sex", and a number of terms related to seagoing and train travel. [...] Thanks to the internet, the spread of English has almost certainly sped up. [...]

Within the anglophone world, that English should be the key to all the world's knowledge and all the world's places is rarely questioned. The hegemony of English is so natural as to be invisible. Protesting it feels like yelling at the moon. Outside the anglophone world, living with English is like drifting into the proximity[6] of a supermassive black hole, whose gravity warps[7] everything in its reach. Every day English spreads, the world becomes a little more homogenous and a little more bland[8]. [...]

The Japanese novelist Minae Mizumura [...] describes English as a "universal language". For Mizumura, what makes it universal is not that it has many native speakers – Mandarin and Spanish have more – but that it is "used by the greatest number of non-native speakers in the world". She compares it to a currency[9] used by more and more people until its utility hits a critical mass and it becomes a world currency. [...]

In the last few decades, as globalisation has accelerated and the US has remained the world's most powerful country, the advance of English has taken on a new momentum. In 2008, Rwanda switched its education system from French to English, having already made English an official language in 14 years earlier. [...] When South Sudan became independent in 2011, it made English its official language despite having very few resources or qualified personnel with which to teach it in schools. The Minister of higher education at the time justified the move as being aimed at making the country "different and modern" [...].

The situation in east Asia is no less dramatic. China currently has more speakers of English as a second language than any other country. Some prominent English teachers have become celebrities, conducting mass lessons in stadiums seating thousands. In South Korea, meanwhile, according to the sociolinguist Joseph Sung-Yul Park, English is a "national religion". Korean employers expect proficiency in English, even in positions where it offers no obvious advantage.

The quest to master English in Korea is often called the *yeongeo yeolpung* or "English frenzy[10]". Although mostly confined to a mania for instruction[11] and immersion[12], occasionally this "frenzy" spills over into medical intervention. As Sung-Yul Park relates: "An increasing number of parents in South Korea have their children undergo a form of surgery that snips off a thin band of tissue[13] under the tongue ... Most parents pay for this surgery because they believe it will make their children speak English better. [...]

There is no evidence to suggest that this surgery in any way improves English pronunciation. The willingness to engage in this useless surgical procedure strikes me, though, as a potent metaphor for English's peculiar status in the modern world. It is no longer simply a tool suited to a particular task or set of tasks [...]. It is now seen as the access code to the global elite. If you want your children to get ahead, then they better have English in their toolkit.

→

ISBN 978-3-425-73646-4

Is the conquest of English really so bad? In the not-too-distant future, thanks to English, the curse of Babel[14] will be undone and the children of men may come together once again, united with the aid of a common tongue. Certainly, that's what English's boosters[15] would have you believe. [...] It's not that English is bad. It's fine! A perfectly nice language, capable of expressing a great many things - and with scores of fascinating regional variants, from Scots to Singapore English. But it is so prevalent. And so hard to escape. [...] "[T]he language that connects the world". Please. There is no reason for any particular language to be worshipped around the world like a golden idol. [...] Is English oppressive? When its pervasive influence silences other languages, or discourages parents from passing on their native languages to their children, I think it can be. [...]

Today it is estimated that the world loses a language every two weeks. Linguists have predicted that between 50 and 90% of the world's 6,000 or so languages will go extinct in the coming century. For even a fraction[16] of these to survive, we're going to have to start thinking of smaller languages not as endangered species worth saving, but as equals worth learning.

In most of the world, it's already too late. [...]

(955 words)

[1] **behemoth** = *Ungeheuer*
[2] **aspirational** = desired, ambitious
[3] **winnower** – to **winnow** = *die Spreu vom Weizen trennen*
[4] **avian pathology** = illnesses of birds
[5] to **mangle** = to ruin
[6] **proximity** = closeness
[7] to **warp** = *krümmen*
[8] **bland** = boring, without colour
[9] **currency** = *Währung*
[10] **frenzy** = extreme excitement
[11] **instruction** = teaching
[12] **immersion** = one specific way of learning a language, being surrounded by the language all the time
[13] **tissue** = *Gewebe*
[14] The story of Babel is a biblical story meant to explain why the world is multilingual. First, all people spoke one language. They planned to build the tower of Babel to reach heaven. God punished them by giving them different languages.
[15] **boosters** = supporters
[16] **fraction** = very small part

ISBN 978-3-425-73646-4

Listening 1: Globalization and regionalization

Listen to Professor Susan Segal Horn talking about the concept of globalization and the question of its inevitability[1]. (2:49)

You will hear the recording twice. First you will have time to read the tasks. After each listening, you will have time to complete your answers.

While listening, fill in the missing information. You do not need to write complete sentences.

1.	Globalization has been made possible by … (name two aspects)	a) b)
2.	How deregulation is defined	
3.	The result of deregulation (name three aspects)	a) b) c)
4.	Three aspects that are positively affected by deregulation	a) b) c)
5.	Two consequences of regionalization	a) b)

[1] **inevitability, inevitable** = *Unausweichlichkeit, unausweichlich*

ISBN 978-3-425-73646-4

Listening/Viewing 2: The impact of globalization

Listen to the beginning of a book presentation about globalization by Professor Ian Goldin. (4:17)

You will hear the recording twice. First you will have time to read the tasks. After each listening, you will have time to complete your answers.

While listening, tick (✓) the correct answer. Sometimes more than one answer is correct.

1. According to Ian Goldin, globalization
- ☐ a) has more good than bad effects.
- ☐ b) might have more negative than positive effects.
- ☐ c) has been one of the most powerful forces in human history.
- ☐ d) has been the most important power influencing human lives.

2. In current British politics there are people who …
- ☐ a) are able to better control the future.
- ☐ b) want to reverse the process of globalization.
- ☐ c) keep in mind the benefits that globalization has brought.
- ☐ d) have realized the negative impact of globalization on the UK.

3. For Goldin, globalization is characterized by …
- ☐ a) an exchange of ideas.
- ☐ b) a precise and clear definition.
- ☐ c) people being more open-minded.
- ☐ d) societies getting linked to each other.

4. Goldin left South Africa because …
- ☐ a) the Berlin Wall came down.
- ☐ b) he was imprisoned and fled.
- ☐ c) he had fought against Apartheid.
- ☐ d) he could not identify with the concept of Apartheid.

5. The political changes in South Africa were initiated by …
- ☐ a) a change in democratization.
- ☐ b) political changes in Eastern Europe.
- ☐ c) the Cold War cascading around the world.
- ☐ d) the democratization of 65 countries worldwide.

ISBN 978-3-425-73646-4

Listening 3: The future of work in a globalized world

Listen to Stijn Broecke from the OECD speaking at a conference about the future of work from an international perspective. (4:19)

You will hear the recording twice. First you will have time to read the tasks. After each listening, you will have time to complete your answers.

While listening, fill in the missing information. You do not need to write complete sentences.

0.	When talking about the future of work, which two other aspects does Stijn Broecke refer to besides "technology"?	a) globalization b) population ageing
1.	What are the two key fears regarding the future of work?	a) b)
2.	According to Broecke, what percentage of jobs might actually be affected by automation?	
3.	According to an OECD survey in the EU, what are people happy about? (name two aspects)	a) b)
4.	According to the same survey, what are people hesitant about? (name two aspects)	a) b)
5.	What are three positive aspects of automation?	a) b) c)
6.	What percentage of the overall economy is made up by platform economy[1]?	
7.	Which two aspects did Canada, as the first country ever, include in their labour force survey?	a) b)

[1] **platform economy** = economic activities that take place through online platforms such as ebay or Airbnb

ISBN 978-3-425-73646-4

Mediation: Withdrawal from globalization

Your friend from the US supports the "America First" movement in her country. She believes America could become independent, given the country's size, its geological diversity, its available natural resources and its economic power. In her last email she wondered whether Germany would also be able to cut itself off from globalization. You decide to write a reply to your friend's question, in which you summarize a corresponding article you have found online.

Globalisierung

Verführerische Isolation

Könnte sich Deutschland aus der Weltwirtschaft zurückziehen? Alles selbst herstellen, statt zu handeln? Kein Industriestaat hat das je gewagt. Aus Gründen.

Von Mark Schieritz, 26. Dezember 2018, Zeit Online

Es ist eine verführerische Vorstellung: einfach die Grenzen schließen und nichts mehr mit den Handelsstreitigkeiten in der Welt zu tun haben. BMW und Mercedes würden ihre Autos in Deutschland verkaufen, wir hätten unsere eigenen Internetsuchmaschinen, Spielzeugfabriken und Textilunternehmen. Aber ist das überhaupt möglich?

Um sich einer Antwort auf diese Frage anzunähern, kann man sich in einem ersten Schritt anschauen, wie viel Geld Deutschland eigentlich im Ausland verdient. Im vergangenen Jahr wurden aus der Bundesrepublik Waren im Wert von 1.279 Milliarden Euro exportiert.

Schätzungen zufolge hängt jeder zweite Arbeitsplatz in der Industrie vom Export ab. Davon könnte man nun die Waren abziehen, die aus dem Ausland nach Deutschland eingeführt werden und künftig im Inland hergestellt würden. Sie haben einen Wert von 1.034 Milliarden Euro. Bleibt eine Differenz von 245 Milliarden Euro. Das ist viel Geld, aber gemessen an der gesamten jährlichen Wirtschaftsleistung von 3.263 Milliarden Euro auch nicht unglaublich viel.

Natürlich ließe sich eine solche Abkopplung nicht auf die Schnelle umsetzen, weil die deutschen Unternehmen in globale Lieferketten integriert sind und ihre Produktionsabläufe radikal umstellen müssten. Es müssten auch erst einmal in ausreichender Zahl Programmierer, Textilingenieure und Spielzeugerfinder ausgebildet werden, denn im Zuge der Globalisierung sind bestimmte Berufsgruppen in Deutschland praktisch komplett verschwunden. Und: Da Deutschland nicht über Öl und andere Bodenschätze verfügt, müssten zumindest diese Rohstoffe eingeführt werden dürfen, sonst wären die Folgen dramatisch.

Unter diesen Voraussetzungen wäre ein weitreichender Rückzug aus der Globalisierung zumindest in der Theorie machbar. Schließlich sind private Unternehmen Meister der Anpassung. Sie würden schon Mittel und Wege finden, um mit der neuen Lage fertigzuwerden.

Aber was würde das mit dem Land machen? An dieser Stelle muss man das Feld der harten Daten und Statistiken verlassen. Es gibt nämlich praktisch keinen modernen Industriestaat, der diesen Weg gegangen ist und als Beispiel dienen könnte. Zwar gibt es Länder wie Südafrika, die mit Sanktionen belegt und deshalb international isoliert wurden. Aber diese Sanktionen wurden in der Regel nach einigen Jahren wieder einkassiert, oder sie waren nicht so streng, dass sie den Handel komplett zum Erliegen brachten.

So lässt sich vielleicht Folgendes sagen: Wenn die Grenzen geschlossen würden, dann müsste das zumindest in der langen Frist nicht unbedingt mit Elend und Massenarbeitslosigkeit einhergehen. Die Deutschen würden sich weiter ernähren, kleiden und fortbewegen wollen. Und das bedeutet, dass es weiterhin für die Bevölkerung genug zu tun gäbe. Und weil Kategorien wie die internationale Wettbewerbsfähigkeit keine Rolle mehr spielten, wäre der Spielraum für eine Umverteilung des erwirtschafteten Wohlstands vermutlich größer.

Das Leben würde aber mit Sicherheit eintöniger. Südfrüchte beispielsweise lassen sich nur unter erheblichem Aufwand im Inland anbauen und würden wahrscheinlich deutlich teurer werden. Bestimmte Dinge – italienische Designermode, neue Medikamente aus den USA – gäbe es in Deutschland wohl überhaupt nicht mehr zu kaufen.

Der größte Nachteil wäre aber vermutlich, dass das Land in der selbst gewählten Isolation wirtschaftlich und gesellschaftlich erstarren würde. Denn Handel bringt vor allem Wandel, er löst Veränderungen aus, verbindet Menschen auf aller Welt und schafft somit ein Umfeld für Innovationen. Das ist zwar manchmal hart, etwa wenn Arbeitsplätze ins Ausland verlagert werden. Dennoch ist es eine wichtige Quelle des Wohlstands.

ISBN 978-3-425-73646-4

Writing: The global "flip-flop trail"

1. **Comprehension:** Outline the global production of flip-flops that Caroline Knowles refers to as the "flip-flop trail" in her article (A).
2. **Analysis:** Examine the given cartoon (B) and contrast it with Knowles' article.
3. **Writing a blog post:** After having read Knowles' article on the "flip-flop trail", you are wondering whether boycotting flip-flops is a good way of helping to end one of "globalisation's darker stories" (l. 55). Based on this article and materials dealt with in class, you decide to discuss boycotting flip-flops in a blog post on a website called "Globalization – a Blessing or a Curse".

(A)

How the flip-flop supply chain uncovers the dark side of globalization

The simplicity of the world's highest-selling shoe defies[1] the complexity of its production – a process involving immeasurable waste, impoverishment and displacement[2]

By Caroline Knowles, 9 July 2018, The Conversation

As you pack for your holidays, don't forget to pack your flip-flops – and treat them with respect. They may have travelled more than you and witnessed things you cannot see. Flip-flops may look simple and cheap, but they are part of a bigger and more complicated story. Flip-flops are the world's highest-selling shoe […]. Uncounted billions of them are made every year, often in small factories in China. […]

Many of us may regard [flip-flops] as beachwear but in some places, they are a prized pair of shoes for everyday use. They also tell stories of how globalisation actually works on the ground, as I discovered in following them along what I call the flip-flop trail[3].

Flip-flops are made from plastics, and so their story begins in the hydrocarbon[4] economy – in the oilfields of the Middle East. The raw material from which they are made is drilled[5] by migrant workers from Syria and southern India, who live in desert camps and work on drilling rigs[6] for 12-hour shifts in searing[7] heat.

Some of the petrochemicals[8] extracted from crude oil[9] are made into little plastic pellets in giant unpeopled plants[10] in the South Korean city of Daesan, an important centre globally producing the building blocks that make all kinds of plastics. These pellets are made by teams of petrochemical workers who prowl[11] the plant checking on the machinery they operate at a distance from computer screens.

The plastic pellets are bought by millions of small and medium-sized flip-flop factories throughout the world in production clusters where labour is cheap – places like Vietnam and various parts of Sub-Saharan Africa. Rural migrants still make them in southeast China, in small factories in industrial villages that sprout up[12] on farmland. Plastic waste is heaped around the countryside like small colourful mountains of acid pink and blue. […]

Flip-flops' biggest markets are in low income countries. Ethiopia, a landlocked[13] state in East Africa, is one of the biggest consumers of cheap flip-flops. Here, I followed the containers of flip-flops from the Somaliland coast and across the Ethiopian border to discover that many of the flip-flop routes are designed to evade import duties. […]

The flip-flop story ends, or so I thought, on a landfill site called Koshe on the outskirts of Addis Ababa[14]. Here I spoke to some of the 200 "scratchers", as they call themselves, who pick up waste materials like metal, wood and plastic that can be sold to recycling plants. […] Often unrecyclable plastic flip-flops will lie in the garbage for more than a hundred years before they decompose[15].

This flip-flop trail pieces together an unfamiliar picture of globalisation as an ad hoc mosaic of shifting connections between lives and ways of getting by, rather than the smooth operation of global commodity[16] chains we have been led to believe in. Connecting […] disposable workers, garbage pickers and the poorest of consumers, this is one of globalisation's darker stories.

(526 words)

[1] to **defy** = to refuse to follow a law or rule
[2] **displacement** = when people are forced to leave the place where they usually live
[3] **trail** = *Spur*
[4] **hydrocarbon** = *Kohlenwasserstoff (zur Herstellung von Plastik)*
[5] to **drill** = to make a deep hole
[6] **drilling rig** = *Bohrturm*
[7] **searing** = extremely hot
[8] **petrochemical** = raw material made from crude oil
[9] **crude oil** = *Erdöl, Rohöl*
[10] **plant** = factory
[11] to **prowl** = *herumstreifen, herumschleichen*
[12] to **sprout up** = to appear suddenly
[13] **landlocked** = without access to the sea
[14] the capital of Ethiopia
[15] to **decompose** = to rot, to decay
[16] **commodity** = a product that is bought and sold

(B)

The World According to Nike

Cartoonist Group

ISBN 978-3-425-73646-4

Listening 1: Globalization at the World Economic Forum

Listen to a report about a shift in perspective on the concept of globalization. (3:29)

You will hear the recording twice. First you will have time to read the tasks. After each listening, you will have time to complete your answers.

While listening, fill in the gaps.

Once a year, in January, Davos sees the return of the World Economic Forum; the perfect place for its wealthy members to (1) ______________________ opportunities, and enjoy a luxury skiing holiday at the same time.
This year, however, when Davos opened its doors once again, the ultra-rich brought with them an atmosphere of (2) ____________, defensiveness and self-reproach.

Above all things, the Davos men and women value economic globalization, and a (3) ________________ suggested this may be under attack.

In particular, members were worried about their plan to (4) ________________ in goods across borders. These fears were caused by the Brexit vote in the UK (the EU is the largest trading bloc in the world), and the (5) ________________ of Donald Trump, who is ardently against major trade agreements, in the US elections.
Now, the upcoming French and German elections could lead to anti-globalization parties (6) ____________________ than they ever have in the past.

Dambisa Moyo is usually an adamant supporter of free trade. However, at a recent panel called Governing Globalization, she (7) ______________ the audience to acknowledge the "significant losses" globalization has caused, which may be impossible to remedy "under the current infrastructure".
Even the head of the (8) ____________________, Christine Lagarde, has asked for "more redistribution".
Despite a long history of (9) __________________ the negative aspects of free trade, the Davos members finally owned up to the fact that globalization causes (10) __________________ wages. If nothing changed, they could only expect the (11) ____________________ to get even worse.

The last 18 months have been full of extreme political changes, caused at least in part by the (12) ____________ to globalization.
Bernie Sanders, in his quest to become the Democratic party candidate, (13) ______________ Hillary Clinton because she supports free trade. Donald Trump made no secret of his plan to (14) ________________ of trade to favour American industry over international trade, under the slogan "Americanism, not globalism".
Areas of the UK which were almost destroyed by (15) ______________ voted overwhelmingly for Brexit. British prime minister Theresa May, whose Conservative party stands for capital and (16) ________________, warned that many Brits believe more globalization will lead to "their jobs being outsourced and [their] wages undercut."

Across Europe, the far right have been condemning the (17) ________________ as well as goods. Marine Le Pen stated during the run-up to the French presidential election that the main issue within the election was the "rampant globalization that is (18) ______________________."

ISBN 978-3-425-73646-4

Listening 2: Facebook and the global community

Listen to radio host Rachel Martin talk to reporter Aarti Shahani about Mark Zuckerberg's essay "Building Global Community". (3:30)

You will hear the recording twice. First you will have time to read the tasks. After each listening, you will have time to complete your answers.

While listening, fill in the missing information. You do not need to write complete sentences.

1.	According to host Rachel Martin, Mark Zuckerberg's essay is about … (name two aspects)	a) b)
2.	According to Zuckerberg, people need to …	
3.	Therefore Facebook should be … (name two aspects)	a) b)
4.	Zuckerberg's essay appeals to …	
5.	What can be read between the lines, according to Aarti Shahani (name two aspects)	a) b)
6.	Two industries that have experienced the dangers of trusting Facebook too much	a) b)
7.	The main problem with the way news are presented on Facebook	
8.	How people have reacted to Zuckerberg's essay	

ISBN 978-3-425-73646-4

Mediation: Jobs of the future

With your social studies class you are taking part in an international school project about the future of work. Using the information from the article below, write a blog post for the project website. In your post, outline the changes in the world of work that are to be expected and introduce the jobs that are likely to be in demand in Germany ten years from now. End your blog post with a general recommendation for your fellow students and invite them to share pieces of information they have also found about the subject.

Diese sechs Jobs sind in zehn Jahren gefragt

Von Lars-Thorben Niggehoff, 22. Februar 2019, Welt online

[...] Jobs, die einst als sicher galten, könnten bald verschwinden. Unterdessen entstehen neue Berufe, die man vor zehn Jahren eher für Fantasiegebilde gehalten hätte. Oder wer hätte 2009 gedacht, dass Menschen heute gutes Geld als Social-Media-Manager verdienen? Laut einer Studie des McKinsey Global Institutes aus dem Jahr 2018 wird es mehrere große Trends geben: Einerseits fallen körperliche und Routinetätigkeiten weg. Denn Maschinen kommen zunehmend ohne Arbeiter aus, die sie bedienen müssen. [...]

Andererseits werden [...] Jobs, die technische Fertigkeiten erfordern, massiv zunehmen. Dazu zählt Datenanalyse in allen ihren Formen. [...]

Welchen Karriereweg sollte ein Jugendlicher heute einschlagen, um in zehn Jahren einen gefragten und sicheren Job zu haben? Sechs Ideen für Berufe und Branchen mit Zukunft:

1. Softwareentwickler

Die Architekten der digitalen Welt von morgen sind die Softwareentwickler. Ob Smartphones, der vernetzte Kühlschrank oder das selbstfahrende Auto: All diese Dinge laufen nicht ohne Software. [...]

Schon heute beklagt der IT-Branchenverband Bitkom, dass tausende Stellen für diese Experten in Deutschland unbesetzt bleiben. Besonders gefragt seien Softwareentwickler, die in Branchen wie der Automobilindustrie oder dem Maschinenbau Themen wie Big Data, Industrie 4.0 und Cloud Computing vorantrieben, sagt Juliane Petrich, Leiterin Bildung bei Bitkom. „Gesucht werden auch Entwickler für Apps und mobile Webseiten." [...] Am besten passen hier Informatik- oder Wirtschaftsinformatikstudiengänge. [...]

2. IT-Sicherheitsexperten

Wenn die Softwareentwickler die Architekten sind, dann sind die IT-Sicherheitsexperten die Polizisten. Unternehmen – aber auch Behörden – suchen händeringend nach qualifizierten Bewerbern. Hackerangriffe haben das Bewusstsein vieler Manager dafür geschärft, dass sie ihre Server und Datennetze nicht einfach ungeschützt lassen dürfen. Doch aktuell fehlen die Fachkräfte. [...] Die beste Grundlage für eine Karriere in diesem Bereich ist ein Informatikstudium. [...]

3. Datenanalysten

Mittlerweile haben auch Unternehmen außerhalb des Silicon Valley erkannt, welchen Mehrwert das Auswerten von Daten mit sich bringen kann. [...] Hier kommen Datenanalysten ins Spiel. Die müssen aus den Daten Prognosen ableiten oder Verbesserungspotenzial für Abläufe im Unternehmen entwickeln. Für den Job werden meist Leute mit Mathematik-, Informatik- oder Statistikstudium gesucht. [...]

4. Ingenieure

Auch ein klassischer Karriereweg hat gute Zukunftsaussichten: „Die Ingenieure werden wichtig bleiben, wir sind ein Industriestandort", prognostiziert Julia Klier, Expertin für das Thema „Future of Work" bei McKinsey und Professorin an der Universität Regensburg. [...] Dem Institut der deutschen Wirtschaft (IW) zufolge ist die Zahl offener Stellen im Ingenieurswesen im vergangenen Jahr um elf Prozent gestiegen. [...] Dem Branchenverband VDE zufolge werden in den nächsten zehn Jahren allein 100.000 Elektroingenieure benötigt. Robotikfachleute wiederum werden in der Fabrik der Zukunft zuhauf gebraucht, etwa in der Autoindustrie, wo Roboter zunehmend Aufgaben von Menschen übernehmen. [...]

5. Ärzte und Gesundheitsmanager

[...] Auch der demografische Wandel verändert die Berufe der Zukunft. Denn gerade die Deutschen werden immer älter [...]. „Um diese Menschen herum werden sich ganz neue Beschäftigungsmöglichkeiten ergeben", sagt McKinsey-Arbeitsexpertin Klier. Nicht nur der Bedarf an Pflegekräften und Physiotherapeuten, sondern auch die Nachfrage an Ärzten wird dadurch steigen. [...]

Wer sich nicht als Mediziner sieht, kann Gesundheitsmanager werden. Dann ist man etwa für die Leitung von Krankenhäusern oder Pflegeheimen verantwortlich. [...]

6. Der Job, den keiner kennt

Nicht vergessen darf man, dass es auch in Zukunft neue Jobs geben wird, die man sich heute noch nicht einmal vorstellen kann. Der IT-Dienstleister Cognizant hat in seiner Studie „21 Jobs of the Future" spekuliert, welche das sein könnten. So könnte es laut der Untersuchung in zehn Jahren Cyber City Analysts geben, die sich nur mit den in einer vernetzten Stadt anfallenden Datenmengen beschäftigen und diese nach Verbesserungsmöglichkeiten durchsuchen. [...]

Auch abseits der Digitalisierung könnten Jobs entstehen. Cognizant hält es etwa für möglich, dass in Zukunft Menschen Geld damit verdienen, dass sie den vielen Älteren Gesellschaft leisten. Das Konzept könnte ähnlich wie etwa das des Fahrdienstvermittlers Uber funktionieren. Begleiter und Rentner würden sich dann per App verbinden.

ISBN 978-3-425-73646-4

Writing: Saeed and Nadia

Read the following extract from the novel *Exit West* (2017) by Mohsin Hamid. The novel is set in an unnamed city increasingly afflicted by terror and unrest. There, two people meet and fall in love: Saeed, a young man from an educated, liberal background and Nadia, who broke away from her traditional family but nevertheless chooses to wear a black robe in public.

1. **Comprehension:** Outline what the extract is about.
2. **Analysis:** Compare Saaed und Nadia's character traits.
3. **Writing an assessment:** The Internet brings the global to the local. Asses its value for the society Saeed and Nadia live in. Refer to the extract as well as to materials dealt with in class.

Nadia and Saeed were, back then, always in possession of their phones. In their phones were antennas, and these antennas sniffed out[1] an invisible world, as if by magic, a world that was all around them, and also nowhere, transporting them to places distant and near, and to places that had never been and would never be. For many decades after independence[2] a telephone line in their city had remained a rare thing, the waiting list for a connection long, the teams that installed the copper wires and delivered the heavy handsets greeted and revered and bribed like heroes. But now wands[3] waved in the city's air, untethered[4] and free, phones in the millions, and a number could be obtained in minutes, for a pittance[5].

Saeed partly resisted the pull of his phone. He found the antenna too powerful, the magic it summoned too mesmerizing, as though he were eating a banquet of limitless food, stuffing himself, stuffing himself, until he felt dazed and sick, and so he had removed or hidden or restricted all but a few applications. His phone could make calls. His phone could send messages. His phone could take pictures, identify celestial bodies[6], transform the city into a map while he drove. But that was it. Mostly. Except for the hour each evening that he enabled the browser on his phone and disappeared down the byways of the internet. But this hour was tightly regulated, and when it ended, a timer would set off an alarm, a gentle, windy chime, as though from the breezy planet of some blue-shimmering science fiction priestess, and he would electronically lock away his browser and not browse again on his phone until the following day [...].

In contrast to Saeed, Nadia saw no need to limit her phone. It kept her company on long evenings, as it did countless young people in the city who were likewise stranded in their homes, and she rode it far out into the world on otherwise solitary, stationary nights. [...] Nadia frequently explored the terrain of social media, though she left little trace of her passing, not posting much herself, and employing opaque usernames and avatars, the online equivalents of her black robes. It was through social media that Nadia ordered the shrooms[7] Saeed and she would eat on the night they first became physically intimate, shrooms still being available for cash-on-demand couriered delivery in their city those days. The police and anti-narcotic agencies were focused on other, more market-leading substances, [...] a fact exploited by a middle-aged local man with a ponytail who ran a small side business [...] and [...] was followed and liked in cyberspace mostly by the young.

In a few months this ponytailed man would be beheaded [...].

But even now the city's freewheeling virtual world stood in stark[8] contrast to the day-to-day lives of most people, to those of young men, and especially of young women, and above all of children who went to sleep unfed[9] but could see on some small screen people in foreign lands preparing and consuming and even conducting food fights with feasts[10] of such opulence that the very fact of their existence boggled the mind[11]. [...]

(533 words)

[1] to **sniff out** *(infml)* = to discover
[2] a reference to the country's colonial past
[3] **wand** = magic stick
[4] **untethered** = unleashed, set free
[5] **pittance** = very little money
[6] **celestial bodies** = *Himmelskörper*
[7] **shrooms** *(infml)* = psychedelic mushrooms
[8] **stark** = obvious, clear
[9] **unfed** = without having eaten
[10] **feast** = *Festmahl*
[11] to **boggle the mind** = to be unbelievable

ISBN 978-3-425-73646-4

Listening: A historic anti-immigration speech

a) Listen to the first part of a report on Enoch Powell's "Rivers of Blood" speech and its reverberations in present day debates over national identity. (4:15)

You will hear the recording twice. First you will have time to read the tasks. After each listening, you will have time to complete your answers.

While listening, fill in the missing information. You do not need to write complete sentences.

1.	When did Enoch Powell give his speech?	
2.	What was the speech about?	
3.	Which aspect of Enoch Powell's speech can be identified in present day debates over national identity?	
4.	What was the Race Relations Act about? (name three aspects)	a) b) c)
5.	Why did immigrants from former colonies come to GB in the first place?	
6.	Wolverhampton was one of the first towns in the UK affected by …	
7.	What was bus driver Tarsem Singh Sandhu, a Sikh, ordered to do or otherwise be not allowed to continue working? (name two aspects)	a) b)
8.	Sandhu being fired led to …	
9.	According to Powell, the middle-aged white man feared that in 15–20 years …	
10.	According to Powell's biographer Simon Heffer, Powell himself feared that immigrant communities …	
11.	What gave the speech its name?	

ISBN 978-3-425-73646-4

b) Now listen to the second part of the report. (2:46)

You will hear the recording twice. First you will have time to read the tasks. After each listening, you will have time to complete your answers.

While listening, match the institutions or people **1** to **6** with the statements **A** to **I**. There are two more statements than you need.

1	The Times of London
2	Many British people
3	Eleanor Smith (2x)
4	Sathnam Sanghera
5	Chris Hannan
6	Uteldra Veronica Warren

A	was attacked after the speech.
B	wonders what Enoch Powell would think about today's Wolverhampton.
C	were afraid of tensions with the immigrant communities.
D	didn't like the way Wolverhampton has moved on.
E	agreed with what Powell said.
F	declared Powell's speech to be very bad.
G	considers today's Wolverhampton as an example of multiculturalism.
H	claims that white people in England feel as though they're a minority.
I	thinks that the debate over Brexit is similar to the discussions at the time of the speech.

1	2	3	4	5	6

ISBN 978-3-425-73646-4

Mediation: National identity

Having discussed the question of British identity in their social studies class, your English friend wonders what it means to be German. In order to provide them with some information, you decide to write an email in which you outline the problems with defining a shared sense of nationality as presented in the article.

◀◀ / ▶▶ https://www

© shutterstock/Andrey_Popov

Auf der Suche nach dem Wirgefühl

Ein Werkstattgespräch: Auf Einladung der Berliner Festspiele, des Tagesspiegels und anderer diskutieren Politiker und Kulturschaffende über die deutsche Identität.

Von Ulrike Scheffer, 17. September 2017, Der Tagesspiegel online

Wer sind wir, was wollen wir sein, wer waren wir je? Kurz: Deutschsein, was ist das eigentlich? Thomas Oberender, Intendant der Berliner Festspiele, ist überzeugt, „dass diese Frage uns alle bedrängt". Doch wie führt man eine Debatte über deutsche Identität oder eine deutsche Leitkultur in Zeiten des Populismus? Wo „draußen ein Herr Gauland von der AfD lauert, der uns alle entsorgen will", wie die Migrationsforscherin Naika Foroutan sagt?

Das Haus der Berliner Festspiele versuchte es am Sonntag, eine Woche vor der Bundestagswahl, mit einer Gedankenwerkstatt. Kooperationspartner sind der Deutsche Kulturrat, der DGB, die Initiative kulturelle Integration und der Tagesspiegel; Chefredakteur Stephan-Andreas Casdorff moderierte. Überraschendes Ergebnis dieses Experiments: Auch viele Zuwanderer in Deutschland sind auf Identitätssuche – und verzweifeln mitunter am Hang ihrer deutschen Mitbürger zur Selbstleugnung. „Wie und womit sollen sie sich da identifizieren?", fragt Naika Foroutan. Das Grundgesetz und formale Regeln für das Zusammenleben – in Deutschland gibt man sich die Hand – reichten als Identifikationsgrundlage nicht. „Es gibt das Bedürfnis nach etwas Übergeordnetem, etwas Verbindendem."

„Wenn Integration funktionieren soll, brauchen wir etwas über den rechtlichen Rahmen hinaus," sagt auch Ali Can. Der junge Deutsche mit türkischen Wurzeln hat eine Hotline für besorgte Bürger eingerichtet und den Verein „Interkultureller Frieden" gegründet.

Ein Viertel aller Deutschen hat einen Migrationshintergund, sagt Sawsan Chebli

Foroutans „Angebot", wie sie sagt, lautet schlicht Solidarität, hergeleitet aus dem Marxismus und der Soziallehre. Für Sawsan Chebli, Kind palästinensischer Flüchtlinge und heute Staatssekretärin im Berliner Senat, kann hingegen aus der gelungenen Aufarbeitung des Nationalsozialismus ein positives Narrativ für die deutsche Zuwanderungsgesellschaft erwachsen. „Wir können daraus den Auftrag ableiten, uns gemeinsam für eine demokratische Kultur und für Menschenrechte einzusetzen." Und: „Wir überfordern Migranten nicht, wenn wir sie in diesen Kampf als Lehre aus dem Holocaust einbinden."

Die Zeiten, in denen die Mehrheitsgesellschaft anderen vorgebe, wie sie zu leben hätten, seien allerdings vorbei, ergänzt Chebli. Ein Viertel aller Deutschen hätte mittlerweile einen Migrationshintergrund. „Schon deshalb kann Deutschsein heute nicht mehr über die Abstammung oder Religion definiert werden." Eine Leitkultur, die Ethnizität und Religion vollständig ausklammert, ist nach Auffassung Naika Foroutans aber ebenfalls nicht mehr zeitgemäß. Für viele seien dies wieder wichtige Bezugspunkte.

Mehr als ein zivilisiertes Miteinander kann es nicht geben, sagt Michael Wolffsohn

AfD und Pegida zum Trotz dominieren bei diesem Werkstattgespräch optimistische Zukunftserwartungen. Allein der deutsch-israelische Historiker und Publizist Michael Wolffsohn will sich dem nicht anschließen. Pessimistisch stimmt ihn vor allem die zunehmende Radikalisierung der „alten neuen Rechten" auf der einen und einer Minderheit von Migranten auf der anderen Seite, die sich bis zum Bürgerkrieg auswachsen könne. Historisch betrachtet sei das allerdings kein Einzelfall. „Migrationskrisen sind nichts Neues. Die Weltgeschichte ist letztlich nichts anderes als eine Geschichte der Migration – die selten friedlich verlief."

Vor diesem geschichtlichen Hintergrund rät Wolffsohn zudem, sich von einem kollektiven Wirgefühl zu verabschieden. Deutschland sei eine im Lauf der Geschichte entstandene Gemeinschaft von Leuten, die zufällig am selben Ort lebten, so seine Argumentation. Selbst die Bayern seien eine Mischung aus Germanen, Kelten und römischen Legionären. Was folgt daraus? „Wir müssen den Mut haben, ins Nichts zu blicken", sagt Michael Wolffsohn. Mehr als ein zivilisiertes Miteinander von Altdeutschen und Neudeutschen, wie er es nennt, könne es nicht geben. „Alles andere ist Illusion."

ISBN 978-3-425-73646-4

Writing: What is "British"?

1. **Comprehension:** Briefly summarize the poem *We're British and We Know It* by Josie Whitehead (A) and the introduction to the book *The How To Be British Collection* by Martyn Ford and Peter Legon (B).
2. **Analysis:** Analyse how both texts define Britishness in terms of structure, style and content.
3. **Writing a blog post:** You have dealt with the question of Britishness in class. While browsing the Internet you have come across a blog with posts and comments on Britishness in the wake of the Brexit referendum. This blog is contributed to and read by people from all over the world. You decide to write a blog post in which you compare Whitehead's poem with Ford and Legon's introduction and critically comment on their depiction of Britishness.

(A)

We're British and We Know It

We're British, and we know it.
We're surrounded by the sea.
We start our day each morning
With our morning cup of tea.

Roast beef and Yorkshire pudding
Go hand in hand of course.
Apple pies or rhubarb crumble –
Not without the custard sauce!

We're British and we know it,
And our countryside's a dream –
And you'll find some English tearooms
Serving scones with jam and cream.

The tinkle[1] of the china[2] cups,
But allow the tea to brew,
Or to mash the tea for some folk –
Well, it just depends on you.

We're British and we know it.
Our history goes way back
And we fight to keep our islands
And we drive our foes all back.

We love our country villages
And cricket on the green,
And the pride in British gardens
Is something to be seen.

You can say that you are British
If you love your fish and chips.
British men don't show emotions –
They just keep stiff upper lips.

To jump the queue is something
That you never, ever do!
It was bound to be the British
Who invented the first queue.

British men just love their football –
It's then you'll hear them shout.
They let off steam, they down their beer,
And stiff upper lips are out.

They support their teams most strongly
And, if it's a winning side ,
You'll see that they are British
As they wave their flags with pride.

British folk are known by everyone
To be tolerant and fair
But they'll quickly rise in combat,
So you foreigners, take care!!

The British pint[3] is known to all
And cricket on the green.
It's Britain where I'm growing old –
With grace – just like our Queen!

Josie Whitehead

(B)

[...] If you are a visitor to our country I expect by now you have realized why we call it **Great** Britain: our long and glorious history; the unspoilt beauty of our landscape; the rich variety of our weather, not to mention our unrivalled achievements in cricket and football. Then there are our cherished traditions: afternoon tea at four, roast beef on Sunday, and warm beer until 11pm. And there's us, with our old-world courtesy[4] and tolerance. Oh, and our sense of humour. I mustn't forget that. We *do* like a good laugh!

As for me, well, I'm so many feet and inches tall, and I weigh so many stones, pounds and ounces. My petrol comes in gallons and my milk in pints – from a milkman. I pay for them, of course, in *pounds sterling*. My home is my castle and I 'Do-it-Myself'. I only hope I live to pay off the mortgage on it. My garden is my recreation and sanctuary[5] to many endangered species, not least of all myself!

[1] **tinkle** = a light ringing sound, [2] **china** = porcelain, [3] **pint** = a unit for measuring an amount of liquid, especially beer or milk (0.568 liters)
[4] **courtesy** = polite behaviour towards other people, [5] **sanctuary** = a peaceful place that is safe and provides protection

ISBN 978-3-425-73646-4

Listening 1: A royal wedding

You will hear a report that was broadcast the day before the wedding between Prince Harry and Megan Markle in 2018. (4:17)

You will hear the recording twice. First you will have time to read the tasks. After each listening, you will have time to complete your answers.

While listening, match the speakers **1** to **7** with the statements **A** to **I**. There are two more statements than you need.

1	Marie Louise Kelly, host
2	Frank Langfitt, NPR's reporter
3	Emma Jones
4	Mike Oke (at the barbershop)
5	Unidentified reporter
6	Prince Harry
7	Mary Brazier

A	is a big fan of Prince Harry and therefore particularly interested in the royal wedding.
B	talks about nude pictures of Prince Harry after a game of strip poker in Vegas.
C	gives an account of people of colour around the globe celebrating the upcoming wedding.
D	introduces the upcoming story as one of a changing Britain and the redemption of a formally naughty prince.
E	explains the unconventionality of Prince Harry's bride by choice.
F	says that the Afro-Caribbean population in Packham and also in Trinidad are celebrating the arrival of diversity within the royal family.
G	opens up about the emotional effects of losing a mother at a young age.
H	is pleased about the royals welcoming Meghan Markle as someone of black heritage into the family.
I	is happy for Prince Harry not to marry another aristocrat, but to live his life and his emotions.

1	2	3	4	5	6	7

ISBN 978-3-425-73646-4

Listening/Viewing 2: Millennials on Britishness

Listen to various young people talking about what they think "Britain" and "Being British" means to them. (2:16)

You will hear the recording twice. First you will have time to read the task. After each listening, you will have time to complete your answers.

While listening, fill in the gaps.

- It fills me with pride to be British. As a (1) ____________________, I'd say we're rather strong and (2) ____________________ in many ways.
- Britain is a collective of countries all cooperating. It's clear we are separate countries, but as a group we (3) ______________________________.
- Britain is my home. Being British, it's clearly part of my (4) ________________. But that doesn't mean I feel (5) ____. My identity is part Irish, part Scottish and part English.
- As a Welsh woman, being "British" feels like a (6) ____________________ identity. I like that all the countries of the United Kingdom share an identity together as well as in our (7) ____________________ countries… that's what I think being British means.
- Britain is full of different cultures, and I think being "British" (8) ______________________ that.
- Compared to other countries, the British are very (9) __________________________________ arriving from other parts of the world.
- Being British means you show (10) ____________________ towards everyone, no matter what.
- (11) __________________________ – especially sharing food from different cultures.
- My main concern with Britishness is manufacturing; we should be trying (12) __________________________ within the country. Nowadays, all our manufacturing is done in other countries, and we should bring businesses back to Britain.
- Britain is only really known for London. All the tourists come here to see the (13) ________________________________, and all the rest of London.
- Britishness is less about the cities and more about the (14) ____________________________. There are also some very British hobbies, like going for a (15) _______________________, and having a cup of tea.
- In terms of human rights, the people are very clever and there's (16) ________________________________. British people are trustworthy.
- The stereotype of Britain is that the people have (17) ___________. Obviously every country has its own culture, but being British in particular comes with certain (18) _______________________.
- Drinking a (19) _________________, eating fish-and-chips… and also being able to understand irony and (20) ______________________.
- The most important thing about being British for me is the (21) ______________________________________.
- Overall, I am (22) ________________________________. I could never imagine being anything else.

 ISBN 978-3-425-73646-4

Mediation: Brexit

Your pen pal from Liverpool wonders how the decision for Brexit has affected Britons living Germany. You have found this article about one of the many Britons who have decided to apply for German citizenship since the referendum in 2016. In an email to your friend, summarize the article and state the reason Ian Bennett from Hamburg decided to become a German citizen.

Engländer in Hamburg: Keinen Bock auf Brexit

Von Bert Beyers, 23. März 2019, NDR.de

„Sie sind bestimmt schon der 20. Brite heute", sagt die Mitarbeiterin im Hamburger Einwohner-Zentralamt zu Ian Bennett und überreicht ihm dem Antrag, um die deutsche Staatsbürgerschaft zu erlangen. Die Zeit drängt, Stichtag ist der 29. März. Das ist der Tag, an dem Großbritannien die EU ursprünglich verlassen wollte. Bis zu diesem Tag können Briten den Antrag in Hamburg stellen. Die Zahl der Anträge auf Einbürgerung von britischen Staatsbürgern ist in diesem Jahr noch mal deutlich gestiegen. Bis Ende Februar waren es fast 200, Tendenz steigend. In Hamburg leben rund 4.000 Staatsbürger mit britischem Pass.

„Wie haben Sie denn den hier reingeschmuggelt?", fragt ein anderer Behördenmitarbeiter – und deutet auf „Polly", den kleinen Hund von Ian Bennett. Nach Polly habe am Eingang des Gebäudes in der Nähe des Wandsbeker Marktplatzes niemand gefragt, sagt er lachend.

Erfolgreich verdrängt

Ian Bennett hat einen Brief von Olaf Scholz in der Tasche. Darin hat der ehemalige Erste Bürgermeister dem Englischlehrer und Übersetzer nahegelegt, die deutsche Staatsbürgerschaft zu erwerben. Das ist nun schon eine Weile her. Scholz ist mittlerweile in Berlin, Ian Bennett immer noch in Hamburg. Er konnte sich bislang nicht zu dem Schritt durchringen. Nun herrscht im Einwohner-Zentralamt Hochbetrieb. „Die haben auch keinen Bock auf Brexit mehr", sagt Ian Bennett. „Ich sowieso nicht." Bislang hat er das Thema erfolgreich verdrängt. Als Engländer werde er fast täglich darauf angesprochen. Langsam nerve es.

Zwei Zuhause

Wenn Ian Bennett zu seinen Eltern nach England fliegt, dann geht es „nach Hause". Zurück nach Hamburg geht es ebenfalls „nach Hause". Die englische Staatsbürgerschaft kann er behalten. Die deutsche Staatsbürgerschaft ist für ihn erstmal ein Papier, das ihm erlaubt, sein Leben wie gehabt weiterzuführen. „Ich fühle mich nicht als Verräter, es ist nur eine Verwaltungsmaßnahme."

Zum ersten Mal war der Engländer 1992 als Austauschschüler in Deutschland, damals im Alter von 17 Jahren. Seit 2005 lebt er nun in Hamburg. Er ist mit einer Deutschen verheiratet. Hamburg ist der gemeinsame Lebensmittelpunkt des Paares, hier wollen sie auch Kinder großziehen.

Die meisten britischen Freunde von Ian Bennett in Hamburg lassen kein gutes Haar am Brexit – und an den Menschen, die dafür gestimmt haben. „Aber das ist auch keine Lösung. Wenn man nur schimpft, hat man kein Verständnis für die Spaltung in England." Er kommt aus der Stadt Wigan in der Nähe von Liverpool. Dort haben mehr als 60 Prozent für den Brexit gestimmt. Die Spaltung geht quer durch Familien, durch Nachbarschaften und Parteien, das ist es, was ihn umtreibt: „Mein Land ist ein bisschen kaputt" – und es sei schwer, nun wieder eine Brücke zwischen den verschiedenen Lagern zu bauen.

Selber hat Ian Bennett nicht an dem Referendum teilgenommen. Er durfte nicht, war schon zu lange in Hamburg. Er hätte es auch nicht gewollt. Für ihn war das eine Sache der Briten auf der Insel. Was ihn traurig stimmt ist, dass die nächste Generation in England es nicht mehr so einfach haben wird, als Europäer in anderen Ländern der EU zu leben, so wie er – das sei schade.

Fünf WM-Titel

An den Hamburgern mag er den respektvollen Umgang miteinander und die Informiertheit der Menschen. Was ihm manchmal fehlt, ist der englische Humor. Mittlerweile sieht er auch Vorteile in der doppelten Staatsbürgerschaft. England war einmal Fußballweltmeister, Deutschland viermal. Er selber bringt es nun also auf fünf Titel.

Bis Ian Bennett kommende Woche seinen Antrag zur Einbürgerung abgibt, muss er noch ein wenig Papierkrieg erledigen: Heiratsurkunde, Einkommensbescheid und vielleicht muss er auch noch einen Test ablegen. Eine der möglichen Fragen hat die Mitarbeiterin im Einwohner-Zentralamt schon verraten: Wie viele Bundesländer hat Deutschland?

ISBN 978-3-425-73646-4

Writing: Scottish novels

1. **Comprehension:** Outline the two contrary positions presented in the article.
2. **Analysis:** Contrast Butlin and Crumey's views on whether it is possible to distinguish Scottish from English writing and analyse how they try to convince the readers of their respective positions.
3. **Writing a comment:** Ron Butlin claims that "all good novels emerge from their native culture". Explain what he means by that and write a comment on this view.

Writing Divided: can you tell a Scottish novelist from an English one?

The First Minister says it is always possible to tell the difference between the work of a Scottish novelist and an English one. Here, two leading writers debate the issue […].

7 July 2011, The Scotsman

It might seem like a parlour game[1], but in a way working out if you can tell a writer is Scottish just by reading what he or she has written goes right to the heart of what nationalism is about. […]

In a recent interview, First Minister Alex Salmond said Scotland had a culture that was distinct and quite separate from England. "Unionism[2] hasn't been based on culture. Obviously there is the same language albeit with different accents, but you couldn't get two more different cultures," he said. "Nobody would mistake a Scottish novelist for an English novelist."

Ah, but can you? Are Scots and English really as predictable as that, so much so that their writers' novels can be so easily categorised? […]

On these pages, two acclaimed Scottish writers take up positions on either side of the debate. […]

© shutterstock/Simple Line

AGREE – Ron Butlin: 'We really cannot mistake them as novelists from anywhere else'

Alex Salmond's remark about nobody mistaking a Scottish novelist for an English one works both ways – and should be celebrated by us all, whichever side of the Border we live on, as all good novels emerge from their native culture.

That is important because it gives a novel depth. Without it, novels would be like a collection of maps that refer to all landscapes equally, or to none at all. Shoddy[3] novels are like this – they have no real context and no significance to anything or anywhere. With no sense of personality, let alone national identity, they often seem written in a kind of universal Google-speak that could mean anything or nothing.

Thankfully, there's more to being a Scottish novelist than being born north of the Border. Forget the 50 words they have for rain and the three languages to shout the odds in, their Scottishness runs deep. Recently it has become crucial to us all.

Alasdair Gray could never be mistaken for an English novelist – just as Dickens created literary London and Balzac Paris, Gray has made Glasgow come alive to the rest of the world, and to us. […]

Let's imagine that James Kelman suddenly revealed to us that he is English. Not a word of his works are changed – the same fractured characters still struggle to discover their dignity amid the same everyday disillusionment and despair. But something would feel very different, wouldn't it? […]

For most of its history Scotland has been a country, but only just, and lack of self-belief was branded onto the Scottish heart at birth. Until recently, that is. With devolution[4], a spring has been put into our step – we're exploring the possibilities of self-confidence. We've become political adolescents – grown up, but not quite. Whatever, we're certainly cultivating attitude!

At some level […] these vital issues of our culture are being examined by Scottish writers.

The politics of this sea-change[5] in our history is too important to be left to party politicians, nor can the arts be entrusted wholesale to mouse-click bureaucrats. Today, as never before, Scottish novelists are speaking to us with real urgency.

We really cannot mistake them as novelists from anywhere else, nor ignore the importance of what they have to tell to us.

DISAGREE – Andrew Crumey: 'Great art serves to bring down boundaries, not raise them'

The First Minister reportedly believes nobody would mistake a Scottish novelist for an English one.

Quite a claim, considering that people have been arguing for years about whether you can tell without prior knowledge if a writer is male or female, black or white, gay or straight. Countless readers have been fooled. Novelists and politicians share one thing: they're good at making things up. If you can work out everything about a

⟶

ISBN 978-3-425-73646-4

novelist from their novels, they're surely doing something wrong.

As a boy, reading *The Hound Of The Baskervilles*, I had no idea that the creator of Sherlock Holmes was born in Edinburgh. No doubt an expert could find some tell-tale[6] sign, but how is the average reader supposed to know that a story about a London-based detective working on a case in Dartmoor was actually written by a Scot?

Alex Salmond's remark was an off-the-cuff[7] comment by someone who has far more important things to think about than novels. More significant, though, is the false premise it rests upon: that a novelist may be English or Scottish, but not both. What about Arthur Conan Doyle? For most of his life he lived in England. If the English want to claim him as one of theirs, they surely have every right.

We do it ourselves. A few years ago, some pundits[8] put together a list of the "100 Best Scottish Books". It included George Orwell's 1984, on the basis that Orwell wrote it while living on Jura[9]. Other Scottish residents who made it onto the list were JK Rowling (born in Gloucestershire), and Bernard MacLaverty (born in Belfast). By the same reckoning, a list of England's best writers could include Ali Smith and Jackie Kay, who both live there.

All of which leaves the idea that you can tell a "Scottish" novelist just by reading them a bit up in the air. [...]

Go to Berlin, ask what sort of writer Kafka was, and you'll be told he was German. In Jerusalem, the answer would be Jewish. In this country we think of Kafka as Czech, though the country he was born in was Bohemia, part of the Austro-Hungarian Empire. The first English translations of his novels were by Edwin and Willa Muir, so maybe *The Trial* should have been in that list of "100 Best Scottish Books". [...]

Every nation has a right to be proud of its cultural products. None has a right to exclusive ownership. [...]

When you read any novel you can't be sure if the writer is Scottish, English, both or neither. What you can decide for yourself is whether or not the book is any good. Cultural figures will always be used as political footballs by people whose agenda is not primarily artistic. But great art serves to bring down boundaries, not raise them.

(1060 words)

[1] **parlour game** = *Gesellschaftsspiel*
[2] **unionism** = *here:* the historical process of making Scotland a part of the United Kingdom
[3] **shoddy** *(infml)* = of poor quality
[4] **devolution** = *here:* the process in the UK of giving more political power to regional parliaments
[5] **sea-change** = a very big and significant change
[6] **tell-tale** = *bezeichnend, verräterisch*
[7] **off-the-cuff** = without thinking
[8] **pundit** = expert
[9] **Jura** = name of a Scottish island

ISBN 978-3-425-73646-4

Listening/Viewing 1: The American Dream

In her show *The Point*, Ana Kasparian asks her guests what the American Dream means to them. (4:10)

You will hear the recording twice. First you will have time to read the tasks. After each listening, you will have time to complete your answers.

While listening, match the speakers **1** to **4** with the statements **A** to **F**. There are two more answers than you need.

1	Kelly Carlin, writer and radio host
2	Fred Karger, political consultant
3	Ryan Singer, comedian
4	Ana Kasparian, host of the show

The American Dream …

A	… is to be able to afford the life you want to have.
B	… changed in the 1980s from a self-centered attitude to a dream which includes everyone.
C	… is the ability to do your dream job even if you earn very little.
D	… changes constantly. Particularly since the 1980s, there has been a noticeable shift from a communal way of thinking to a rather egotistical one.
E	… is about improving people's lives gradually.
F	… is something every nation in the world aspires to.

1	2	3	4

ISBN 978-3-425-73646-4

Listening 2: Being black in Princeton

Listen to former First Lady of the United States Michelle Obama reading from her memoir *Becoming*, published in November 2018. In the extract, she describes starting college at the prestigious Princeton University in the 1980s. (4:27)

You will hear the recording twice. First you will have time to read the tasks. After each listening, you will have time to complete your answers.

While listening, fill in the missing information. You do not need to write complete sentences.

1.	The groups of people Michelle spent time with as a student (name two)	a) b)
2.	What Michelle did in her free time (name two activities)	a) b)
3.	What the university administration wanted the students to do	
4.	On college campuses, the "burden of assimilation" is carried by …	
5.	The challenges many non-white students faced (name two aspects)	a) b)
6.	The number of roommates Michelle had	
7.	With regard to white students, Michelle describes her younger self as …	
8.	What the mother of Cathy, one of Michelle's roommates, asked the university to do	
9.	The reason Cathy's mother contacted the university	
10.	Cathy's family background (name two aspects)	a) b)
11.	What Cathy eventually did	

ISBN 978-3-425-73646-4

Mediation: A German entrepreneur

Your American friend is taking part in a school project about the American Dream. You have found an article about the German entrepreneur Dirk Roßmann. You want to persuade your friend that Germany can also be a land of opportunity. In an email to your friend, summarize the article, focusing on the advice Dirk Roßmann gives to the pupils of his former school.

Dirk Roßmann besucht seine alte Schule

Der erfolgreiche Unternehmer Dirk Roßmann hat in seiner früheren Schule, der Berufsbildenden Schule 11, aus seinem Buch gelesen und den Schülern erklärt, dass gute Noten und unternehmerischer Erfolg nicht unbedingt zusammenhängen.

Von Saskia Döhner, 2. Mai 2019, Hannoversche Allgemeine

Auch nach 58 Jahren ist das Gefühl immer noch da – der Respekt vor Schule. Der Unternehmer Dirk Roßmann ist zurückgekehrt an die Schule, an der er zwischen 1961 und 1964 seinen Berufschulabschluss als Drogist gemacht hat. Er sei nie gern zur Schule gegangen, erzählt der Unternehmer den rund 500 Schülern in der voll besetzten Aula der Berufsbildenden Schule 11. „Schule war nicht so mein Ding." Wobei die Zeit an der Berufsschule schon okay gewesen sei, wie der heute 72-Jährige sagt.

Zu dumm für die Mittelschule?

Die schlechten Erinnerungen stammen von früher. Von der Volksschule, von der Mittelschule, der Werner-von-Siemens-Schule, die er schon nach einem halben Jahr auf Anraten seines Lehrers wieder verlassen hatte. Der Junge sei einfach nicht gescheit genug für diese Schulform, habe der Lehrer damals seiner Mutter gesagt, berichtet Roßmann. „Heute führe ich ein Unternehmen mit 56.000 Mitarbeitern und mache fast zehn Milliarden Euro Umsatz im Jahr." Das würde er seinem Lehrer gern mal ins Gesicht sagen, fügt der „Drogeriekönig" hinzu. Die Schüler applaudieren lang und anhaltend.

Heute Unternehmer mit 56.000 Mitarbeitern

Es sei schon richtig, dass seine Leistungen in der Schule früher „sauschlecht" gewesen seien, sagt Roßmann. Ein Tipp hat er an die Jugendlichen: „Lernt richtig Englisch, das braucht man, wenn man ins Ausland reist." Ein bisschen Rechnen zu können, sei auch gut, meint er. Noch wichtiger aber sei: „Geben Sie nie zu früh auf", rät er den Jugendlichen, „es ist fast alles möglich, wenn man kein Erfolg hat oder es Gegenwind gibt, dann kein Bock mehr zu haben, das geht nicht", stellt er klar. Seine Frau, mit der er seit 37 Jahren verheiratet sei, sage immer: „Wenn sich dich vorn rausschmeißen, musst du von hinten wieder reingehen." Auch sein Unternehmen habe in den neunziger Jahren vor der Insolvenz gestanden, dann sei es irgendwann wieder aufwärtsgegangen, erzählt Roßmann. [...]

„Geld, um frei zu sein"

Dass man in der Schule fürs Leben lerne, sei Quatsch. Lernen müsse man sein Leben lang, sagt der Unternehmer, nicht nur in der Schule. Menschen sollten sich für die Welt interessieren, in der sie lebten.

Roßmann liest aus seinem Buch „ ... und dann bin ich auf den Baum geklettert." „Als ich zur Welt kam, lag diese in Trümmern", sagt er. Im September 1946 wurde Dirk Roßmann geboren, der Zweite Weltkrieg war erst im Mai 1945 beendet worden. Seine Mutter Hilde gehörte zu den ersten Frauen, die in Hannover den Führerschein machten. Die Familie mütterlicherseits hatte ein Pelzgeschäft, das war Großbürgertum, die Familie seines Vaters war ärmer, Kaufleute aus einfachen Verhältnissen. Geld sei in seiner Kindheit immer knapp gewesen. Umso wichtiger sei es ihm schon als kleiner Junge gewesen, Geld zu besitzen, nicht zum Horten wie Dagobert Duck, sondern zum Ausgeben, um sich aus den Abhängigkeiten zu befreien: „Ich wollte nie Befehlsempfänger sein." Ihm sei klar geworden, dass er selbstständig sein wollte. „Der Mensch braucht Geld, um fei zu sein."

ISBN 978-3-425-73646-4

Writing: Upward mobility

You are an intern at the *Pacific Standard* magazine and have to decide on a suitable cartoon to accompany Tom Jacobs' article, which will be published on the magazine's website.

1. **Comprehension:** Briefly summarize Tom Jacobs' article below.
2. **Analysis:** Analyse cartoons **A** and **B** (on the next page).
3. **Writing an evaluation:** Write an email to the editors in which you evaluate if either of the cartoons goes well with the article.

◂◂ / ▸▸ https://www

New Research Debunks[1] the Upward Mobility Myth

You're far more likely to hold a high-status occupation if your parents did the same.

By Tom Jacobs, 6 September 2018, Pacific Standard

In America, if you're ambitious and work hard, you can move up the socioeconomic ladder. At least, that's the truism[2] we all grew up believing.

But new research suggests such social mobility is far from the norm. It finds you are significantly more likely to hold a high-status (which usually means higher-paying) job if your parents held similarly prestigious positions.

"Your circumstances at birth – specifically, what your parents do for a living – are an even bigger factor in how far you get in life than we had previously realized," Michael Hout, the New York University sociologist who conducted the study, said in announcing the results. "Generations of Americans considered the United States to be a land of opportunity. This research raises some sobering[3] questions about that image."

Hout utilized data on 20,856 Americans who participated in the General Social Survey between 1994 and 2016. The occupations of participants and their parents were ranked by "social standing" on a 100-point socioeconomic index, ranging from physician (93 points) to flight attendant (53) to shoe shiner (nine).

"American workers face dramatically different opportunities, depending on their parents' occupations," Hout reports in the *Proceedings of the National Academy of Sciences.*

Specifically, he found half of the Americans surveyed whose parents held top-tier[4] occupations worked in jobs ranked at 76 or higher on that 100-point scale. Half of those whose parents' jobs were in the bottom tier were in jobs that scored 28 or under.

"Father's and mother's status were both significant factors in people's occupational success," Hout adds, "but father consistently had more influence."

The strong influence of one's parents' jobs on one's own occupation remained consistent for the entire period he examined (1994 to 2016). So why is the image of mom and dad being outdone[5] by their offspring so pervasive[6]?

Hout argues we have been misled by the fact that, for the Baby Boomer generation, pretty much everybody experienced upward mobility as part of the post-World War II economic boom. "Ninety percent of young adults earned more than their parents did, and 60 percent worked in higher-status occupations," he notes. This was due to "broad economic growth and occupational transformation, not from equal chances to take advantage of opportunity," he writes. The waning of these trends in recent decades, he adds, has "unmasked" the reality that people from lower socioeconomic backgrounds have a tough time moving up.

The social stagnation this study suggests is even more problematic since blue-collar jobs[7] are not providing the sort of robust paychecks they once did. Perhaps it's time to stop blindly believing that America makes it easy to move up in the world, and start implementing efforts to make that mirage[8] a reality.

(478 words)

[1] to **debunk** = to prove that an idea is wrong
[2] **truism** = a well-known idea
[3] **sobering** = serious
[4] **top-tier** = of the highest level or quality
[5] to **outdo** = to be better or more successful than someone else
[6] **pervasive** = *allgegenwärtig*
[7] **blue-collar jobs** = jobs in which manual or physical work is done
[8] **mirage** = an unrealistic hope or wish

ISBN 978-3-425-73646-4

A

"Remind me again, Dad. Why did you want me to get that college degree?"

B

ISBN 978-3-425-73646-4

Listening 1: No miracles

Listen to part of an interview with Casey Gerald about his book *There Will Be No Miracles Here* and the concept of the American Dream. (5:01)

You will hear the recording twice. First you will have time to read the tasks. After each listening, you will have time to complete your answers.

While listening, tick (✓) the correct answer. Sometimes more than one answer is correct.

1. Growing up in Texas, Casey Gerald
- ☐ a) had a tough time having no mother or father.
- ☐ b) took drugs and ended up in prison, but managed to raise himself.
- ☐ c) had the support of his parents who helped him to achieve success.
- ☐ d) basically had to take care of himself because his parents weren't able to.

2. In his memoir *There Will Be No Miracles Here*, Gerald gives an insight into …
- ☐ a) the struggles of being on your own.
- ☐ b) his life at Yale and Harvard universities.
- ☐ c) the bumpy road to getting an MBA from Yale.
- ☐ d) the hardships of growing up black and homosexual.

3. When a groundskeeper[1] approached Gerald after a ceremony in the stadium, he …
- ☐ a) felt proud to be a black football player.
- ☐ b) felt honored and respected by the people around him.
- ☐ c) realized that he was a role model for the black community.
- ☐ d) looked at the people staring at him and didn't know what to do.

4. According to Gerald, his story makes people …
- ☐ a) believe that success is like a conveyor belt[2].
- ☐ b) believe that everyone can achieve success.
- ☐ c) realize that only a few can become successful.
- ☐ d) realize that they're going from nothing to nowhere.

5. Gerald explains that …
- ☐ a) the American Dream is an illusion.
- ☐ b) the road to the American Dream is difficult.
- ☐ c) pretending to live the American Dream makes him a fraud.
- ☐ d) not admitting that he is living the American Dream makes him a liar.

6. The example of a 22-year-old boy being selected to become a Rhodes scholar shows …
- ☐ a) that working hard pays off.
- ☐ b) the dilemma of being seen as a symbol.
- ☐ c) that even people from rough neighbourhoods are able to become successful.
- ☐ d) that people have to overcome their personal worries to become a symbol of society.

7. In his book, Gerald generally …
- ☐ a) advocates being held up as a standard to other people.
- ☐ b) makes his readers aware of the kind of people that are held up as a standard of society.
- ☐ c) complains about how society reacts towards people who are held up as a standard of society.
- ☐ d) questions why people who dislike being held up as a standard of society still promote that concept to others.

8. With regard to the discussion about the culture at Yale and similar institutions, Gerald states …
- ☐ a) they fail at forming independent people.
- ☐ b) they educate students and enable them to develop freely.
- ☐ c) they prepare students for a life as an influential member of society.
- ☐ d) they are extraordinarily good at bringing out the best in their students.

[1] **groundskeeper** *(AE) = Platzwart*
[2] **conveyor belt** = *Fließband*

 ISBN 978-3-425-73646-4

Listening 2: White supremacy and terrorism

Listen to a radio interview on global extremism and the growing threat of white power groups. (3:46)

You will hear the recording twice. First you will have time to read the task. After each listening, you will have time to complete your answers.

While listening, complete the sentences.

1.	According to host Garcia-Navarro's next guest, law enforcement needs to …	
2.	Ali Soufan is a …	
3.	In the past, he investigated both …	a) b)
4.	He is interviewed about …	
5.	According to Ali Soufan, right-wing extremists and Islamic extremists are similar in …	a) b) c)
6.	Terror groups tend to cultivate …	
7.	According to Soufan, right-wing extremists have not been made …	
8.	This is the case despite the fact that we see …	
9.	The Soufan Center has issued a report …	
10.	According to Soufan, Russian propaganda has shifted from supporting ….	
11.	Soufan believes that any terrorist attack is …	
12.	He thinks that seeing terrorist attacks is particularly hard when they happen …	

ISBN 978-3-425-73646-4

Mediation: Black Lives Matter in Germany

At his college, your former American exchange partner attends a course dealing with the Black Lives Matter movement in the US. In his course, he has learned that there is also a German branch of this movement fighting racism towards people of colour. He has asked you to give him some insight into the movement in Germany.
On the basis of an article you have found, you decide to write an email to your friend. This email should explain the reasons a German branch of the Black Lives Matter movement was set up, including why it is necessary, historical aspects, the present-day situation with regard to racism in Germany, and how to fight this racism.

◂◂ / ▸▸ https://www

„Anstand reicht nicht“

Ein deutscher Ableger der Black-Lives-Matter-Bewegung prangert Rassismus an. Für Schwarze ist das schmerzhafter Alltag, sagt die Aktivistin Josephine Apraku.

Interview: Vanessa Vu, 24. Juni 2017, Zeit Online

ZEIT ONLINE: Die Black-Lives-Matter-Bewegung kennt man vor allem aus den USA, Auslöser war unter anderem die dortige Polizeigewalt gegen Schwarze. Warum organisieren Sie unter demselben Namen eine Demonstration in Deutschland?

Josephine Apraku: Rassismus ist auch in Deutschland lebendig und für viele schwarze Menschen schmerzhafter Alltag. Sie haben zum Beispiel nicht den gleichen Zugang zu Bildung, zum Arbeits- und Wohnungsmarkt. Sie werden bei Polizeikontrollen überproportional häufig aus dem Verkehr gezogen, erfahren rassistische Gewalt. Und ihnen wird ihre Identität als Deutsche aberkannt.

ZEIT ONLINE: Was meinen Sie damit?

Apraku: In den USA steht es zum Beispiel gar nicht so infrage, dass Schwarze eine US-Staatsbürgerschaft haben. Begriffe wie *Black American* sind ganz selbstverständlich. Schwarze Menschen in Deutschland werden hingegen auch nach vielen Generationen nicht als deutsch gedacht. Der Begriff Afrodeutsch ist für viele ein Widerspruch. In ihrer Logik kann man nicht schwarz und deutsch sein.

ZEIT ONLINE: Andererseits werden in den USA Schwarze auf offener Straße erschossen. Das klingt nicht nach einem Staat, den man sich in puncto Antirassismus zum Vorbild nehmen sollte.

Apraku: Wenn wir uns mit dem Thema Rassismus beschäftigen, hierarchisieren wir schnell die Gewalt – als wäre Widerstand erst notwendig, wenn reales Leben bedroht ist. Ich glaube, dass es sich immer lohnt, sich für Gleichberechtigung und gleiche Teilhabe einzusetzen. Wenn zum Beispiel die Menschenrechte von einer Freundin nicht gewahrt werden, dann sind das immer auch meine Menschenrechte. [...]

ZEIT ONLINE: Die diesjährige Black-Lives-Matter-Demo haben Sie und fünf Mitstreiterinnen organisiert, gemeinsam bilden Sie ein feministisches Frauenkollektiv. Gehört das für Sie zusammen, Feminismus und Antirassismus?

Apraku: Es geht nicht anders. Unterschiedliche Formen von Diskriminierung sind miteinander verwoben und wirken zusammen: Ich beispielsweise erfahre sowohl in Bezug auf mein Frau-Sein als auch als im Hinblick auf mein Schwarz-Sein Diskriminierung. In Teilen ergeben sich daraus spezifische Marginalisierungen, die gleichermaßen sexistisch und rassistisch sind. Weil unsere Identitäten komplex sind, muss es unser Widerstand auch sein.

[...]

ZEIT ONLINE: Sehen Sie eine ähnliche Entwicklung der Bürgerrechtsbewegung in den USA und in Deutschland?

Apraku: Rassismus in Deutschland hat eine andere Geschichte und andere Auswirkungen. Ich denke da an die preußische Beteiligung am Versklavungshandel, an Deutschlands Verhalten in der Kolonialzeit und die NS-Zeit, die Völkermorde an den Nama, Ovaherero, Damara und San in Namibia. Schwarze Menschen spüren noch heute die Nachwirkungen der Kolonialzeit.

ZEIT ONLINE: Inwiefern?

Apraku: Es gibt einen unkritischen Umgang mit der Vergangenheit. In Berlin gibt es zum Beispiel das sogenannte Afrikanische Viertel, ein Kolonialviertel. Initiativen kämpfen seit Jahren dafür, einige der Straßennamen umzubenennen. Das Berliner Straßengesetz versteht Straßennamen als Ehrungen. Einige der Namen erinnern an Kolonialisten, zum Beispiel Adolf Lüderitz oder Gustav Nachtigal, der in

→

ISBN 978-3-425-73646-4

⏪ / ⏩ https://www

der Geschichtsliteratur beschönigend und als Afrikaforscher verklärt wird. Im Grunde haben wir also momentan Denkmäler, die Rassisten ehren.

[...]

Ich verstehe auch nicht die Angst vor der Auseinandersetzung mit dem Thema Rassismus oder allgemein die Angst vor einer Erschütterung des Selbstbildes. Als deutsche Staatsbürgerin und Akademikerin bin auch ich in vielerlei Hinsicht privilegiert. Das Problem beginnt damit, dass diese Privilegien nicht als solche erkannt werden und es keinen verantwortungsvollen Umgang mit dieser begünstigten Position gibt. Ich habe auch wenig Verständnis dafür, wenn Menschen komplexe Realitäten vereinfachen und zum Beispiel pauschal alle Schwarzen oder *people of color* für kriminell halten. Das ignoriert etwa, dass Geflüchtete oft zutiefst prekäre Aufenthaltszustände haben, zum Teil nicht arbeiten dürfen und eigene Überlebensstrategien entwickeln, die nach aktueller Rechtsprechung als kriminell gelten. Kriminalität entsteht nicht im Vakuum.

ZEIT ONLINE: Wie kommen wir aus dem Dilemma raus?

Apraku: Mit Privilegien entstehen Gewinner, und wo Gewinner sind, sind auch Verlierer. Das ist ein strukturelles Problem. Viele argumentieren aber kleinteilig. Sie sagen: Das war doch jetzt dieser eine Vorfall, das hat doch nichts mit uns zu tun. Dahinter steckt die Idee, dass Rassismus nicht die Norm ist, sondern eine Abweichung. Also Rechtsextreme, die im schlimmsten Fall Geflüchtetenunterkünfte anzünden, aber auf gar keinen Fall die Gesellschaft selbst. Dabei müssten wir selbst schauen: Inwiefern sind wir in gewisse Strukturen involviert und durch diese begünstigt, und welche Verantwortung ergibt sich daraus?

ZEIT ONLINE: Ist es nicht etwas zu viel verlangt, wenn alle Leute sich mit gesellschaftlichen Strukturen auseinandersetzen sollen? Reicht nicht ein bisschen Anstand im Umgang miteinander aus?

Apraku: Nein, Anstand reicht nicht aus. Und das ist es auch nicht, wofür ich und all diejenigen, mit denen ich arbeiten darf, eintreten. Wir arbeiten an unterschiedlichsten Punkten für nachhaltige Veränderungen. Das kann etwa in Form von Netzwerken gegen Diskriminierung in Schulen und Kitas sein, in Form von Stadtrundgängen, die einen Einblick geben in die deutsche Beteiligung an der Besetzung und Ausbeutung der ehemaligen Kolonien. Letztlich arbeiten wir an struktureller Veränderung.

ZEIT ONLINE: Träumen Sie manchmal von einer Revolution?

Apraku: Ich träume nicht. Ich versuche, so wie alle, mit denen ich arbeite, echte Veränderung zu bewirken.

ISBN 978-3-425-73646-4

Writing: Oprah Winfrey for president?

You are an intern at the *The Guardian* newspaper and have to decide on a suitable cartoon to accompany Emine Saner's article on Oprah Winfrey.

1. **Comprehension:** Briefly summarize Emine Saner's article below.
2. **Analysis:** Analyse cartoons **A** and **B** (on the next page).
3. **Writing an evaluation:** Write an email to the editors in which you evaluate if either of the cartoons goes well with the article.

Oprah Winfrey: from poverty to America's first black billionaire ... to #Oprah2020?

Succeeding Donald Trump as US president would be an incredible climax to a true rags to riches life story that fostered her trademark compassion.

By Emine Saner, 12 January 2018, The Guardian

[...]

This week, there has been fevered speculation that Winfrey might run for president of the US. And that she might win – one poll found 48% of US voters would choose Winfrey, with 38% voting for Trump.

[...]

The suggestion [to run for presidency] has been made to Winfrey over the years, and she has repeatedly said she'd never do it, though her stance has softened, particularly since the election of another politically inexperienced TV star. "I never considered the question even a possibility," she said in an interview in December 2016. "I thought, 'Oh gee, I don't have the experience, I don't know enough.' And now I'm thinking, 'Oh'." If Winfrey did become president, it would be the incredible climax to a story that already seems impossible.

"Oprah's narrative – this triumphant narrative of coming from a hardscrabble[1], traumatic, abusive [background] – and becoming one of the wealthiest women, the wealthiest black woman, and creating her own empire is the quintessential American story as we envision it," says Leah Wright Rigueur, assistant professor of public policy at the Harvard Kennedy School of Government [...].

Winfrey was born in 1954 in Mississippi, to a teenage mother, but raised by her grandmother. At six she was sent to live with her mother, who worked long hours as a cleaner. When she was nine, Winfrey was raped by a cousin, and over the next few years she was sexually abused by other men. She went to live with her father in Nashville at 14, hiding the fact she was pregnant and gave birth to a son two months early. He died soon afterwards.

Living with her father and stepmother provided stability and high expectations – her father expected good grades at school. When she was 17, Winfrey won a beauty pageant[2] sponsored by a local radio station. Someone at the station, perhaps noticing her smooth, warm voice, asked her to read a news report on tape and she did it so well, she was offered a part-time job [and started her career].

[...]

["Our talkshow People Are Talking] became a sensation," says [her co-moderator and friend Richard] Sher. [...] The word I would use to describe her is: compassionate. One of the reasons she gave up news and went into talk was whenever she did a story of children killed in a fire, or children murdered and abused, she would cry and cry. [...] She wore her heart on her sleeve, and people really loved that about her. She could relate, and still does, to the person who doesn't have a penny to their name and a person who has billions."

[Later on she got her own TV show], The Oprah Winfrey show, [which] was syndicated nationally. [...] By the time she ended her talkshow in 2011, leaving to set up her own cable channel, she had become a billionaire, and one of the most powerful women in the world. She has been credited with everything from liberalizing US culture to reinvigorating[4] America's publishing industry with her book club, to influencing Barack Obama's victory, following her endorsement[4].

[...] "In my career, what I've always tried my best to do [...]," said Winfrey in her [Golden Globe] speech, "is to say ... how we experience shame, how we love and how we rage, how we fail, how we retreat, persevere, and how we overcome."

America's relationship with Winfrey is complex, says Christina Greer, associate professor of political science at Fordham University [...]. "She is the first black billionaire, so in the black community she holds a special place because she has shown the promise of going from abject[5] poverty to unimaginable success." As a woman "she's shown that it is possible to become a millionaire, and then a billionaire, without having a husband who does it for you." Winfrey has been with her partner Stedman Graham since 1986, but they never married. [...] "[A common] phrase used about her is that she 'transcends race' because in the US, to 'transcend race' means that you're accepted and embraced by whites", [says Janice Peck, professor of media studies at the University of Colorado Boulder. Yet, Greer concludes by saying:] "I know she's a lot more inclusive than our current president, and for many people that's enough. I just think that one great speech should not catapult someone to a presumptive nominee when we already have a lot of qualified women."

[...]

→

ISBN 978-3-425-73646-4

In her Golden Globes speech, she talked about abuse suffered by generations of women and touched on what kept them down, particularly poor women and women of color. [...] "I think Oprah does understand the idea of inequalities that are built into the system," says Wright Rigueur. [...]

Winfrey has always symbolized possibility and we've become excitable at the prospect of President Oprah because it seems like the inevitable, desirable conclusion to her story. But though her delivery was presidential, her words said something else. "She is essentially saying we need to offer people on the ground platforms in order to fix inequality and broken systems," says Wright Rigueur, rather than look to this one woman. "I think we have to be very wary of putting our projections of what we need and what we want at this moment onto Oprah."

(918 words)

[1] **hardscrabble** = involving hard work and struggle
[2] **beauty pageant** = a beauty contest
[3] to **reinvigorate** = to give new energy or strength to sth
[4] **endorsement** = a statement of support for a political candidate
[5] **abject** = extremely unpleasant and degrading

A

B

ISBN 978-3-425-73646-4

Listening: Chinua Achebe's legacy

a) Listen to the first part of a report on Nigerian writer Chinua Achebe (1930–2013) and his classic novel *Things fall apart* from 1958. (2:27)

You will hear the recording twice. First you will have time to read the tasks. After each listening, you will have time to complete your answers.

While listening, complete the sentences.

1.	According to professor Nwando Achebe, *Things fall apart* was the first type of book that …	
2.	Nwando Achebe is Chinua Achebe's …	
3.	*Things fall apart* was the first book that began …	
4.	Chinua Achebe grew up in …	
5.	As a child he won …	
6.	When reading novels about Africa from a European perspective, he found himself …	
7.	He realized that literature …	
8.	According to Chinua Achebe, the inadequacy of novels about Africa written by Europeans is due to the fact that …	
9.	For him, language doesn't mean just words but also …	
10.	After realizing the problem with novels from a European perspective, he felt …	

ISBN 978-3-425-73646-4

b) Listen to the second part of the report. (4:15)

You will hear the recording twice. First you will have time to read the tasks. After each listening, you will have time to complete your answers.

While listening, tick (✓) the correct answer. Sometimes more than one answer is correct.

1. At first, Chinua Achebe had difficulties
- ☐ a) typing his novel.
- ☐ b) writing the novel.
- ☐ c) getting his novel published.
- ☐ d) convincing his friend of the quality of the novel.

2. When Alan Hill first read Achebe's story, he
- ☐ a) was fascinated by it.
- ☐ b) made sure that it got published.
- ☐ c) tossed it the corner of the room.
- ☐ d) was worried about possible racist reactions.

3. Okonkwo, one of the protagonists of the book,
- ☐ a) is a rather feminine character.
- ☐ b) upholds tradition in his society.
- ☐ c) is a rather masculine character.
- ☐ d) challenges tradition in his society.

4. According to Nwando Achebe, Christianity
- ☐ a) was a vehicle for colonialism.
- ☐ b) stood in contrast to colonialism.
- ☐ c) incorporated the Igbo gods and goddesses.
- ☐ d) marginalized the female aspects of Igbo religion.

5. When the Achebe family moved to the United States, Nwando
- ☐ a) only spoke Igbo at school.
- ☐ b) experienced a lot of racism at school.
- ☐ c) wanted her father to tell stories at school.
- ☐ d) made her father tell stories on the way to school.

c) Now listen to the third part of the report. (2:13)

You will hear the recording twice. First you will have time to read the tasks. After each listening, you will have time to complete your answers.

While listening, fill in the missing information. You do not need to write complete sentences.

1.	What a young man from South Africa told Nwando Achebe about her father's books (name two aspects)	a) b)
2.	What Chinua Achebe's work meant to Nelson Mandela	
3.	What Mandela said to Chinua Achebe when they first met	
4.	What Chinua Achebe wanted to tell fellow Africans with his work, according to his daughter (name two aspects)	a) b)

ISBN 978-3-425-73646-4

Mediation: A road trip through Nigeria

You are part of an international online community that is interested in travelling to Africa after finishing school. You have come across the following blog post about a recent trip to Nigeria. For the online forum, write a summary of the blog post and give a short evaluation as to whether Maxi Brommer's descriptions make you want to travel to Nigeria.

◀◀ / ▶▶ https://www

Der Alptraum jedes Afrikafahrers heißt Nigeria. Ein Land so groß wie Deutschland, Frankreich und Belgien zusammen. Auf der Westroute ist es unmöglich zu umfahren. Will man von Europa nach Südafrika führt kein Weg daran vorbei. [...]

Mein Ziel ist ein kleines Hotel mitten im Zentrum [der Stadt Lagos], wo ich Dave treffen will. Lagos ist eines der größten Ballungsgebiete der Welt, 25 Millionen Menschen sollen nach Schätzungen hier leben, auf einem Radius von 80 Kilometern. [...] Bisher ist noch kein Verkehr zu sehen und ich beginne mich schon zu wundern, ob das alles nur Mythen waren, die ich gehört habe. Plötzlich springen hinter Bäumen am Straßenrand zehn Jugendliche auf die Fahrbahn und schieben Nagelbretter vor meine Reifen. Mein Puls schnellt nach oben, aber es ist nur eine Straßengang. Sie fordern 100$, aber da sie keine Waffen haben, mache ich ihnen klar, jetzt Militär vom letzten Checkpoint zur Hilfe zu holen. Ich bin inzwischen total abgestumpft [...].

Der Verkehr wird zunehmend dichter und dichter und kommt etwa 50 Kilometer vor der Stadt vollständig zum Erliegen. Es ist das komplette Chaos, Stoßstange reiht sich an Stoßstange, teilweise würde ich meine Fahrertür nicht aufbekommen, so dicht stehen die Autos. Menschen klettern über die Motorhauben, dazwischen Motorradtaxis, deren Fahrer ihre Maschinen über Autos hinweg heben. Alle Fahrzeuge stehen Kreuz und Quer, es wird geschrien, nach zwei Stunden bin ich mit meinen Nerven am Ende, dazu hat es nahezu 40 Grad im Auto. Links und rechts die Slums von Lagos, hier will ich nicht aussteigen müssen und wie ich später erfahre, ist die Anzahl der bewaffneten Überfälle in diesem Viertel auch tagsüber extrem hoch. Die Autos stecken fest, sind somit gefangen und Banditen hilflos ausgeliefert.

Ich passiere Müllberge, so groß, dass kleine Dörfer auf ihnen errichtet wurden. Hütte reiht sich an Hütte, Kindern wühlen im Müll, es riecht nach verbranntem Plastik [...].

Über 200 Millionen Menschen leben in Nigeria und die Regierung hat längst die Kontrolle über viele ihrer Zuständigkeiten verloren. Der Kampf gegen den Terror frisst einen großen Teil ihrer Aufmerksamkeit, die eigentlich an ganz anderen Stellen dringend gebraucht wird. [...]

Ich gucke in den Rückspiegel, mit Sirenen kündigt sich ein Konvoi an. Drei SUVs mit verdunkelten Scheiben wühlen sich durch den Verkehr. An der Front ein Pickup mit Soldaten auf der Ladefläche, drei davon laufen mit Baseballschlägern voran und dreschen auf alle Autos ein, die nicht sofort eine Gasse freimachen. In Nigeria herrscht Anarchie. Für mich eine Welt, die ich zuvor noch nirgends so gesehen habe. Für die restlichen Leute einfach nur Alltag in Lagos.

Nach neun Stunden erreiche ich Victoria Island, eine der vielen Inseln der Stadt, wo ich Dave treffe. Es ist das Viertel der westlichen Welt und solange man es nicht verlässt, könnte man meinen, man befindet sich in Accra oder Dakar. Hier gibt es alles, was teuer und luxuriös ist. Modernste Hotelketten, exquisite Restaurants, angesagte Nachtklubs. [...] Um zwei Uhr habe ich genug gesehen und fahre zurück zum Hotel. [...]

Es sind anstrengende Tage. Der Wecker klingelt morgens um 4.30 Uhr, wir brechen in der Morgendämmerung auf und fahren bis zum Einbruch der Dunkelheit. Ohne eine Pause zu machen, schaffen wir jeden Tag 10–11 Stunden. [...] Nach einem weiteren Tag werden die Militärposten langsam weniger, genauso wie die Menschen. Auch die Landschaft verändert sich, es wird kühler und grüner. Affen springen vor mir über die Straßen. Wir schrauben uns kleine Bergstraßen nach oben, es ist wunderschön und zum ersten Mal genieße ich Nigeria in vollen Zügen. [...] Die Leute sind extrem nett, die Gegend ist so abgelegen, hier gibt es keine Rebellen oder sonstige Bösewichte. Wir machen uns auf den Weg die Grenze Kameruns auf einem kleinen off-road Track in den Bergen zu überqueren. Der Pfad ist teilweise extrem ausgesetzt und kann von Autos nicht mehr befahren werden. Zum Glück reite ich eine wilde Bergziege, die nahezu mühelos über alle Felsen springt. Wir passieren kleine Dörfer, Kinder rennen uns schreiend hinterher. Wir dürfen in einem kleinen Dorf campen [...].

Nigeria war unglaublich intensiv für mich, in einer noch nie dagewesenen Dimension. Es fühlt sich an, als hätte ich zehn verschiedene Versionen des Landes durchquert, so unterschiedlich waren die Leute und Regionen von Tag zu Tag.

Von kantig und harsch in Lagos bis sanftmütig und willkommend in den Bergen im Nordosten.

Eins ist aber überall gleich – es herrscht eine unglaubliche Energie. So viel Bewegung. So viel Leben.

So muss der Wilde Westen damals in Amerika gewesen sein.

ISBN 978-3-425-73646-4

Writing: From Nigeria to Britain

Read the following extract from the novel *The Other Hand* (2008) by Chris Cleave. The novel centres around the story of Little Bee, who is a young girl from Nigeria and Sarah O'Rourke, a magazine editor from Surrey. After two years of being held in a British detention centre, Little Bee is illegally released. She travels to Sarah and her husband Andrew, whom she met two years previously on a beach in the Niger Delta. The following extract is taken from the beginning of the novel.

1. **Comprehension:** Sum up the extract at hand.
2. **Analysis:** Analyse the way in which Little Bee reflects upon her experiences in the United Kingdom by considering her use of stylistic devices.
3. **Writing a discussion:** Discuss Little Bee's statement that globalization is a "human triumph" against the backdrop of your knowledge about global challenges in today's postcolonial world.

Most days, I wish I was a British pound coin instead of an African girl. Everyone would be pleased to see me coming. Maybe I would visit with you for the weekend and then suddenly, because I am fickle[1] like that, I would visit with the man from the corner shop instead – but you would not be sad because you would be eating a cinnamon bun[2], or drinking a Coca Cola from the can, and you would never think of me again. We would be happy, like lovers who met on holiday and forgot each other's names. A pound coin can go wherever it thinks it will be safest. It can cross deserts and oceans and leave the sound of gunfire and the bitter smell of burning thatch behind. [...]

How I would love to be a British pound. A pound is free to travel to safety, and we are free to watch it go. This is the human triumph. This is called, *globalization*. A girl like me gets stopped at immigration, but a pound can leap the turnstiles[3] and dodge[4] [...] those big men with their uniform caps, and jump straight into a waiting airport taxi. *Where to, sir?* Western civilization, my good man, and make it snappy[5].

See how nicely a British pound coin talks? It speaks with the voice of Queen Elizabeth the Second of England. Her face is stamped upon it, and sometimes when I look very closely, I can see her lips moving. I hold her up to my ear. What is she saying? *Put me down this minute, young lady, or I shall call my guards.*

If the Queen spoke to you in such a voice, do you suppose it would be possible to disobey? I have read that the people around her – even Kings and Prime Ministers – they find their bodies responding to her orders before their brains can even think why not. Let me tell you, it is not the crown and the scepter that have this effect. Me, I could pin a tiara[6] on my short fuzzy hair, and I could hold up a scepter in one hand, like this, and police officers would still walk up to me in their big shoes and say, *Love the ensemble, madam, now let's have a quick look at your ID, shall we?* No, it is not the Queen's crown and scepter that rule in your land. It is her grammar and her voice. That is why it is desirable to speak the way she does. That way you can say to police officers, in a voice as clear as the Cullinan diamond[7], *My goodness, how dare you?*

(446 words)

[1] **fickle** = constantly changing your mind about sth
[2] **cinnamon bun** = *Zimtbrötchen*
[3] **turnstile** = *Drehkreuz*
[4] to **dodge** = to avoid
[5] **make it snappy** *(phrase)* = hurry up
[6] **tiara** = *Diadem*
[7] The biggest diamond ever found. It was found in South Africa. The diamond has been property of the British monarchs since 1907.

ISBN 978-3-425-73646-4

Listening: India's rising middle class

a) Listen to the first part of a report on the new middle class in the Indian city of Pune (2:11)

You will hear the recording twice. First you will have time to read the tasks. After each listening, you will have time to complete your answers.

While listening, fill in the missing information. You do not need to write complete sentences.

1.	The groups of people getting off the bus in Pune (name three)	a) b) c)
2.	One of Pune's growing economic sectors	
3.	What Pune used to be	
4.	The size of Pune today	
5.	What Ram and Jyothi are planning to buy	
6.	What Indian middle-class people are now typically doing (name three aspects)	a) b) c)
7.	Possible downsides of India's economic boom (name two)	a) b)

ISBN 978-3-425-73646-4

b) Listen to the second part of the report. (5:00)

You will hear the recording twice. First you will have time to read the tasks. After each listening, you will have time to complete your answers.

While listening, tick (✓) the correct answer. Sometimes more than one answer is correct.

1. For hundreds of millions of Indians, the economic boom means that

- ☐ a) life doesn't change very much.
- ☐ b) they can imagine a better future.
- ☐ c) they are free to buy American products.
- ☐ d) they have the chance to do things that Westerners take for granted.

2. For Ram Kashi, one of the best aspects of moving to CyberCity is

- ☐ a) to be able to walk a short distance to work.
- ☐ b) to live close to other modern Indian families.
- ☐ c) the combination of housing and shopping offered there.
- ☐ d) to live only a two-minute walk away from city centre of Pune.

3. According to former CEO and writer Gurcharan Das, the middle class

- ☐ a) consists of around 500–600 million Indians.
- ☐ b) makes up around 30 % of the Indian population.
- ☐ c) makes up around 50 % of the Indian population.
- ☐ d) is now the fastest-growing part of India's society.

4. The "Indian Dream" is

- ☐ a) similar to the American Dream.
- ☐ b) a better education for the next generation.
- ☐ c) to get a job in one of the economy's fast-growing sectors.
- ☐ d) made up of the same aspirations of people anywhere in the world.

5. 25,000 $

- ☐ a) is the top middle-class salary in India.
- ☐ b) equates to about 100,000 $ in the US.
- ☐ c) is the average middle-class salary in India.
- ☐ d) doesn't get you very far in India's boom towns.

ISBN 978-3-425-73646-4

c) Now listen to the third part of the report. (3:31)

You will hear the recording twice. First you will have time to read the tasks. After each listening, you will have time to complete your answers.

While listening, fill in the missing information. You do not need to write complete sentences.

1.	Why food prices worldwide have gone up in the past years (name two reasons)	a) b)
2.	What has changed for many Indians with regard to food (name two aspects)	a) b)
3.	The resources affected by the economic rise of India and China (besides food) (name two)	a) b)
4.	What the citizens of India want	
5.	The economic boom in India and China makes Americans think about …	
6.	The difficulties India still faces (name two)	a) b)

ISBN 978-3-425-73646-4

Mediation: Mumbai

Imagine you are an exchange student at an English grammar school. In your geography class, you discuss "megacities" in India. You have come across this article about the history of Mumbai with its more than 18 million inhabitants. Write a presentation about Mumbai based on the information from the article.

[...] Mumbai ist die vielfältigste, reichste und wohl auch extremste Stadt Indiens. Wolkenkratzer, Blechhütten, Diätkliniken, Yuppies, Religionsführer, Müllsammler. In der dicht besiedelten Stadt begegnen sich Arm und Reich tagtäglich. Mumbai hat die höchste Slumrate Indiens, und in der Stadt findet sich das größte Elendsviertel Asiens: In dem innerstädtischen Slum Dharavi leben über 500.000 Menschen, eine Stadt in der Stadt.

„Bom Bahia" – die gute Bucht

Nach wie vor ist Mumbai vielen als Bombay bekannt. Das mag nicht verwundern, denn über 400 Jahre trug die Hafenstadt diesen Namen: Abgeleitet von „bom bahia", was auf portugiesisch gute Bucht heißt. So nannten die Portugiesen eine der Inseln als sie Anfang des 16. Jahrhunderts mit ihren Schiffen an der Westküste Indiens landeten. 1995 beschloss die Regierung des Bundesstaates Maharashtra, dessen Landeshauptstadt Bombay ist, die Umbenennung: Mumbai sollte die Millionenmetropole von nun an heißen, benannt nach der hinduistischen Lokalgöttin Mumbadevi.

Mumbai nahm seinen Anfang auf sieben sumpfigen Inseln entlang der Küste am Arabischen Meer. Die von Fischern bewohnte Region erlebte wechselnde Herrscher. Ab 1384 gehörte ein Teil zum Sultanat Gujarat bis Anfang des 16. Jahrhunderts die Portugiesen das Küstengebiet eroberten. Das Sultanat war militärisch geschwächt und beugte sich: Im Vertrag von Bassein erwarb 1534 Portugal das heutige Gebiet rund um Mumbai. 1661 ging das Küstengebiet als Mitgift der portugiesischen Prinzessin Katharina von Braganza an ihren Ehemann, den englischen Thronfolger Karl II. Dieser verpachtete wenige Jahre später das ehemalige Bombay an die Britische Ostindien-Kompanie. Eine Handelsniederlassung wurde gegründet und der Aufstieg der Stadt zum Handelszentrum begann.

Bombay wurde das „Tor nach Indien"

Unter den Briten kam es zu umfangreichen Landgewinnungsmaßnahmen: Durch Aufschüttungen wurden die Inseln nach und nach miteinander verbunden und es entstand eine kohärente Landmasse, deren Spitze als längliche Halbinsel ins Arabische Meer hineinragt. Darauf findet sich heute das Stadtzentrum Mumbais. Ab 1860 wurde die erste Eisenbahn Indiens im heutigen Bundesstaat Maharashtra gebaut: Die ersten Teilstücke verbanden das Hinterland mit Bombay und machten die Stadt zum „Tor nach Indien". Der Hafen wurde zum zentralen Umschlagplatz für Baumwolle aus dem Hinterland auf dem Weg nach England. Ende des 19. Jahrhunderts war die Stadt neben Kalkutta zu einem der wichtigsten Handelszentren Indiens avanciert, mit über 800.000 Einwohnerinnen und Einwohnern. Als erste indische Stadt erhielt Bombay 1872 eine Stadtverwaltung, die Bombay Municipal Corporation.

Nach und nach gewann die Stadt auch als Industriestandort an Bedeutung, zunächst vor allem im Bereich der Textilindustrie. 1911 besuchten König George V und Königin Mary von England Bombay. Ihnen zu Ehren wurde kurz darauf das „Gateway of India" gebaut, ein imposanter Torbogen am Hafen und bis heute Wahrzeichen der Stadt. Als 1915 Gandhi nach Indien zurückkehrte, ging er nach Bombay und machte die Stadt zu einer wichtigen Basis für seinen gewaltfreien Widerstand gegen die britische Kolonialmacht. 1947 erfolgte die Unabhängigkeit Indiens und die Teilung des Subkontinents. Die letzten britischen Truppen verließen durch das „Gateway of India" die ehemalige Kolonie.

Nach der Unabhängigkeit nahm das Bevölkerungswachstum des heutigen Mumbais beständig zu. Immer mehr Menschen strömten aus dem Hinterland wie auch aus anderen Bundesstaaten in die Metropole. In den 1970er Jahren wuchs die Bevölkerung um fast vier Prozent jährlich: Bereits 1980 lebten fast neun Millionen Menschen im heutigen Mumbai. Nach und nach dehnte sich die Stadt nach allen Seiten hin aus. Zu „Greater Mumbai" gehört heute Mumbai Stadt, das auf der Halbinsel liegt, sowie die Vororte auf der Insel Salsetta. Die Megastadt Mumbai umfasst jedoch längst auch angrenzende Städte wie Thane, Kalyan oder Navi Mumbai: Satellitenstädte, die umso schneller wuchsen, je unerträglicher die Siedlungsdichte in den innerstädtischen Gebieten wurde. [...]

ISBN 978-3-425-73646-4

Writing: A new age in Bangalore

Read the following extract from the novel *The White Tiger* (2008) by Aravind Adiga. The novel centres around the story of Balram Halwai, who was born into a poor family in rural India but who manages to work his way up to become a chauffeur in Delhi. He murders his employer, Mr Ashok, steals seven hundred thousand rupees from him and uses the money to establish himself as an entrepreneur in Bangalore, a thriving metropolis whose growth is based on IT companies and call centres. The novel consists of seven emails written by Balram who calls himself "The White Tiger". His emails are addressed to Wen Jiabao, the Chinese premier, who will visit Bangalore to meet Indian business people and to learn the secret behind their economic success.

1. **Comprehension:** Describe the "New Bangalore" as seen by Balram Halwai.
2. **Analysis:** Analyse the way in which Balram reflects upon his own past and future in the New Bangalore by considering his use of stylistic devices and syntax.
3. **Writing a discussion:** Discuss Balram's vision of a New Bangalore against the background of your knowledge of globalization.

Now, Your Excellency[1], [...] although my story is done, and my secrets are now your secrets, if you allow me, I would leave you with one final word. [...]

When I drive down Hosur Main Road, when I turn into Electronics City Phase 1 and see the companies go past, I can't tell you how exciting it is to me. General Electric, Dell, Siemens – they're all here in Bangalore. And so many more are on their way. There is construction everywhere. Piles of mud everywhere. Piles of stone. Piles of bricks. The entire city is masked in smoke, cement dust. It is under a veil. When the veil is lifted, what will Bangalore be like?

Maybe it will be a disaster: slums, sewage, shopping malls, traffic jams, policemen. But you never know. It may turn out to be a decent city, where humans can live like humans and animals can live like animals. A new Bangalore for a new India. And then I can say that, in my own way, I helped to make New Bangalore.

Why not? Am I not part of all that is changing in this country? Haven't I succeeded in the struggle that every poor man here should be making – the struggle not to take the lashes[2] your father took, not to end up in a mound of indistinguishable bodies that will rot in the black mud of Mother Ganga[3]? True, there was the matter of murder – which is a wrong thing to do, no question about it. It has darkened by soul. All the skin-whitening creams sold in the markets of India won't clean my hands again.

But isn't it likely that everyone who counts in this world, including our prime minister (including *you*, Mr Jiabao), has killed someone or other on their way to the top? Kill enough people and they will put up bronze statues to you near Parliament House in Delhi – but that is glory, and not what I am after. All I wanted was the chance to be a man – and for that, one murder was enough.

What comes next for me? I *know* that's what you're wondering. [...] You see, I'm always a man who sees "tomorrow" when others see "today". The whole world will come to Bangalore tomorrow. Just drive to the airport and count the half-built glass-and-steel boxes as you pass them. Look at the names of the American companies that are building them. And when all these Americans come here, where do you think they're all going to sleep? On the road?

Anywhere there's an empty apartment, I take a look at it, I wonder, *How much can I get from an American for this in 2010?* If the place has a future as the home of an American, I put down payment on it at once. The future of real estate is Bangalore, Mr Jiabao. You can join the killing if you want – I'll help you out!

After three or four years in real estate, I think I might sell everything, take the money, and start a school – an English-language school – for poor children in Bangalore. A school where you won't be allowed to corrupt anyone's head with prayers and stories about God or Ghandi – nothing but the facts of life for these kids. A school full of White Tigers, unleashed on Bangalore! We'd have this city at our knees, I tell you. I could become the Boss of Bangalore. [...]

(577 words)

[1] Balram is addressing Wen Jiabao, China's head of government between 2003 and 2013
[2] **lash** = *Peitschenhieb*
[3] **Mother Ganga** = the Ganges River

ISBN 978-3-425-73646-4

Listening 1: Politics through the eyes of Shakespeare

Listen to radio host Scott Simon talking to renowned Shakespeare scholar Stephen Greenblatt about his book *Tyrant*. (4:45)

You will hear the recording twice. First you will have time to read the tasks. After each listening, you will have time to complete your answers.

While listening, fill in the missing information. You do not need to write complete sentences.

1.	One of the topics Shakespeare deals with in his plays, according to Simon Scott	
2.	Stephen Greenblatt's intention for writing his book *Tyrant*	
3.	What fascinated Shakespeare about tyrants (name two aspects)	a) b)
4.	Why people fall for tyrants, according to Shakespeare (name two aspects)	a) b)
5.	How Shakespeare envisioned a route out of catastrophic leadership (name three aspects)	a) b) c)

ISBN 978-3-425-73646-4

Listening/Viewing 2: Why study Shakespeare today?

Listen to Professor Ewan Fernie talking about why students should come to the UK to study Shakespeare. (2:24)

You will hear the recording twice. First you will have time to read the task. After each listening, you will have time to complete your answers.

While listening, fill in the gaps.

People may wonder why we (1) ____________________ with Shakespeare – and the basic yet

(2) __________________________ answer is because Shakespeare's characters appear more real to us, more

(3) __________________________ than any others have throughout the whole of (4) ______________________________.

Throughout the centuries, Shakespeare has been (5) ______________________________________ within revolutions

of every kind.

In the 19th century, Chartists in England hoped to (6) ____ the vote for

the first time – Shakespeare was (7) ______________________________________ in this struggle. A chartist named

Thomas Cooper founded a Shakespearean Association of Leicester Chartists, where they used a Shakespearean

Chartist (8) __________________; one such hymn was "The lion of freedom is come from his den". Cooper had learnt

Hamlet (9) __________________________, proving this wasn't just a

(10) ____ for him. He believed Shakespeare's plays

(11) ______________________________________ a better world, with a fairer political system.

Shakespeare was a source of inspiration for many (12) ________________________________, including Nelson

Mandela, who left a signature next to a passage in *Julius Caesar* about not fearing death; this shows an

(13) _____________________________ between Shakespeare and the (14) _____________________________.

This link has been made throughout history.

Now is an (15) _____________________________ to come to the UK to study Shakespeare; in this

(16) _____________________________, Shakespeare is constantly (17) _________________________________ to fit with

today's new, multicultural and more

(18) _____________________________. In fact, studying Shakespeare in the UK is the (19) _________________ you

could do to extend your (20) _____________________________ Shakespeare.

ISBN 978-3-425-73646-4

Listening/Viewing 3: Shakespeare in virtual reality games

Listen to a report by BBC reporter Jane O'Brien about re-imagining Shakespeare's plays in virtual reality (VR) games. (2:53)

You will hear the recording twice. First you will have time to read the tasks. After each listening, you will have time to complete your answers.

While listening, fill in the missing information. You do not need to write complete sentences.

1.	What you need in order to play the VR game *Play the Knave* (name three aspects)	a) b) c)
2.	What the modern technology brings back in terms of acting	
3.	What VR players can select before playing *Play the Knave* (name three aspects)	a) b) c)
4.	The original intention behind developing the VR game	
5.	An advantage of *Play the Knave*, according to first student	a) b)
6.	An advantage of *Play the Knave*, according to second student	
7.	A positive aspect of the VR game, according to third student	
8.	Where the Folger Theatre is located	
9.	When the Folger Theater was built	
10.	What is going to happen to the Folger Theatre	
11.	Why it is not surprising that Shakespeare goes virtual reality	

ISBN 978-3-425-73646-4

Listening 4: High school students perform *Romeo and Juliet*

Listen to a group of high school students in Watertown, NY, talk about their upcoming performance of *Romeo and Juliet* in the school's cafeteria. (2:40)

You will hear the recording twice. First you will have time to read the tasks. After each listening, you will have time to complete your answers.

While listening, match the speakers **1** to **5** with the statements **A** to **G**. There are two more statements than you need.

1	Frank
2	Eliana
3	Stormy
4	Andrea
5	Amanda

A	thinks Shakespeare's language lets you be more imaginative than today's everyday language.
B	likes the way Juliet ignores her family's advice and follows her heart.
C	likes that Shakespeare describes the world as it is.
D	thinks Romeo is a strange character who is difficult to play.
E	believes that Romeo doesn't make the right choices for Juliet and himself.
F	believes Juliet doesn't know what is good for her.
G	likes Shakespeare's language because it allows room for different interpretations.

1	2	3	4	5

ISBN 978-3-425-73646-4

Mediation 1: Shakespeare in Weimar

You are taking part in an international school project called "Global Shakespeare". Your task is to write a blog post for the project's website. Based on an article you have found, you describe how Shakespeare's work found its way to Germany and the relationship between Weimar and Shakespeare.

Wie Shakespeares Denkmal in den Weimarer Ilmpark kam

Wieland machte den Engländer durch seine Übersetzungen bekannt. Vor 150 Jahren wurde die Deutsche Shakespeare Gesellschaft in Weimar gegründet.

Wolfgang Hirsch, 24. April 2016, Thüringer Allgemeine

Landauf, landab will man sich Shakespeares nicht erwehren. In Großbritannien feiert man den Nationaldichter mit stolzem Eifer, in London zeigt die British Library eine fulminante Ausstellung, und in Shakespeares Globe, erst recht daheim in Stratford-upon-Avon drängeln sich Literatur-Touristen aus der ganzen Welt. [...]

Hierzulande veranstaltet soeben die Deutsche Shakespeare Gesellschaft ihre Frühjahrstagung zum modischen Thema „Shakespeare's Green Worlds" in Bochum – leider geschichtsvergessen in der falschen Stadt. Denn gegründet wurde diese renommierte Vereinigung 1864, vor auf den Tag genau 150 Jahren, in Weimar – und das nicht grundlos. Denn von Ilm-Arkadien aus nahm die deutschsprachige Rezeption des Dramatikers erst ihren Lauf. Kaum zu glauben: Bis tief ins 18. Jahrhundert war das Genie bei uns eine unbekannte Größe. Kein Vorwurf, es mangelte ja an Übersetzungen. [...]

Der Jenaer Germanistik-Professor Klaus Manger weiß nur zu gut, wer Abhilfe schuf: Kein Geringerer als Christoph Martin Wieland, der Stammvater der Deutschen Klassik, hat als erster in gehörigem Umfang die Dramen des Engländers ins Deutsche übersetzt. Zwischen 1762 und 1766 erschienen in Zürich 22 Dramen in einer achtbändigen Ausgabe. Manger [...] fügt fairerweise an, dass sich erste Hinweise auf Shakespeares Format bereits in Lessings „Hamburgischer Dramaturgie" finden und dass schon Goethe und Herder sich von Straßburg aus um angemessene Weihen des gewesenen Handschuhmachersohns bemühten. Aber auch er findet es naturgemäß erstaunlich, dass mit Wieland, Goethe und Herder sich alsbald das Dreigestirn der deutschen Shakespeare-Renaissance in Weimar einfand. [...]

Wielands Vorbild und die Kritik daran lässt erst die Romantiker auf den Plan treten; die Schlegel/Tieckschen Übertragungen, denen man nicht zu Unrecht attestiert, sie hätten derbe Zotigkeiten mit Rücksicht auf die höheren Töchter unter der Leserschaft geglättet, galten bei uns lange Zeit als Standard. Inzwischen gibt es eine Reihe moderner Übersetzungen respektive Nachdichtungen, zum Beispiel von Erich Fried, Rudolf Schaller oder Peter Stein. Doch Manger hält fest an seinem Ideal und schwärmt zum Beispiel von den poetischen Kräften in Wielands Fassung des „Sommernachtstraums": „Es gibt keinen größeren Dichter, der das so ins Schweben bringt."

© shutterstock/marako85

Selbstverständlich war auch das Weimarische Hoftheater keine shakespearefreie Zone. So geschah es folgerichtig, dass am 8. April 1864 – dem Geburtstag der Großherzogin Sophie – sich ein „Verein der Shakespeare-Freunde" konstituierte, um den Todes- und auch mutmaßlichen Geburtstag des Idols aus elisabethanischen Zeiten zu begehen. Hoftheaterintendant Franz von Dingelstedt inszenierte einen Zyklus von Historiendramen, und nicht zuletzt dies wirkte offenbar so inspirierend, dass sich am nämlichen Tage die Shakespeare-Gesellschaft als die somit älteste literarische Vereinigung Deutschlands in Weimar gründete.

Seit je versteht man sich in der Klassikstadt auf die Kunst, aus einer einmal etablierten Dichterverehrung immer wieder Kapitalien zu schlagen. Ergo errichtete man zum 40. Jubiläum der Gesellschaft und 340. Geburtstag des Dichters im Park an der Ilm ein Shakespeare-Denkmal – als erstes auf dem europäischen Kontinent. Der Berliner Bildhauer Otto Lessing schlug die Skulptur aus noblem Carrara-Marmor und gab der sitzenden Ganzkörperfigur Schriftrolle und Rose, Narrenkappe und Totenschädel als sprechende Attribute bei. [...] Just am 23. April 1904 wurde das Denkmal feierlich eingeweiht [...]. Dem ist nur hinzuzufügen, dass in unseren Tagen die Klassik Stiftung Weimar der seit 1998 zum Unesco-Weltkulturerbe zählenden Statue obwaltet.

ISBN 978-3-425-73646-4

Mediation 2: Shakespeare on German stages

Your English pen pal is working on an essay about Shakespeare's global appeal and asks you whether Shakespeare is played in German theatres. You have found an interesting article explaining why producers in Brandenburg still put on Shakespeare's plays. In an email to your pen pal, outline the reasons each producer provides for staging Shakespeare.

Darum spielen wir Shakespeare

William Shakespeare, der vor vier Jahrhunderten starb, ist immer noch das Maß aller Dinge. Was macht sein Werk so brisant und aktuell, dass er immer noch der beliebteste Dramatiker ist?
Die MAZ [Märkische Allgemeine Zeitung] hat sich unter vier Brandenburger Theatermachern umgehört.

Karim Saab, 23. April 2016, Märkische Allgemeine

[...]

Das sagen Brandenburgs Theatermacher

Shakespeares Werk ist deshalb so relevant geblieben, weil die Erfindung der Dampfmaschine und des Internets das Panoptikum der menschlichen Gefühle und Charaktere nicht aufheben konnte. Doch lassen wir die Fachleute zu Wort kommen! Wir haben die vier Theater in Brandenburg gefragt, warum sie immer noch und immer wieder Shakespeare spielen.

Mario Holetzeck, Schauspieldirektor am Staatstheater Cottbus:

„Shakespeare. Ein Star in ruheloser Zeit. Ein Genie? Das Wunder einer dauerhaften Lebendigkeit? Shakespeare ist der Wahnsinn. Ist die Rache. Ist der Verrat. Der Mord. Ist die Spionage. Ist der Hass. Der Zweifler. Verachtung. Wut. Intrige. Die reine absolute Liebe.

Er ist anders! Er stellt uns ständig vor Überraschungen. Wir können nicht aufhören, Neues in ihm zu entdecken, weil sein Drama uns immer wieder von einer neuen Seite her packt und uns dazu zwingt, nach anderen Antworten zu suchen. Wir tauchen in eine Welt der Vergangenheit ein und sind konfrontiert mit einer Welt der Gegenwart. Mit Shakespeare, der im 21. Jahrhundert angekommen ist. Obwohl sich sein 400. Todestag jährt, ist er aktueller denn je. Er hält uns einen Spiegel vor, in dem wir Eigenes wiedererkennen. Eine gute Shakespeare-Aufführung geht an keinem spurlos vorüber. Hamlet – an dem wir gerade arbeiten – ist eine Theatererfahrung wert!" [...]

Tobias Wellemeyer, Intendant des Hans-Otto-Theaters in Potsdam:

„Shakespeare hat wie kein anderer das Theater geprägt: Ohne ihn kein Goethe, kein Schiller, kein Brecht. Schauen Sie in unseren Spielplan, auch Huxleys „Schöne neue Welt" kommt nicht ohne Shakespeare aus. Wie kein anderer hat er poetisch, geistvoll und komplex die Abgründe des Menschen beschrieben. Gnadenlos zeigt er das Ringen des Einzelnen um Glück und seine Verstrickung in Machtmechanismen. Er zeigt Despoten im Aufstieg und Fall, menschliche Verkommenheit, schwache Helden, starke Frauen, dunkle Clowns. Mit seinen einzigartigen Beschreibungen der Liebe ist uns Shakespeare auch heute ganz nah: Qual und Genuss, Begehren, Eifersucht und Hass – all diese Facetten hat er in seinen Stücken und Sonetten meisterhaft ausgeleuchtet. Schöner und drastischer hat das vielleicht keiner nach ihm geschafft. Was Bach für die Musik bedeutet oder Michelangelo für die bildende Kunst, ist Shakespeare für Theater und Dichtkunst. [...]

Reinhard Simon, Intendant der Uckermärkischen Bühnen Schwedt:

„Die Texte William Shakespeares – zu denen ja nicht nur die Theaterstücke gehören – sind nach wie vor von ungeheurer poetischer und rhetorischer Kraft. Insbesondere die Theaterstücke sind für ein breites Publikum geschrieben, das seine Kritik gewohnt war, sofort und unmissverständlich zum Ausdruck zu bringen: Die Tragödie birgt mitunter brachial humoristische Szenen, wie die Komödie tieftragische Momente enthält. Shakespeare gelingt es dadurch, jedem etwas zu bieten und dabei noch Figuren von großer Komplexität zu zeichnen, die in ihrer Zuspitzung auch für unsere Gegenwart noch interessant sind und Diskussionsstoff bieten. Dadurch bleiben seine Stücke in jeder Epoche aufs Neue prägnant und aktuell. Sie unterscheiden nicht, trennen nicht, sondern bilden zugespitzt Leben ab – in seiner ganzen komplexen Farbigkeit. Und sie rühren an unser Innerstes, denn dass es Shakespeare gelingt, nur mit Worten sämtliche Gefühle zu evozieren, ist der Kern seines Geheimnisses, denke ich." [...]

Igor Holland-Moritz, Dramaturg an der Neuen Bühne Senftenberg:

„400 Jahre nach William Shakespeares Tod sind aus seiner Feder 38 Stücke und sechs Versdichtungen überliefert, darunter die berühmten 154 Sonette. Diese schiere Menge allein lässt schon ahnen: Man kommt einfach nicht an ihm vorbei. Shakespeare wurde in über 100 Sprachen übersetzt – schon sehr früh ins Deutsche und über die Jahre immer wieder neu – vom Romantiker Schlegel über Frank Günther und Thomas Brasch bis, jüngst sehr prominent, Feridun Zaimoglu. Es scheint, jede Zeit hat ihre Shakespeareübersetzung. Dabei ist der Dichter in seiner Beschreibung des Menschlichen zeitlos. Es bleibt wohl so, dass weiterhin er unsere Geschichten schreibt.

Nicht ohne Grund haben wir uns in Manuel Soubeyrands erster Spielzeit als Intendant in Senftenberg gleich „Romeo und Julia" vorgenommen. Dieser energiegeladene Sturm der Gefühle ist ja nicht nur eine der schönsten Liebesgeschichten überhaupt. Mitreißend und verführerisch wie der Gedanke, dass Liebe stärker als der Tod ist, verkörpert das Stück auch das Wechselhafte und das überernsthafte Pathos der Jugend und mithin unser nach Jugendlichkeit, großen Erlebnissen und Sensationen gierendes Heute." [...]

ISBN 978-3-425-73646-4

Writing 1: A sonnet

1. **Comprehension:** Briefly outline what each quatrain and the couplet are about.
2. **Analysis:** Analyse the sonnet with regard to the portrayal of the lover and the contradictory presentation of the relationship between speaker and lover. In doing so, focus on how the structure, imagery and stylistic devices complement the content.
3. **Comment:** While browsing the Internet you have come across a blog titled "Shakespeare is dead!" in which students complain about the difficulties they experienced when dealing with Shakespeare at school. One statement in particular has sparked your interest: "Shakespearean sonnets are not contemporary and should not be taught in schools anymore." Comment on this statement in the comment section of the blog. Refer to materials dealt with in class.

Sonnet 141

In faith, I do not love thee with mine eyes,
For they in thee a thousand errors note;
But 'tis my heart that loves what they despise,
Who in despite of view is pleased to dote[1];
Nor are mine ears with thy tongue's tune delighted,
Nor tender feeling, to base touches prone[2],
Nor taste, nor smell, desire to be invited
To any sensual feast with thee alone:
But my five wits[3] nor my five senses can
Dissuade[4] one foolish heart from serving thee,
Who leaves unsway'd[5] the likeness of a man[6],
Thy proud hearts slave and vassal[7] wretch[8] to be:
Only my plague thus far I count my gain,
That she that makes me sin awards me pain.

William Shakespeare (1609)

[1] to **dote** (on sb) = to love sb very much
[2] to **base touches prone** = likely to suffer from sth unpleasant or regrettable
[3] **five wits** = common sense
[4] to **dissuade** = to persuade sb not to take a particular course of action
[5] **unswayed** = unmoved, not impressed
[6] **the likeness of a man** = sb who looks like a man but is not one
[7] **vassal** = follower of a king or lord in exchange for land and protection
[8] **wretch** = a person who experiences something unpleasant

ISBN 978-3-425-73646-4

Writing 2: Variation on a sonnet

The romantic comedy *10 Things I Hate About You* (1999) is based on William Shakespeare's comedy *The Taming of the Shrew* (1593). Both the names of the protagonists, Katharina (Kat) und Bianca, and major storylines from Shakespeare's comedy were reused and adapted for a modern American high school setting. The film also alludes to various other Shakespearean elements. In the film, Kat confesses her true feelings for Patrick by reciting a homework assignment, which was to rewrite Shakespeare's Sonnet 141.

1. **Comprehension**: Summarize Kat's version of the sonnet.
2. **Analysis**: Critically analyse Kat's version of the sonnet by first examining her sonnet and then contrasting it with the regular Shakespearean sonnet form.
3. **Comment**: This is how Kat's teacher introduced the homework assignment:
   "Let's open our books to page 73, Sonnet 141 and listen up: [he freely recites the first quatrain of the Shakespearean sonnet in a modern rap version sticking to the original lines]

   In faith, I do not love thee with mine eyes,
   For they in thee a thousand errors note;
   But 'tis my heart that loves what they despise,
   Who in despite of view is pleased to dote;

Now, I know Shakespeare's a dead white guy but, he knows his shit, so we can overlook that. I want you all to write your own version of this sonnet."

You have come across a blog called "How to teach Shakespeare" and decide to contribute to the discussion with a comment piece which critically evaluates the approach Kat's teacher uses in the film *10 Things I Hate About You*. You may also refer to materials dealt with in class and your own experiences as a student.

10 Things I Hate About You

I hate the way you talk to me,
And the way you cut your hair.
I hate the way you drive my car.
I hate it when you stare.
I hate your big dumb combat boots,
And the way you read my mind.
I hate you so much, that it makes me sick.
It even makes me rhyme.
I hate the way you're always right.
I hate it when you lie.
I hate it when you make me laugh –
Even worse when you make me cry.
 I hate it when you're not around and the fact that you didn't call.
 But mostly I hate the way I don't hate you – not even close, not even a little bit, not even at all.

ISBN 978-3-425-73646-4

Lösungen und Erwartungshorizont für eine gute inhaltliche Leistung

Listening 1: First woman on Canadian bank notes Webcode: WES-73646-01

1. women to the $5, $10 and $20 notes/Harriet Tubman to the 20$ bill
2. nominate women who could be on a future bank note
3. over 20,000
4. six months (so far)
5. a) dead for at least 25 years, b) made a contribution to Canadian society
6. a black businesswoman/a black businesswoman-turned civil libertarian/a woman who (in 1946) defied whites-only segregation in a Nova Scotia movie theatre
7. a poet of Aboriginal heritage
8. the first woman in Canada to receive a bachelor's degree in Electrical Engineering
9. held Canadian records in the running and standing broad jump and the discus
10. a feminist and pioneer in the fight for suffrage in Quebec
11. Queen Elizabeth II

Listening 2: Border crossings into Canada Webcode: WES-73646-02

1a, 2d, 3c, 4b, 5d, 6c, 7b, 8d, 9b, 10b

Listening 3: Apology to Canada's LGBTQ community Webcode: WES-73646-03

1. acknowledged
2. persecution
3. undercover operations
4. networks of informants
5. big raids
6. ruined
7. psychiatric therapy
8. corruption by the Soviet Union
9. hundred million dollars in compensation
10. anti-homophobia campaigns
11. formal apology and compensation
12. re-impose a ban
13. transgender
14. Aboriginal people and First Nations people

Mediation: Emigrating to Canada

A friend of yours from Ireland is planning to live and work in Canada after finishing school. You are thinking of joining them and searched the Internet for reports by people who have left Germany for Canada. You have come across this blog post on the downsides of living and working abroad. Write an email to your friend about the challenges of emigrating to Canada based on what Irene, the blogger, has written.

	Der Schüler/Die Schülerin ...
Umsetzung der Aufgabenstellung	erfüllt weitgehend die Erfordernisse einer *Mediation*-Aufgabe: • Verzicht auf wortwörtliche Übersetzungen • Entnahme der nötigen Informationen aus dem deutschen Text (Textsorte: Persönlicher Blogeintrag) zum Verfassen eines eigenen Textes (Textsorte: E-Mail)
Textsortenspezifik	setzt die textsortenspezifischen Merkmale für *email* weitgehend um: • Betreff • Anrede • Einleitung, die in das Thema und die Situation ein-/hinführt (Auswandern, Leben und Arbeiten im Ausland) • inhaltlich aspektorientierte Strukturierung • zusammenfassender Schluss, der die Situation aufgreift und adäquat persönlich endet • Schlussgrußformel

	Der Schüler/Die Schülerin ...
Situationsangemessenheit und Adressatenbezug	schreibt weitgehend situationsangemessen und adressatenbezogen: • an einen Freund/eine Freundin • es geht um eine persönliche Entscheidung von großer Tragweite
Text- und Problemverständnis	kann das Thema des Blogs bzw. der E-Mail ggfs. in größere Zusammenhänge (*individual life decisions, living and working abroad/emigration, identity*) einordnen.
Darstellung und Gliederung	stellt die Herausforderungen einer Auswanderung nach Kanada auf Basis des Blogs sensibel und überwiegend nachvollziehbar dar.

Gesamteindruck	Die inhaltliche Leistung entspricht in vollem Maße den Anforderungen der Aufgabe.

Mögliche inhaltliche Aspekte:

- *not easy to find a job: usually 2–3 years job experience expected; you have to be willing to make compromises, since you can't live in Canada without income for very long (life is expensive)*
- *not that easy to find friends*
- *if you are a family person, you'll miss your family*
- *you'll feel lonely, even if you meet new people*
- *at times you'll feel guilty for being so far away from your family*

Writing: Multicultural Canada

Read the following extract from a speech given by Canadian writer Erna Paris at the University of Toronto, as published on the website of the Canadian newspaper *The Globe and Mail*. Then complete the tasks below.

1. Comprehension: Point out what defines Canadian identity today and describe how that view has developed over the years.

	Der Schüler/Die Schülerin ...
Umsetzung der Aufgabenstellung	kann benennen, was kanadische Identität ausmacht und beschreiben, wie sich diese Identität im Laufe der Jahre herausgebildet hat.
Text- und Problemverständnis	durchdringt die Textvorlage weitgehend.
Darstellung und Gliederung	verfasst einen strukturierten und kohärenten Text, der überwiegend den Erfordernissen der Operatoren *point out* und *describe* entspricht: • Herausarbeiten der Aspekte, die kanadische Identität heute ausmachen • Ausführliche Beschreibung der historisch-politischen Entwicklung dahin

Gesamteindruck	Die inhaltliche Leistung entspricht in vollem Maße den Anforderungen der Aufgabe.

Mögliche inhaltliche Aspekte:

What defines Canadian identity today:
- *multiculturalism instead of just biculturalism (English-French)*
- *Canadians define themselves as citizens of a multi-ethnic, multi-religious society*
- *multiculturalism as shared identity*
- *multiculturalism is seen as second most valuable aspect of being proud of Canada*
- *integration instead of assimilation works well*
- *shows in growing numbers of university attendance and intermarriage*
- *leaves people their core identity*
- *emphasis on citizenship*
- *no single culture defines the country → Canadian identity is fairly loose*

ISBN 978-3-425-73646-4

How that view has developed over the years:
- *1930s: immigrants were rejected as "unassimilable"*
- *1960s and early 1970s saw nationalism and violence*
- *Oct. 8, 1971, prime minister Pierre Trudeau introduced capital-M multiculturalism to the House of Commons*
- *2006: multiculturalism second place of what Canadians are proud of*
- *2015: Environics poll: immigrants are good citizens*
- *2017: Canadians comfortable with diversity*
- *Canadian leaders of both major parties had historically promoted both immigration and citizenship*
- *reason for success: no overriding cultural identity to assimilate to*
- *in contrast to populism and intolerance increasing elsewhere*

2. Analysis: Analyse Paris' use of rhetorical devices in order to get her message across.

	Der Schüler/Die Schülerin ...
Umsetzung der Aufgabenstellung	führt die im Sinne der Aufgabenstellung relevanten Informationen weitgehend präzise aus.
Text- und Problemverständnis	durchdringt die Textvorlage weitgehend.
Darstellung und Gliederung	verfasst einen strukturierten, kohärenten und durchgängig lesbaren Text, der überwiegend den Erfordernissen des Operators *analyse* entspricht: • Analyse der rhetorischen Mittel und deren Wirkung auf die Leser/innen • Untermauerung durch relevante Beispiele aus dem Text (Zitate und Textverweise)

Gesamteindruck	Die inhaltliche Leistung entspricht in vollem Maße den Anforderungen der Aufgabe.

Mögliche inhaltliche Aspekte:

- ***repetition/choice of words:*** *use of different words for basically the same ideas:*
  - *"smart", "shrewd", "agility" → to emphasize the idea that the introduction of multiculturalism was an intelligent move*
  - *"spoke up", "audacious" → to show that the introduction of multiculturalism was courageous*
  - *"compromise", "accommodation" → to show that Canada is sensible and not prone to radicalism*
- *use of **rhetorical questions** → to engage the audience, to make them agree with what is said*
- *use of **first person pronouns:** "I" → to show that the speaker was also sceptical towards the concept of multiculturalism at first; "we" → to emphasize shared experience and shared responsibility to preserve Canada's multicultural identity*
- ***humour**, e.g. "were we really supposed to don national garb and sing and dance for one another?" → makes the speech lighter and more entertaining for the audience*
- ***comparison** with medieval Spain ("Hispania", "Andalusia") → to evoke a time and place that is often associated with diversity and religious tolerance*
- ***use of statistics** → to ground the speaker's arguments in facts*
- ***contrast** → by showing that intolerance is on the rise in other countries, the Canadian way of doing things appears particularly precious and worthy of preserving*

3. Creative writing: Imagine you are a Canadian with an immigrant background visiting your relative in Germany. Your relative is complaining about their difficult situation in Germany becoming really and fully integrated. You tell him/her about your experiences in Canada, what would have to change in Germany and what your relative could do. Write their dialogue.

	Der Schüler/Die Schülerin ...
Umsetzung der Aufgabenstellung	kann sich so weit in die Situation eines Kanadiers/einer Kanadierin und eines Deutschen/einer Deutschen mit Migrationshintergrund hineinversetzen, um einen weitgehend glaubwürdigen Dialog zu verfassen.

ISBN 978-3-425-73646-4

	Der Schüler/Die Schülerin ...
Textsortenspezifik	setzt die textsortenspezifischen Merkmale für *dialogue* um: • Sprecher kommen abwechselnd zu Wort • Ziel des Gesprächs: Verständnis für Anliegen und Suche nach Lösungsmöglichkeiten • Verweise auf Kenntnis der Situation von Einwanderern in Deutschland und Kanada • Vorschläge für Politiker erörtern (Bezug zu Textinformationen) • Notwendige Haltung beschreiben, die gelingende Integration unterstützt (*show causes and effects*) • Evtl. Beispiele aus eigener Erfahrung
Situationsangemessenheit und Adressatenbezug	schreibt weitgehend situationsangemessen: • Persönliches Gespräch unter Verwandten • zwangloses, persönliches Register
Text- und Problemverständnis	zeigt im Rahmen des Dialogs, dass er/sie die Frage der Integration ggfs. in größere Zusammenhänge stellen kann (*multiculturalism, national identity, history of immigration to Germany, recent public debates on migration and integration*)
Darstellung und Gliederung	verfasst einen Text, der den Erfordernissen von *creative writing* überwiegend entspricht: eigenständige Entwicklung eines fiktiven Gesprächs

Gesamteindruck	Die inhaltliche Leistung entspricht in vollem Maße den Anforderungen der Aufgabe.

Mögliche inhaltliche Aspekte:

Person complaining about lack of integration in Germany:
- *doesn't feel he/she fully belongs to German society*
- *Germany doesn't see itself as a country of immigration*
- *other cultures might be accepted but not considered part of German culture*
- *increase in xenophobia and nationalist polemic following the arrival of more than a million refugees in 2015*

Person visiting from Canada:
- *describes positive experiences in Canada*
- *shows understanding for relative's situation but also for Germany's geography and history, which are very different to Canada's (densely populated, location in the middle of Europe, historically not a typical country of immigration)*
- *for integration to work, Germany could also embrace multiculturalism and open up towards other cultures*
- *however, people with immigrant background should also try to identify with Germany*
- *possible advice for relative: mingle more with Germans, show an interest in "German" way of life*

ISBN 978-3-425-73646-4

Erwartungshorizont für eine gute sprachliche Leistung

Für die Einschätzung der sprachlichen Leistung schriftlicher Arbeiten kann folgende Tabelle eine Orientierung bieten.

Die Bewertung der sprachlichen Leistung erfolgt auf der Grundlage der in der Tabelle genannten Kriterien ganzheitlich über die in der linken Spalte genannten Teilaspekte hinweg; es werden also keine Einzelnoten zu diesen Teilaspekten gebildet. Die Gewichtung der einzelnen Kriterien innerhalb der Kategorien hängt von den Anforderungen der jeweiligen Aufgabenstellung ab.

	Der Schüler/Die Schülerin ...
Kommunikative Textgestaltung Textaufbau Textsortenspezifik Situationsangemessenheit und Adressatenbezug (Register)	• verfasst einen weitgehend zielgerichteten, strukturierten und kohärenten Text. • setzt die geforderten Textsortenmerkmale weitgehend überzeugend um. • schreibt weitgehend situationsangemessen und mit gelungenem Adressatenbezug.
Ausdrucksvermögen, Verwendung sprachlicher Mittel Eigenständigkeit Wortschatz Idiomatik Satzbau Umgang mit Materialien/ Belegtechnik	• verfasst eine eigenständige Darstellung. • verwendet sowohl allgemeinen als auch themenspezifischen Wortschatz weitgehend treffsicher und variabel. • verwendet weitgehend angemessene idiomatische Strukturen. • formuliert mit weitgehend variablem und funktionalem Satzbau unter Verwendung angemessen komplexer Strukturen. • verwendet Zitate weitgehend funktional und bettet diese weitgehend korrekt in den Textfluss ein. • kennzeichnet Zitate/Textverweise weitgehend korrekt.
Sprachrichtigkeit Lexik Grammatik/Syntax Orthografie Verständlichkeit	• drückt sich lexikalisch, grammatisch, syntaktisch und orthografisch weitgehend korrekt aus. • drückt sich verständlich aus: Sprachliche Verstöße beeinträchtigen die Verständlichkeit nicht.

Gesamteindruck	Die sprachliche Leistung entspricht in vollem Maße den Anforderungen der Aufgabe.

ISBN 978-3-425-73646-4

Lösungen und Erwartungshorizont für eine gute inhaltliche Leistung

Listening 1: Ireland's historic vote on abortion Webcode: WES-73646-04

1. to repeal the 8th amendment of their constitution
2. This is the end of Irish exceptionalism./The Ireland of absolutes is dead and gone.
3. a) to compensate for its troubles/for the fact that it exported so many of its people,
   b) to show that is was an exceptionally holy, Catholic place.
4. because the Irish people embrace/recognize their reality/they feel they don't need to be special anymore
5. like freaks in their own country
6. traditional people/people of faith
7. (kind of) culture wars
8. a small society/an intimate society/they agree about more things than they disagree
9. a battle between tradition and modernity
10. they won't/they are ideologically motivated and will continue to make their point
11. a popular vote of all Irish people/it shows what the (vast) majority of Irish people want

Listening 2: The Scots Irish Webcode: WES-73646-05

1. London
2. a pro-British, Unionist party
3. Ulster Scots
4. British
5. a) many of the (original) British colonists in Northern Ireland came from Scotland, b) Northern Ireland and Scotland are (geographically) very close to each other/people go back and forth all the time
6. occupiers
7. Catholic Irish went to Scotland
8. they looked for work
9. Glasgow
10. a) Irish nationalism, b) Unionism

Mediation: Discussions on abortions

Ireland is known for its Catholic conservatism in many private issues such as sex, partnership or abortion. Recently, Ireland has voted in a referendum to reform the country's strict abortion laws, which had effectively banned all terminations. Your Irish friend Sarah is preparing a panel discussion at school about how other countries are dealing with the topic of abortion. She has asked you for a contribution telling her how Germans think about that issue. You have found the following article on *Spiegel Online*. Send Sarah an email, telling her which aspects of the topic are recently discussed in Germany, according to Valerie Höhne's article.

	Der Schüler/Die Schülerin ...
Umsetzung der Aufgabenstellung	erfüllt weitgehend die Erfordernisse einer *Mediation*-Aufgabe: • Verzicht auf wortwörtliche Übersetzungen • Entnahme der nötigen Informationen aus dem deutschen Text (Textsorte: Kommentar) zum Verfassen eines eigenen Textes (Textsorte: informative E-Mail an eine(n) gleichaltrige(n) Freund(in))
Textsortenspezifik	setzt die textsortenspezifischen Merkmale für *email* weitgehend um.
Situationsangemessenheit und Adressatenbezug	schreibt weitgehend situationsangemessen und adressatenbezogen: • breite Schulöffentlichkeit • Bezug zum Thema im Werte- und Normenunterricht • neutrales Register: informativ-kritisch
Text- und Problemverständnis	kann das Thema ggfs. in größere Zusammenhänge *(self-determination, feminism, ethic and moral values, culture wars)* einordnen.

ISBN 978-3-425-73646-4

	Der Schüler/Die Schülerin ...
Darstellung und Gliederung	stellt die in Deutschland komplizierte rechtliche Lage hinsichtlich Abtreibungen (rechtswidrig, aber straffrei in den ersten drei Monaten nach erfolgter Beratung; Werbeverbot; neuer Kompromiss der Bundesregierung) sowie die öffentliche Diskussion zu dem Thema weitgehend nachvollziehbar dar.

Gesamteindruck	Die inhaltliche Leistung entspricht in vollem Maße den Anforderungen der Aufgabe.

Mögliche inhaltliche Aspekte:

- *the recent discussion about abortions has been triggered by a new political compromise which makes it possible for doctors to inform that they conduct abortions (information has been viewed as advertisement and advertisement for abortions is illegal according to article 219a)*
- *the discussion is dominated by strict opponents of abortion on the one side and those who believe that abortions should be allowed without any limitations on the other*
- *two problems the compromise wants to address:*
  - *no list of places for pregnant women to turn to*
  - *offering abortions openly is illegal → punishment of doctors who do so*
- *according to the author, the discussion about article 219a doesn't address the core of the matter: the continuing illegality of abortions according to article 218. This is what should be discussed on a broad basis.*

Writing: Irish youth and Catholicism

1. Comprehension: Summarize the article below.

	Der Schüler/Die Schülerin ...
Umsetzung der Aufgabenstellung	kann eine selbstständig formulierte, strukturierte und zusammenhängende Zusammenfassung des Artikels unter Beachtung relevanter Textsortenmerkmale verfassen, indem nur wesentliche Informationen weitgehend präzise wiedergegeben werden.
Textsortenspezifik	setzt die textsortenspezifischen Merkmale für *summary* weitgehend um: • Einleitungssatz (Genre, Titel, Autor, Quelle, Publikationsjahr, Thema) • *present tense* • eigene Worte, keine Zitate, keine Verweise • keine Nacherzählung • keine Wertung
Text- und Problemverständnis	durchdringt die Textvorlage weitgehend.
Darstellung und Gliederung	verfasst einen strukturierten, kohärenten und durchgängig lesbaren Text, der überwiegend den Erfordernissen des Operators *summarize* entspricht: straffe Darstellung der wesentlichen Aspekte des Textes

Gesamteindruck	Die inhaltliche Leistung entspricht in vollem Maße den Anforderungen der Aufgabe.

Mögliche inhaltliche Aspekte:

- *Ireland, the Catholic Church and the young people of Ireland have changed since Pope John Paul II visited Ireland in 1979: abuse scandals, fallen church attendance, fewer priests*
- *many young Catholics questions the Church or even turn away from it*
- *esp. the Church's stance towards the LBGT+ community troubles young Irish people*
- *others agree with the Church on that matter and feel there is a stigma attached to being religious*
- *there are priests, such as Fr Chris O'Donnell in Dublin, who reach out to young people and want the Church to be more inclusive*

ISBN 978-3-425-73646-4

2. Analysis: Explain the changing attitudes of the Irish young towards Catholicism.

	Der Schüler/Die Schülerin ...
Umsetzung der Aufgabenstellung	führt die im Sinne der Aufgabenstellung relevanten Informationen weitgehend präzise aus.
Text- und Problemverständnis	durchdringt die Textvorlage weitgehend.
Darstellung und Gliederung	verfasst einen Text, der den Erfordernissen des Operators *explain* überwiegend entspricht: • Erklärung für die veränderten Einstellungen gegenüber der katholischen Kirche (*show causes and effects*) • Untermauerung durch sinnvolle und prägnante Beispiele aus dem Text (u. a. Verwendung von Zitaten)

Gesamteindruck	Die inhaltliche Leistung entspricht in vollem Maße den Anforderungen der Aufgabe.

Mögliche inhaltliche Aspekte:

- *changing society means more freedom for young people to have different beliefs to their family's*
- *scientific knowledge makes young people question the teachings of the Church*
- *some turn away from the Church due to the scandals associated with it and due to its stance towards LGBT+ people*

3. Writing a discussion: Should religions change with their societies or should they remain institutions of tradition in an ever faster changing world? Discuss by giving examples from the text and materials studied in class.

	Der Schüler/Die Schülerin ...
Umsetzung der Aufgabenstellung	führt die im Sinne der Aufgabenstellung relevanten Informationen weitgehend präzise aus.
Textsortenspezifik	setzt die textsortenspezifischen Merkmale für *discussion* um: • die Argumente beider Seiten werden ausgewogen dargestellt • die Argumente werden mit passenden Beispielen belegt • aus dem Hauptteil heraus begründetes Fazit
Text- und Problemverständnis	• durchdringt die Textvorlage weitgehend. • kann das Thema des Artikels bzw. der Diskussion ggfs. in größere Zusammenhänge (*religion in liberal societies, identity, values, moral orientation*) einordnen.
Darstellung und Gliederung	• erfüllt mit seinen/ihren überwiegend klaren und logischen Ausführungen die Erfordernisse des Operators *discuss*: Ausgewogene Behandlung der Pro/Contra-Argumente mit Fazit

Gesamteindruck	Die inhaltliche Leistung entspricht in vollem Maße den Anforderungen der Aufgabe.

Mögliche inhaltliche Aspekte:

Arguments in favour of change:
- *religions are part of societies and should therefore evolve with them; otherwise they run the risk of becoming irrelevant*
- *by changing they can offer even more valuable orientation for people, because they address current problems and questions*
- *through change, religions not only remain relevant for believers but also attract young people to represent them*

Arguments against change:
- *in an ever faster changing world, there should be some things people can rely on to stay the same*
- *by changing, religions run the risk of becoming arbitrary and subject to trends*
- *continuity as such offers orientation and stability*

ISBN 978-3-425-73646-4

Erwartungshorizont für eine gute sprachliche Leistung

Für die Einschätzung der sprachlichen Leistung schriftlicher Arbeiten kann folgende Tabelle eine Orientierung bieten.

Die Bewertung der sprachlichen Leistung erfolgt auf der Grundlage der in der Tabelle genannten Kriterien ganzheitlich über die in der linken Spalte genannten Teilaspekte hinweg; es werden also keine Einzelnoten zu diesen Teilaspekten gebildet. Die Gewichtung der einzelnen Kriterien innerhalb der Kategorien hängt von den Anforderungen der jeweiligen Aufgabenstellung ab.

	Der Schüler/Die Schülerin ...
Kommunikative Textgestaltung Textaufbau Textsortenspezifik Situationsangemessenheit und Adressatenbezug (Register)	• verfasst einen weitgehend zielgerichteten, strukturierten und kohärenten Text. • setzt die geforderten Textsortenmerkmale weitgehend überzeugend um. • schreibt weitgehend situationsangemessen und mit gelungenem Adressatenbezug.
Ausdrucksvermögen, Verwendung sprachlicher Mittel Eigenständigkeit Wortschatz Idiomatik Satzbau Umgang mit Materialien/ Belegtechnik	• verfasst eine eigenständige Darstellung. • verwendet sowohl allgemeinen als auch themenspezifischen Wortschatz weitgehend treffsicher und variabel. • verwendet weitgehend angemessene idiomatische Strukturen. • formuliert mit weitgehend variablem und funktionalem Satzbau unter Verwendung angemessen komplexer Strukturen. • verwendet Zitate weitgehend funktional und bettet diese weitgehend korrekt in den Textfluss ein. • kennzeichnet Zitate/Textverweise weitgehend korrekt.
Sprachrichtigkeit Lexik Grammatik/Syntax Orthografie Verständlichkeit	• drückt sich lexikalisch, grammatisch, syntaktisch und orthografisch weitgehend korrekt aus. • drückt sich verständlich aus: Sprachliche Verstöße beeinträchtigen die Verständlichkeit nicht.

Gesamteindruck	Die sprachliche Leistung entspricht in vollem Maße den Anforderungen der Aufgabe.

ISBN 978-3-425-73646-4

Lösungen und Erwartungshorizont für eine gute inhaltliche Leistung

Listening 1: Delivery robots Webcode: WES-73646-06

1D, 2A, 3B, 4C

Listening 2: Real-life cyborgs Webcode: WES-73646-07

1. one of the founders of the Cyborg Foundation/a cyborg himself
2. feels like he *is* technology
3. he is colour-blind
4. it allows Neil to hear and sense colours/it transposes the frequency of light into the frequency of sound
5. through an operation/his head was drilled four times to integrate the antenna
6. like it is part of his body/feels like a new body part
7. a) infrared colours/light, b) ultraviolet colours/light, c) colours from other places in the world (due to Bluetooth technology)
8. RFID-chips implanted in both of his hands
9. a) unlock his car, b) unlock his computer
10. through brain stimulators
11. *two of these aspects:* advanced capabilities that biology never gave humans/let people do things that animals can do/let people do what no human can do
12. *three of these aspects:* a light/a microphone/a chatting tool/a hands-free phone/a new telephone/something to do with Google Glass/something used for filming
13. more wearable technology/wearing tech will become normal/people will start accepting the unity of cybernetics and organisms

Mediation: Artificial intelligence

You have dealt with artificial intelligence as an important force of the digital revolution. While browsing the Internet you have come across a German article that indicates that artificial intelligence is becoming increasingly creative. You decide to share your new insight with an international science community for high school students by posting on their website. Write a blog post which informs the community about advances in AI, its market value and the critical concern that is associated with its development.

	Der Schüler/Die Schülerin ...
Umsetzung der Aufgabenstellung	erfüllt weitgehend die Erfordernisse einer *Mediation*-Aufgabe: • Verzicht auf wortwörtliche Übersetzungen • Entnahme der nötigen Informationen aus dem deutschen Text (Textsorte: Artikel aus einer Tageszeitung) zum Verfassen eines eigenen Textes (Textsorte: Blogeintrag)
Textsortenspezifik	setzt die textsortenspezifischen Merkmale für *blog post* weitgehend um: • Titel • Einleitung, die auf das Thema hinführt • Gliederung in Absätzen • zusammenfassender Schluss, der eine Frage aufwirft und die Leserschaft auffordert, den Beitrag zu kommentieren bzw. ihre Meinung kundzutun
Situationsangemessenheit und Adressatenbezug	schreibt weitgehend situationsangemessen und adressatenbezogen: • interessierte Online Community Gleichaltriger • Register: freundlich und informell • Verwendung der 1. Person
Text- und Problemverständnis	kann das Thema des Artikels ggfs. in größere Zusammenhänge (*chances and risks of new technologies*) einordnen.
Darstellung und Gliederung	kann die Entwicklung künstlicher Intelligenz im kreativen Bereich, wie z. B. in den bildenden und darstellenden Künsten, differenziert und überwiegend klar und logisch darstellen.

ISBN 978-3-425-73646-4

Gesamteindruck	Die inhaltliche Leistung entspricht in vollem Maße den Anforderungen der Aufgabe.

Mögliche inhaltliche Aspekte:

Advances in AI:
- *artistic work, like painting, writing books and poems, composing pieces of music and helping musicians to come up with original lyrics, is now autonomously conducted by AI*

AI's market value:
- *a painting created by AI was auctioned for more than $400,000 at Christie's*
- *Sony Music, Warner Music Group and Abbey Road Studios invest in AI start-ups*
- *IBM and Google also sell AI programs that compose music*

The critical concern that is associated with AI's development:
- *AI influences and changes people's listening habits through personalized recommendations based on preferences (Spotify), by playing mood related music (Alexa) or by adapting music to given contexts (AI Music)*
- *the quality of creative work by AI is open to critical debate*
- *the question of whether AI itself or its programmers are the composers of a piece of creative work is contested*
- *the unique characteristic of creativity is called into question*
- *concerns about humans being replaced by AI*

Writing: Machines taking over

Imagine you are taking part in an international school project on the potential and risks of new technologies. You have come across an article about an automated vending machine (A) and a cartoon about robots taking over human jobs (B). You decide to write an article for the project's website entitled "Machines taking over business: a blessing or a curse?"

1. Comprehension: State what the "Clifton Speedy Shop" is and also name its advantages.

	Der Schüler/Die Schülerin ...
Umsetzung der Aufgabenstellung	kann benennen, um was für ein Geschäft es sich bei „Clifton Speedy Shop" handelt und welche Vorteile es birgt.
Text- und Problemverständnis	durchdringt die Textvorlage weitgehend.
Darstellung und Gliederung	erfüllt mit seinen/ihren klaren und logischen Ausführungen überwiegend die Erfordernisse der Operatoren *state* und *name*: knappe Darstellung der wichtigsten Aspekte.

Gesamteindruck	Die inhaltliche Leistung entspricht in vollem Maße den Anforderungen der Aufgabe.

Mögliche inhaltliche Aspekte:

What "Clifton Speedy Shop" is:
- *a traditional looking, medium-sized shop without any shop assistants*
- *it sells all kinds of items needed for daily life*
- *cash and credit card payments are possible*
- *the machine sends emails about sold articles to its owner and inventor (Peter Fox) so that he can stock the machine accordingly*

Advantages:
- *calculable opening hours/no dependency*
- *since there are no stores in Clifton, the machine provides a local shopping facility, which is appreciated by Clifton's residents, because other shopping facilities are far away and only reachable by car*

- *holidaymakers in the cottages (nearby) can get supplies without having to use the local pub as a rather limited shopping possibility; this in turn takes the pressure off the local pub*

2. Analysis: Analyse the most striking pictorial elements in the cartoon with reference to the given topic.

	Der Schüler/Die Schülerin ...
Umsetzung der Aufgabenstellung	kann den Cartoon als diskontinuierlichen Text differenziert im Sinne der Aufgabenstellung beschreiben und wesentliche Bildelemente themenbezogen analysieren.
Text- und Problemverständnis	weist eine weitgehend treffende Beschreibung und Auswertung des Cartoons nach und zeigt so ein überwiegend differenziertes Text- und Problemverständnis.
Darstellung und Gliederung	verfasst einen eigenständigen, strukturierten, kohärenten und durchgängig lesbaren Text, der den Erfordernissen des Operators *analyse* überwiegend entspricht: • präzise, nachvollziehbare Beschreibung, die Lokalisierungsphrasen beinhaltet • bildliche Elemente und deren Funktion/Bedeutung werden im Kontext des Cartoons erläuternd benannt

Gesamteindruck	Die inhaltliche Leistung entspricht in vollem Maße den Anforderungen der Aufgabe.

Mögliche inhaltliche Aspekte:

Description:
- *cartoon is focusing on robots making the human workforce redundant*
- *on the left of the cartoon, a woman is sat behind a desk; the sign below her reads "Now Hiring"*
- *the woman is smiling politely and is dressed professionally; above her are two business charts, which reveal to the reader that this is a professional office*
- *on the right of the cartoon is a figure who appears to be a robot because they have an antenna on their head, and though its body parts roughly resemble those of a human, the body is comprised of geometric shapes, such as a square head, and screws and bolts*
- *this robot has a mouth and nose, indicating that it is capable of speech and based on humans; the robot also carries a briefcase which makes it seem more professional and demonstrates that this robot is in an office/ job centre to find a job of its own*
- *at the bottom of the image is the caption, "I'm not particular. I'll take any job that will replace a human."*
- *the robot has its mouth open, suggesting this statement was spoken by the robot, and it appears to be the robot's response to a question asked by the woman behind the next regarding which jobs the robot is interested in*

Analysis:
- *the focus of this cartoon is clearly the idea that robots could take over any human job, as is indicated by the caption; the idea that the robot specifically wants jobs which will allow it to "replace a human" implies that robots are able to think and have opinions, and that this robot wants to deliberately make humans redundant*
- *the robot in the cartoon represents all robots and machines, and this desire to disrupt the lives of humans portrays new technology as evil; the cartoon relates to the fear that many people have that, with the increase of technology and robotics, humans will no longer be seen as necessary within the job market*
- *the contrast between the soft, rounded lines used to draw the human woman and the hard lines and shapes which make up the body of the robot highlight the differences between humans and robots; however, the robot's mouth and nose appear almost human, which implies that robots are at least as smart and capable as humans.*
- *additionally, the briefcase suggests that robots are ready and willing to take over human jobs as soon as possible*
- *overall, the message of the cartoon is that we should fear robots and new technology, as this scientific progress will prevent most humans from being able to find jobs*

3. Writing an article: Write an article in which you discuss the automatic vending machine and the robot in the office within the context of "Machines taking over business: a blessing or a curse?" with concrete references to materials A and B. You may also refer to materials dealt with in class.

	Der Schüler/Die Schülerin ...
Umsetzung der Aufgabenstellung	kann einen selbstständig formulierten, adressatengerechten und strukturierten, zusammenhängenden Artikel gemäß der Aufgabenstellung unter Beachtung der Textkonvention verfassen, indem sich der Artikel argumentativ mit unterschiedlichen Positionen bezüglich *machines taking over as a blessing or a curse* differenziert auseinandersetzt.
Textsortenspezifik	setzt die textsortenspezifischen Merkmale für *article* um: • Titel; Autorschaft • Einleitung • Hauptteil mit pro/contra-Diskussion • resümierender Schluss mit einer klaren Position
Situationsangemessenheit und Adressatenbezug	schreibt weitgehend situationsangemessen und adressatenbezogen: • breite Schulöffentlichkeit • neutrales, nicht allzu formelles Register
Text- und Problemverständnis	• weist ein weitgehend differenziertes Textverständnis im Sinne der Aufgabenstellung nach, indem unter Bezugnahme auf das vorliegende sowie im Unterricht behandelte Material detailliert und widerspruchsfrei die eigene Meinung überzeugend dargelegt wird.
Darstellung und Gliederung	erfüllt mit seinen/ihren klaren und logischen Ausführungen überwiegend die Erfordernisse des Operators *discuss*: • ausgewogene Darstellung der Probleme und Vorteile der Automatisierung in Geschäften und Betrieben • Unterstützung der Argumente durch Beispiele aus den Textvorlagen und dem Unterrichtsstoff • Fazit

Gesamteindruck	Die inhaltliche Leistung entspricht in vollem Maße den Anforderungen der Aufgabe.

Mögliche inhaltliche Aspekte:

Blessing:
- *in remote areas machines taking over the human workforce can be a blessing (e.g. a locally reachable shopping facility for older people, reliable opening hours)*
- *robots/machines can eliminate human mistakes due to automated standardization*
- *using cost-efficient robots increases revenue*
- *if robots are smarter than humans, they are likely to be able to do human jobs more efficiently*

Curse:
- *people experience being made redundant with all the negative economic, social and psychological consequences that come with unemployment*
- *likely that there will be fewer jobs for humans in future*
- *human isolation due to a lack of real communication*
- *if robots develop the ability to think and have opinions, as suggested in the cartoon, they may try to deliberately disrupt or destroy human lives*

ISBN 978-3-425-73646-4

Erwartungshorizont für eine gute sprachliche Leistung

Für die Einschätzung der sprachlichen Leistung schriftlicher Arbeiten kann folgende Tabelle eine Orientierung bieten.

Die Bewertung der sprachlichen Leistung erfolgt auf der Grundlage der in der Tabelle genannten Kriterien ganzheitlich über die in der linken Spalte genannten Teilaspekte hinweg; es werden also keine Einzelnoten zu diesen Teilaspekten gebildet. Die Gewichtung der einzelnen Kriterien innerhalb der Kategorien hängt von den Anforderungen der jeweiligen Aufgabenstellung ab.

	Der Schüler/Die Schülerin ...
Kommunikative Textgestaltung Textaufbau Textsortenspezifik Situationsangemessenheit und Adressatenbezug (Register)	• verfasst einen weitgehend zielgerichteten, strukturierten und kohärenten Text. • setzt die geforderten Textsortenmerkmale weitgehend überzeugend um. • schreibt weitgehend situationsangemessen und mit gelungenem Adressatenbezug.
Ausdrucksvermögen, Verwendung sprachlicher Mittel Eigenständigkeit Wortschatz Idiomatik Satzbau Umgang mit Materialien/ Belegtechnik	• verfasst eine eigenständige Darstellung. • verwendet sowohl allgemeinen als auch themenspezifischen Wortschatz weitgehend treffsicher und variabel. • verwendet weitgehend angemessene idiomatische Strukturen. • formuliert mit weitgehend variablem und funktionalem Satzbau unter Verwendung angemessen komplexer Strukturen. • verwendet Zitate weitgehend funktional und bettet diese weitgehend korrekt in den Textfluss ein. • kennzeichnet Zitate/Textverweise weitgehend korrekt.
Sprachrichtigkeit Lexik Grammatik/Syntax Orthografie Verständlichkeit	• drückt sich lexikalisch, grammatisch, syntaktisch und orthografisch weitgehend korrekt aus. • drückt sich verständlich aus: Sprachliche Verstöße beeinträchtigen die Verständlichkeit nicht.

Gesamteindruck	Die sprachliche Leistung entspricht in vollem Maße den Anforderungen der Aufgabe.

ISBN 978-3-425-73646-4

Lösungen und Erwartungshorizont für eine gute inhaltliche Leistung

Listening 1: Dystopian novel *The Water Cure* Webcode: WES-73646-08 (Ausschnitt: 00:00–04:22)

1b, 2d, 3a, 4b, 5d, 6d, 7a, 8d, 9c, 10b

Listening 2: Facial recognition technology Webcode: WES-73646-09

1. a) implications of facial recognition software, b) emerging use of artificial intelligence (in local policing)
2. *two of these aspects*: misidentification/innocent people could be pursued by the police/chance of fatal consequences
3. to help officers make better decisions
4. seeing differences in darker faces
5. (to dig a layer deeper and) understand the benefits and risks
6. *DNA technology:* helped wrongfully convicted people being exonerated; *facial recognition:* a) reduce prejudice in policing, b) help catch dangerous people
7. a) people make use of such technologies for their convenience, b) questions of what privacy means are raised

Mediation: "Designer babies"

Your former American exchange partner is currently working on an essay for his social studies class on "designer babies" and is wondering how this issue is treated in Germany. Having read an interesting article about this subject, you decide to write him an email in which you outline He Jiankui's alleged scientific achievement and corresponding responses by politics, churches, and experts in the field of ethics.

	Der Schüler/Die Schülerin ...
Umsetzung der Aufgabenstellung	erfüllt weitgehend die Erfordernisse einer *Mediation*-Aufgabe: • Verzicht auf wortwörtliche Übersetzungen • Entnahme der nötigen Informationen aus dem deutschen Text (Textsorte: Zeitungsartikel) zum Verfassen eines eigenen Textes (Textsorte: E-Mail)
Textsortenspezifik	setzt die textsortenspezifischen Merkmale für *email* weitgehend um: • Betreff • Anrede • Einleitung, die in das Thema und die Situation ein-/hinführt (Hes mutmaßliche HIV-resistente „Designerbabys") • inhaltlich aspektorientierte Strukturierung (Reaktion der Politik, der Kirche(n), der Ethikexperten) • zusammenfassender Schluss, der die Situatione (*essay for social studies*) aufgreift und adäquat persönlich endet • Schlussgrußformel (ggfs. inkl. guter Wünsche für das Essay)
Situationsangemessenheit und Adressatenbezug	schreibt weitgehend situationsangemessen und adressatenbezogen: • persönlicher Freund • eher neutrales, sachliches Register ob des Themas
Kulturspezifik	kann ggfs. kulturspezifische Aspekte und Begriffe (deutsche Minister und Ministerien, Evangelischer Pressedienst, katholische und evangelische Kirchen in Deutschland) weitgehend nachvollziehbar erläutern bzw. verständlich umschreiben.
Text- und Problemverständnis	kann das Thema des Artikels ggfs. in größere Zusammenhänge (*ethical questions/problems with new technologies*) einordnen.
Darstellung und Gliederung	kann alle im Sinne der Aufgabenstellung wichtigen Informationen überwiegend präzise und situations- bzw. adressatenorientiert wiedergeben.

Gesamteindruck	Die inhaltliche Leistung entspricht in vollem Maße den Anforderungen der Aufgabe.

ISBN 978-3-425-73646-4

Mögliche inhaltliche Aspekte:

He Jiankui's alleged scientific achievement:
- *Chinese scientist He Jiankui has manipulated the genome of embryos via genetic scissors/CRISPR and these embryos have now presumably developed into born HIV resistant babies*

Political responses:
- *the Federal Ministry of Education and Research condemns He Jiankui's manipulation as clear boundary crossing*
- *Federal Minister of Health, Jens Spahn, deplores He's achievement, believing that man should not play god by experimenting with the human genome. He demands Europe to invest large sums of money into research in order to reach the top position to establish standards which are constant with European values*

Responses from the churches:
- *Protestant news outlet regards He's action as a violation of established ethical standards for medical research*
- *the president of the German Protestant church, Heinrich Bedford-Strohm, issues the warning of getting human breeding started*
- *a Catholic ethics expert demands similar protection standards for biogenetics as we have for human rights*

Responses by ethics experts:
- *co-chairman of the German Ethics Council criticizes the application of CRISPR as consequences of genome editing are incalculable*
- *the Protestant social ethics expert Ulrich H. J. Körtner questions in how far society can be involved in the debate on these complexities of biopolitics and bioethics stating that scientific freedom does and must have ethical limits*

Writing: *The forever kitten*

Read the following extract from the short story *The forever kitten* (2005) by Peter F. Hamilton and complete the tasks. The story is about Joe Gordon, a wealthy venture capitalist who lives with his wife Fiona and their two daughters in a mansion. While their younger daughter, Heloise, is an adorably cute, innocent and well-behaved child, their older teenaged daughter, Saskia, has gone completely astray. She has quit school, consumes drugs, steals from her parents, shoplifts and, thus, has often been arrested by the police. Consequently, she causes her parents great trouble, which leads to frustration and even health issues for Fiona.

1. Comprehension: Summarize the extract.

	Der Schüler/Die Schülerin …
Umsetzung der Aufgabenstellung	führt die im Sinne der Aufgabenstellung relevanten Informationen weitgehend präzise um.
Textsortenspezifik	setzt die textsortenspezifischen Merkmale für *summary* um: • Einleitungssatz (Genre, Titel, Autor/in, Quelle, Publikationsjahr, Thema) • *present tense* • eigene Worte, keine Zitate, keine Verweise • keine Nacherzählung • keine Wertung
Text- und Problemverständnis	durchdringt die Textvorlage weitgehend.
Darstellung und Gliederung	verfasst einen strukturierten, kohärenten und durchgängig lesbaren Text, der überwiegend den Erfordernissen des Operators *summarize* entspricht: straffe Darstellung der wesentlichen Aspekte des Textes

Gesamteindruck	Die inhaltliche Leistung entspricht in vollem Maße den Anforderungen der Aufgabe.

Mögliche inhaltliche Aspekte:

- *the dystopian short story "The Forever Kitten", written by Peter F. Hamilton, is about a doctor, who hast just been released from custody, and his investor, the venture capitalist Joe Gordon, negotiating their project on stopping the human ageing process*
- *to avoid a prison sentence and to continue the ethically forbidden project the doctor has to leave the country*
- *it becomes apparent that the doctor has unknowingly been successful in creating a never aging kitten*
- *Joe Gordon aims at the possibility of human rejuvenation*
- *having a wayward teenaged daughter, who causes the family a lot of distress, Gordon wants the doctor to carry out the necessary procedures to keep his daughter Heloise at her five-year-old stage*

2. Analysis: Analyse the narrative perspective and the atmosphere it creates.

	Der Schüler/Die Schülerin ...
Umsetzung der Aufgabenstellung	kann die Erzählperspektive und Atmosphäre der Kurzgeschichte durch Analyse expliziter und impliziter Elemente überwiegend klar deuten und dabei wesentliche Aspekte ausführen und mit relevanten Details und Beispielen stützen.
Text- und Problemverständnis	weist ein dokumentiertes, weitgehend differenziertes Textverständnis im Sinne der Aufgabenstellung nach.
Darstellung und Gliederung	verfasst einen Text, der den Erfordernissen des Operators *analyse* überwiegend entspricht: • sachgemäßer Aufbau und eigene Schwerpunktsetzung mit folgerichtigem Ergebnis (→ Einleitung – Hauptteil – Schluss) • Benennung und Analyse von *narrative perspective* und *atmosphere* • *present tense* • treffende Zitate, Verweise, Belege • pointierte Darstellung

Gesamteindruck	Die inhaltliche Leistung entspricht in vollem Maße den Anforderungen der Aufgabe.

Mögliche inhaltliche Aspekte:

Narrative perspective:

- *first-person narrator with a limited point of view, as the story is told from the doctor's perspective and the reader knows only what this character thinks, knows, sees or hears ("I never thought I'd be so entranced by anything as simple as horse chestnuts", ll. 1–3)*
- *the narrative perspective makes the reader identify with the doctor, even though he is has committed a crime, ("I smiled over at Heloise ...", l. 68)*
- *the first person narrator seems to have conflicted feelings about his research: on the one hand he is a scientist through and through and wants to carry on with the project of human rejuvenation ("'I can do it,' I said through clenched teeth. 'I can.'", ll. 61f.), on the other hand he doesn't like the idea that the investor wants to make a lot of money with it ("I recognized the greed in his eyes: it wasn't pleasant.", ll. 52f.)*

Atmosphere:

- *the narrator employs vivid, expressive words e.g. "mansion", "lush", "ornate" → evokes an atmosphere of great wealth and comfort around the Gordon family*
- *at the same time he uses numerous scientific expressions (e.g. "stasis-regeneration", "stabilized its cellular structure", "human rejuvenation", , "practical application", , "mammal reaches sexual maturity", "modification") → this is to show that he is a scientist through and through and is interested in his research for scientific as opposed to monetary reasons*
- *throughout the narration constant contrasts are created between the untouched innocent nature ("horse chestnuts", l. 3, "the smile on her face ... was angelic", ll. 26f., "fluffy light fur", l. 30) and the scientific procedure of human rejuvenation (see above) → illustrates the doctor's dilemma, adds to the shock the reader experiences when reading about Gordon's request*

ISBN 978-3-425-73646-4

- *all in all, there is an atmosphere of something forbidden, fundamentally wrong and potentially very dangerous happening (meddling with nature, experimenting with children)*

3.
a) Writing an article: You are taking part in the international school project "How far should scientific research go?" You have decided to write an article for the project website. In your article, discuss whether there should be limits to scientific research and if so, who should define them. Refer to Hamilton's short story and to materials dealt with in class.

	Der Schüler/Die Schülerin ...
Umsetzung der Aufgabenstellung	kann einen selbstständig formulierten, adressatengerechten und weitgehend strukturierten, zusammenhängenden Artikel gemäß der Aufgabenstellung unter Beachtung der Textkonvention verfassen, indem sich der Artikel argumentativ mit unterschiedlichen Positionen bezüglich *limits to scientific research* differenziert auseinandersetzt.
Textsortenspezifik	setzt die textsortenspezifischen Merkmale für *article* um: • Titel; Autorschaft • Einleitung • Hauptteil mit pro/contra-Diskussion • zusammenfassender, resümierender und klar positionierender Schluss
Situationsangemessenheit und Adressatenbezug	schreibt situationsangemessen und adressatenbezogen: • breite Schulöffentlichkeit • neutrales, informatives Register
Text- und Problemverständnis	weist ein weitgehend differenziertes Textverständnis im Sinne der Aufgabenstellung nach, indem unter Bezugnahme auf das vorliegende sowie im Unterricht behandelte Material detailliert und widerspruchsfrei die eigene Meinung überzeugend dargelegt wird.
Darstellung und Gliederung	erfüllt mit seinen/ihren klaren und logischen Ausführungen überwiegend die Erfordernisse des Operators *discuss*: • ausgewogene Darstellung der Argumente für und wider einer Beschränkung wissenschaftlicher Forschung • Unterstützung der Argumente durch Beispiele aus der Kurzgeschichte und dem Unterrichtsstoff • Fazit

Gesamteindruck	Die inhaltliche Leistung entspricht in vollem Maße den Anforderungen der Aufgabe.

Mögliche inhaltliche Aspekte:

Arguments against limits to scientific research:
- *scientific progress can only thrive if there are no limits as to what is allowed, e.g. look at the historical role of the Church in thwarting scientific progress*
- *if societies decide to sanction certain scientific procedures, they will be carried out anyway, either illegally (as in the short story) or in societies with less scruples and regulations*
- *we might run the risk of being overtaken by other societies who have fewer regulations than we do*

Arguments in favour of limits to scientific research:
- *the dignity of the human being stands above all scientific progress; the cruel and deadly experiments with humans in the Third Reich have shown what boundless scientific research can lead to*
- *societies shouldn't pursue science just for the sake of it (as the doctor in the short story seems to do); it first has to be proven that the benefits of scientific research outweigh the disadvantages and potential risks*
- *we as society have to engage in an inclusive discourse as to where the limits should be; it shouldn't be decided only by experts*

ISBN 978-3-425-73646-4

b) Creative writing: The short story has an open end. Continue the story, finding a suitable ending.

	Der Schüler/Die Schülerin ...
Umsetzung der Aufgabenstellung	kann nach der Lektüre des Auszugs die Perspektive des Ich-Erzählers einnehmen und die Kurzgeschichte weitgehend glaubwürdig zu Ende schreiben.
Textsortenspezifik	setzt die textsortenspezifischen Merkmale für Ende einer Kurzgeschichte um: • Auflösung des für eine *short story* typischen Konflikts • Dialoge • Beobachtungen und Gedanken des Ich-Erzählers
Situationsangemessenheit und Adressatenbezug	schreibt weitgehend situationsangemessen und adressatenbezogen: • Leserschaft der Kurzgeschichte • Art und Sprache möglichst im Stil der Vorlage
Text- und Problemverständnis	durchdringt die Textvorlage weitgehend, sodass eine glaubwürdige Fortführung der Kurzgeschichte gelingt.
Darstellung und Gliederung	verfasst einen Text, der den Erfordernissen von *creative writing* überwiegend entspricht: Verfassen eines eigenständigen und kreativen Endes der Kurzgeschichte.

Gesamteindruck	Die inhaltliche Leistung entspricht in vollem Maße den Anforderungen der Aufgabe.

Mögliche inhaltliche Aspekte:

- *the doctor is shocked by Gordon's words but then decides to throw caution to the winds; he agrees to satisfy Gordon's wish as it would give him the opportunity to try out his procedure on a human being*
- *the doctor wrestles with himself but then suddenly sees how morally corrupted Gordon's proposal is; he decides to leave Gordon even if it means that he will face jail*

ISBN 978-3-425-73646-4

Erwartungshorizont für eine gute sprachliche Leistung

Für die Einschätzung der sprachlichen Leistung schriftlicher Arbeiten kann folgende Tabelle eine Orientierung bieten.

Die Bewertung der sprachlichen Leistung erfolgt auf der Grundlage der in der Tabelle genannten Kriterien ganzheitlich über die in der linken Spalte genannten Teilaspekte hinweg; es werden also keine Einzelnoten zu diesen Teilaspekten gebildet. Die Gewichtung der einzelnen Kriterien innerhalb der Kategorien hängt von den Anforderungen der jeweiligen Aufgabenstellung ab.

	Der Schüler/Die Schülerin …
Kommunikative Textgestaltung Textaufbau Textsortenspezifik Situationsangemessenheit und Adressatenbezug (Register)	• verfasst einen weitgehend zielgerichteten, strukturierten und kohärenten Text. • setzt die geforderten Textsortenmerkmale weitgehend überzeugend um. • schreibt weitgehend situationsangemessen und mit gelungenem Adressatenbezug.
Ausdrucksvermögen, Verwendung sprachlicher Mittel Eigenständigkeit Wortschatz Idiomatik Satzbau Umgang mit Materialien/ Belegtechnik	• verfasst eine eigenständige Darstellung. • verwendet sowohl allgemeinen als auch themenspezifischen Wortschatz weitgehend treffsicher und variabel. • verwendet weitgehend angemessene idiomatische Strukturen. • formuliert mit weitgehend variablem und funktionalem Satzbau unter Verwendung angemessen komplexer Strukturen. • verwendet Zitate weitgehend funktional und bettet diese weitgehend korrekt in den Textfluss ein. • kennzeichnet Zitate/Textverweise weitgehend korrekt.
Sprachrichtigkeit Lexik Grammatik/Syntax Orthografie Verständlichkeit	• drückt sich lexikalisch, grammatisch, syntaktisch und orthografisch weitgehend korrekt aus. • drückt sich verständlich aus: Sprachliche Verstöße beeinträchtigen die Verständlichkeit nicht.

Gesamteindruck	Die sprachliche Leistung entspricht in vollem Maße den Anforderungen der Aufgabe.

Lösungen und Erwartungshorizont für eine gute inhaltliche Leistung

Listening 1: Fake news Webcode: WES-73646-10

1a, 2b, 3c, 4a, 5d, 6d, 7b, 8c, 9d, 10d

Listening 2: Teenagers and their phones Webcode: WES-73646-11

1. address addiction/compulsive use
2. gaming disorder is mental health condition/behavioural addiction
3. fear tech overuse more than sex or drug abuse
4. *three of these aspects:* problems at work/in relationships/with sleep/fights at home/lying/depression/anxiety/ADHD
5. track smartphone use/find out how often you pick up phone
6. make more money when people are online
7. likes it/enjoys using it/does something to her/causes anxiety
8. fear of missing out (FOMO)/fear of being scrutinized/fear that every post is examined
9. gets up at one or two at night to use smartphone/stays up all night to use smartphone/snapchatting with friends at night
10. does not know what she can do about it/(does not know she is online)
11. more than half/more than 50 %
12. a) need it for school, b) stay in contact with friends

Mediation: A scandal in journalism

Together with your American partner school, your English class is working on a project about journalism today. You have come across the following article about a journalistic scandal in Germany's famous news magazine *Der Spiegel*. Write an article for the project website about this scandal, focusing on criteria of journalistic quality that were ignored.

	Der Schüler/Die Schülerin ...
Umsetzung der Aufgabenstellung	erfüllt weitgehend die Erfordernisse einer *Mediation*-Aufgabe: • Verzicht auf wortwörtliche Übersetzungen • Entnahme der nötigen Informationen aus dem deutschen Text (Textsorte: Artikel aus einer Wochenzeitung) zum Verfassen eines eigenen Textes (Textsorte: Web-Artikel)
Textsortenspezifik	setzt die textsortenspezifischen Merkmale für *website article* weitgehend um: • klare Gliederung • Überschrift und Zwischenüberschriften • Einleitung • interessanter Einstieg • Hauptteil mit Sinnabschnitten • Schluss
Situationsangemessenheit und Adressatenbezug	schreibt weitgehend situationsangemessen und adressatenbezogen: • informierte Schulöffentlichkeit • neutrales Register: informativ-kritisch • Verweis auf Schulprojekt • interessante Darstellung für Mitschüler
Kulturspezifik	kann relevante kulturspezifische Aspekte nachvollziehbar erläutern (ggfs. Bedeutung des *Spiegels* in der deutschen Presselandschaft)
Text- und Problemverständnis	kann das Thema des Artikels ggfs. in größere Zusammenhänge (*media, fake news*) einordnen.
Darstellung und Gliederung	stellt den Skandal sowie die journalistischen Verstöße eigenständig und überwiegend klar und logisch dar.

ISBN 978-3-425-73646-4

Gesamteindruck	Die inhaltliche Leistung entspricht in vollem Maße den Anforderungen der Aufgabe.

Mögliche inhaltliche Aspekte:

Scandal:
- *Young, award-winning journalist worked for the news magazine* Der Spiegel *and others*
- *admitted having faked articles, manipulated dialogues, made up stories and protagonists*
- *his motivation: wanted to create perfect stories that were better than reality*
- *scandal was revealed in 2018, journalist quit his job*
- *following this scandal, news magazine* Der Spiegel *is experiencing a crisis*

Criteria of journalistic quality that were ignored:
- *thorough research*
- *quality material*
- *facts that are beyond doubt*
- *reflective texts*
- *news magazines have responsibility to search for and present truth; no need to be faster than other media*

Writing: Too much information

Read the following excerpt from the non-fiction book *The Organized Mind* (2014) by American-Canadian author Daniel Levitin and complete the tasks.

1. Comprehension: Outline the challenges of the information age as they are presented in the text.

	Der Schüler/Die Schülerin ...
Umsetzung der Aufgabenstellung	kann die im Auszug geschilderten Herausforderungen unseres Informationszeitalters umreißen.
Text- und Problemverständnis	durchdringt die Textvorlage weitgehend.
Darstellung und Gliederung	erfüllt mit seinen/ihren klaren und logischen Ausführungen überwiegend die Erfordernisse des Operators *outline*: • knappe Darstellung • keine Zusatzinformation zum Text • *present tense* • keine Zitate und Textverweise • keine Kommentare

Gesamteindruck	Die inhaltliche Leistung entspricht in vollem Maße den Anforderungen der Aufgabe.

Mögliche inhaltliche Aspekte:

- *masses of information*
- *difficulty of organizing data*
- *competition of attention, less resources for important decisions, people overwhelmed, unable to focus*
- *more work, less time*
- *faster development of products → need to constantly learn new tech-related things*
- *globalization: information from all parts of the world, keeping brains busy, less resources for things that are important for us personally*
- *less accuracy of news and information, false news, unclear what is true and what is not*
- *no time to do research, random quality of information*

ISBN 978-3-425-73646-4

2. Analysis: Analyse how the author tries to convince the readers of his opinion. Consider his choice of words and stylistic devices.

	Der Schüler/Die Schülerin ...
Umsetzung der Aufgabenstellung	führt die im Sinne der Aufgabenstellung relevanten Informationen weitgehend präzise um.
Text- und Problemverständnis	durchdringt die Textvorlage weitgehend.
Darstellung und Gliederung	verfasst einen klaren und kohärenten Text, der den Erfordernissen des Operators *analyse* überwiegend entspricht: • Untersuchung von Wortwahl und sprachlichen Mitteln sowie deren Wirkung auf den Leser • Untermauerung durch sinnvolle und prägnante Beispiele aus dem Text • Zitate und Textverweise

Gesamteindruck	Die inhaltliche Leistung entspricht in vollem Maße den Anforderungen der Aufgabe.

Mögliche inhaltliche Aspekte:

Choice of words:

- ***positive terms:*** *"key resource", "improve society", "enjoy personal and economic growth" → stress that information is something beneficial in principle*
- ***negative terms/semantic field*** **fight***: "struggle", "confronted with", "have trouble with", "processing makes us tired", "serious problem" → show the downsides of an information overload, frame the handling of too much information as a fight*
- ***drastic/vivid descriptions:*** *"unprecedented amount" → appeal to emotions*
- ***informal/colloquial words:*** *"come to grips", "stuff is competing" → reader can relate, everyday situations, not too academic impression*

Stylistic devices:

- ***anaphora:*** *"Sometimes these authorities are worthy of our trust, sometimes not." → stresses difficulty of situation, puts emphasis on it, draws attention to key words*
- ***parallelism:*** *"more work, more changes", "new software, new buttons, new menus (...), new icons", "Whom to believe, what is true, what has been modified, what has been vetted" → stresses impact and range of questions*
- ***contrast:*** *"Instead of more time, most of us have less." → shows dilemma and difficulty*
- ***first person plural****; use of "we" throughout article: "we are confronted ...", "Many of us ..." → involves readers, creates the notion of mutual understanding, author part of the group, presupposes that readers share these problems, establishes a relationship, reader can relate*
- ***rhetorical question:*** *"Why is information overload such a serious problem now?" → raises interest, involves readers, really rather a kind of statement*
- ***enumeration:*** *"where we shop and what we buy ... and the weather on Mars", "take notes, make to do lists ...", "We hear about revolutions ... we see images ... and hear languages ...", "we rely on trusted authorities, newspapers, the cab driver" → shows extent of problem, emphasizes number of activities/amount of information, range of possibilities, gives examples, partly satirical (random people whom to trust, unimportant facts)*
- ***personification:*** *"all this stuff is competing" → simplifies matters by reducing complexity, making it less abstract*
- ***metaphor/image/symbol:*** *"information explosion", "information shot at us", "brains are hungrily soaking in", "accuracy and authoritativeness have become clouded" → draw attention to the arguments made, illustrate*
- ***exaggeration:*** *"traffic jams in Singapore ... weather on Mars"→ draws attention to the extent of the problem by highlighting the ridiculous, makes article entertaining to read*
- ***claims:*** *"We don't have the time or the expertise to do research on every little decision." → no room for doubts or questions, author implies that readers agree with him, appeals to general knowledge*
- ***quote experts/authorities:*** *"former Boeing scientist and New York Times writer" → the author backs up his own arguments, eliminates doubts*
- ***reference to statistics/research:*** *"information scientists have quantified this ... e.g. 21,274 television stations ... → supports arguments by incredible numbers*
- ***climax:*** *"more information than ever before in human history" → makes clear extent of situation*

ISBN 978-3-425-73646-4

All in all, the article is informative yet entertaining:
- *reader can relate*
- *examples from our everyday lives*
- *not too academic, informative, entertaining*
- *opening eyes, reader becomes aware of problem*

3. Writing a discussion: On his website, Daniel Levitin says that he would enjoy hearing from his readers. Write an email to him in which you discuss the benefits and problems of digital media from your own point of view.

	Der Schüler/Die Schülerin ...
Umsetzung der Aufgabenstellung	führt die im Sinne der Aufgabenstellung relevanten Informationen weitgehend präzise um.
Textsortenspezifik	setzt die textsortenspezifischen Merkmale für *email* weitgehend um: • Betreff • Anrede • Anlass der E-Mail (was der Verfasser/die Verfasserin diskutieren möchte) • Hauptteil in Abschnitte geteilt (dabei optional: Bezüge zum Sachbuch in Form von kurzen Zitaten oder Beispielen) • Schluss • Abschiedsformel
Situationsangemessenheit und Adressatenbezug	schreibt weitgehend situationsangemessen und adressatenbezogen: • E-Mail an den Autor eines Sachbuchs • Register: höflich, förmlich
Text- und Problemverständnis	• durchdringt die Textvorlage weitgehend. • kann das Thema des Artikels bzw. der E-Mail ggfs. in größere Zusammenhänge (*news, digital media*) einordnen.
Darstellung und Gliederung	erfüllt mit seinen/ihren klaren und logischen Ausführungen überwiegend die Erfordernisse des Operators *discuss*: • ausgewogene Darstellung der Probleme und Vorteile der digitalen Medien • Unterstützung der Argumente durch Beispiele (z. B. aus dem eigenen Leben) • Fazit

Gesamteindruck	Die inhaltliche Leistung entspricht in vollem Maße den Anforderungen der Aufgabe.

Mögliche inhaltliche Aspekte:

Benefits:
- *makes it easy to communicate*
- *vast information, greater knowledge base*
- *possible to pick out things that are interesting for you*
- *entertainment*

Problems:
- *possibilities to identify fake news: people are often not skilled enough*
- *distraction*
- *addiction*
- *bullying*

Erwartungshorizont für eine gute sprachliche Leistung

Für die Einschätzung der sprachlichen Leistung schriftlicher Arbeiten kann folgende Tabelle eine Orientierung bieten.

Die Bewertung der sprachlichen Leistung erfolgt auf der Grundlage der in der Tabelle genannten Kriterien ganzheitlich über die in der linken Spalte genannten Teilaspekte hinweg; es werden also keine Einzelnoten zu diesen Teilaspekten gebildet. Die Gewichtung der einzelnen Kriterien innerhalb der Kategorien hängt von den Anforderungen der jeweiligen Aufgabenstellung ab.

	Der Schüler/Die Schülerin ...
Kommunikative Textgestaltung Textaufbau Textsortenspezifik Situationsangemessenheit und Adressatenbezug (Register)	• verfasst einen weitgehend zielgerichteten, strukturierten und kohärenten Text. • setzt die geforderten Textsortenmerkmale weitgehend überzeugend um. • schreibt weitgehend situationsangemessen und mit gelungenem Adressatenbezug.
Ausdrucksvermögen, Verwendung sprachlicher Mittel Eigenständigkeit Wortschatz Idiomatik Satzbau Umgang mit Materialien/ Belegtechnik	• verfasst eine eigenständige Darstellung. • verwendet sowohl allgemeinen als auch themenspezifischen Wortschatz weitgehend treffsicher und variabel. • verwendet weitgehend angemessene idiomatische Strukturen. • formuliert mit weitgehend variablem und funktionalem Satzbau unter Verwendung angemessen komplexer Strukturen. • verwendet Zitate weitgehend funktional und bettet diese weitgehend korrekt in den Textfluss ein. • kennzeichnet Zitate/Textverweise weitgehend korrekt.
Sprachrichtigkeit Lexik Grammatik/Syntax Orthografie Verständlichkeit	• drückt sich lexikalisch, grammatisch, syntaktisch und orthografisch weitgehend korrekt aus. • drückt sich verständlich aus: Sprachliche Verstöße beeinträchtigen die Verständlichkeit nicht.

Gesamteindruck	Die sprachliche Leistung entspricht in vollem Maße den Anforderungen der Aufgabe.

ISBN 978-3-425-73646-4

Lösungen und Erwartungshorizont für eine gute inhaltliche Leistung

Listening 1: Losing your accent Webcode: WES-73646-12

1b, 2a, 3d, 4b, 5c, 6a, 7d, 8c, 9c, 10d, 11b

Listening 2: Technology and the future of English Webcode: WES-73646-13 (Ausschnitt: 03:20–07:35)

1. translate a language into every other language
2. computer technology
3. San Francisco/Silicon Valley
4. *two of these aspects:* computerized translation/computerized linguistics/artificial intelligence/voice recognition technology/machine translation
5. taught people standardized English/Netflix: 100+ million users/Google: 500+ million users
6. language interactions back and forth, e.g. English and Mandarin
7. CEO/founder (of "Gridspace")/entrepreneur
8. computer software/language software/ realistic computer communication
9. conversational speech/how human conversation works/to build a machine that speaks like a human
10. to answer calls/call centres/agencies
11. complicated questions/topic gets too complicated/(sometimes computer cannot understand/understanding varieties)
12. challenging/hard/software trying to do their best to recognize it/has difficulties
13. more people start to use system/system will improve by re-training/adaptations to accents

Mediation: Language learning

Your American host brother, who is going to college, is planning to spend a semester in Japan. He sent you an email, asking for your opinion. Using the information from the following interview, write an email to him, focusing on how to make most of the semester in terms of language learning.

	Der Schüler/Die Schülerin ...
Umsetzung der Aufgabenstellung	erfüllt weitgehend die Erfordernisse einer *Mediation*-Aufgabe: • Verzicht auf wortwörtliche Übersetzungen • Umschreibung von Begriffen, die sich nur schwer ins Englische übertragen lassen (z. B. WG) • Entnahme der nötigen Informationen aus dem deutschen Text (Textsorte: Sachtext, Interview) zum Verfassen eines eigenen Textes (Textsorte: E-Mail)
Textsortenspezifik	setzt die textsortenspezifischen Merkmale für *email* weitgehend um. • Betreff • Anrede • Einleitung, die in das Thema und die Situation ein-/hinführt (Auslandsjahr, Spracherwerb im Ausland) • inhaltlich aspektorientierte Strukturierung • zusammenfassender Schluss, der die Situation aufgreift und adäquat persönlich endet • Schlussgrußformel
Situationsangemessenheit und Adressatenbezug	schreibt weitgehend situationsangemessen und adressatenbezogen: • Austauschbruder • Register: neutral, informell • Bezugnahme auf Anfrage
Kulturspezifik	Erläuterung relevanter kulturspezifischer Aspekte: ggfs. Erasmus-Studierende (*Erasmus – scholarship programme for European students*)

ISBN 978-3-425-73646-4

	Der Schüler/Die Schülerin ...
Text- und Problemverständnis	kann das Thema des Artikels ggfs. in größere Zusammenhänge (*language learning, English as a global language*) einordnen.
Darstellung und Gliederung	stellt Tipps zum Spracherwerb in einem Auslandssemester eigenständig und überwiegend klar und logisch dar.

Gesamteindruck	Die inhaltliche Leistung entspricht in vollem Maße den Anforderungen der Aufgabe.

Mögliche inhaltliche Aspekte:

Semester abroad as a great way to learn a foreign language; a large majority of students find this an important aspect when they go abroad

How to make the most of your stay abroad in terms of language learning:

- *be motivated*
- *start learning language before semester abroad:*
  - *learn some basic vocabulary, e.g. with a language learning app*
  - *start learning a language in an intensive course or with a tandem partner*
- *while in Japan:*
  - *talk Japanese all the time*
  - *if the other person answers in English, insist on Japanese*
  - *try not to be scared of making mistakes*
  - *try to overcome shyness*
  - *surround yourself with locals, not only with foreign students*
  - *ideas to get in contact: freshmen parties, local bars, shared flats,*
  - *take a language course at the university*

Writing: Global English

1. Comprehension: Outline the dominance of the English language as it is presented in the article.

	Der Schüler/Die Schülerin ...
Umsetzung der Aufgabenstellung	führt die im Sinne der Aufgabenstellung relevanten Informationen weitgehend präzise aus.
Text- und Problemverständnis	durchdringt die Textvorlage weitgehend.
Darstellung und Gliederung	erfüllt mit seinen/ihren klaren und logischen Ausführungen überwiegend die Erfordernisse des Operators *outline*: • knappe Darstellung • keine Zusatzinformation zum Text • *present tense* • keine Zitate und Textverweise • keine Kommentare

Gesamteindruck	Die inhaltliche Leistung entspricht in vollem Maße den Anforderungen der Aufgabe.

Mögliche inhaltliche Aspekte:

- *number of speakers*
- *infiltration of other languages*
- *speed*
- *primacy*

ISBN 978-3-425-73646-4

- *attraction*
- *no alternative*
- *other languages are going extinct*

2. Analysis: Analyse the stylistic devices the author uses and the effect they have on the reader.

	Der Schüler/Die Schülerin ...
Umsetzung der Aufgabenstellung	führt die im Sinne der Aufgabenstellung relevanten Informationen weitgehend präzise um.
Text- und Problemverständnis	durchdringt die Textvorlage weitgehend.
Darstellung und Gliederung	verfasst einen klaren und kohärenten Text, der den Erfordernissen des Operators *analyse* überwiegend entspricht: • Untersuchung von Wortwahl und sprachlichen Mitteln sowie deren Wirkung auf den Leser • Untermauerung durch sinnvolle und prägnante Beispiele aus dem Text • Zitate und Textverweise
Gesamteindruck	Die inhaltliche Leistung entspricht in vollem Maße den Anforderungen der Aufgabe.

Mögliche inhaltliche Aspekte:

Stylistic devices:

- ***parallelism, gradation:*** *"But it is so prevalent. And so hard to escape." → stresses impact, increase in intensity*
- ***first person singular:*** *"I think it can be", "strikes me" → clear personal position*
- ***rhetorical question:*** *"Is the conquest of English really so bad?", "Is English oppressive?" → involves readers*
- ***enumeration:*** *"Last minute, fitness, group sex", "Dialects crushed, languages forgotten, literatures mangled" → shows extent of problem, emphasizes number of activities/amount of information, amount of problem, partly satirical*
- ***comparison/simile:*** *"Protesting feels like yelling at the moon", "Living with English is like drifting into the proximity of a supermassive black hole", likening English to a currency, "smaller languages not as endangered species worth saving" → simplifies complicated matters by referring to everyday problem/other extreme*
- ***personification:*** *"Behemoth, bully, loudmouth, thief", "taking over the planet", "inescapable", "Everywhere it goes, it leaves behind a trail of the dead", "English was a great importer of words", "world is threatened by English", "survive", "silences other languages" → simplifies matters by reducing complexity, making it less abstract*
- ***metaphor/image/symbol:*** *"infiltrated", "English should be the key to all the world's knowledge", "frenzy spills over", "no longer simply a tool", "access code to global elite", "language to be worshipped around the world like a golden idol", "hard to escape", "gravity" → makes article more interesting, illustrates*
- ***claims:*** *"There is no reason…"→ no room for doubts or questions, author implies that readers agree with him, appeal to general knowledge*
- ***quote experts/authorities:*** *Japanese novelist, sociolinguist, literary critic → author backs up his own arguments, eliminates doubts*
- ***reference to statistics/research:*** *400 million people, a billion, 59 countries, between 50 and 90 % → supports arguments*
- ***reference to Bible:*** *"Curse of Babel, children of men may come together once again, united" → here rather ironic, satirical*

3. Writing a comment: Readers are invited to post a comment on *The Guardian* website. Write a text in which you comment on the author's critical remark that English "is now seen as the access code to the global elite. If you want your children to get ahead, then they better have English in their toolkit." Refer to your own experiences and materials studied in class.

	Der Schüler/Die Schülerin ...
Umsetzung der Aufgabenstellung	führt die im Sinne der Aufgabenstellung relevanten Informationen weitgehend präzise um.
Textsortenspezifik	setzt die textsortenspezifischen Merkmale für *comment on a website* weitgehend um: • Anlass für den Kommentar (Bemerkung des Autors, die man kommentieren möchte) • strukturierter und pointierter Kommentar • eigener Standpunkt wird deutlich • Untermauerung der eigenen Meinung mit eigenen Erfahrungen und Hintergrundwissen • Schlusswort • Name und Wohnort (optional)
Situationsangemessenheit und Adressatenbezug	schreibt weitgehend situationsangemessen und adressatenbezogen: • informierte, internationale Leserschaft der Webseite des *Guardians* • Register: formal, neutral
Text- und Problemverständnis	durchdringt die Textvorlage weitgehend und kann das Thema des Artikels bzw. der E-Mail ggfs. in größere Zusammenhänge (*English as a global language*) einordnen.
Darstellung und Gliederung	erfüllt mit seinen/ihren klaren und logischen Ausführungen überwiegend die Erfordernisse des Operators *comment*: Begründete Darlegung des eigenen Standpunktes

Gesamteindruck	Die inhaltliche Leistung entspricht in vollem Maße den Anforderungen der Aufgabe.

Mögliche inhaltliche Aspekte:

Agree:
- personal experiences with English as a lingua franca
- personal experience: support/pressure from parents
- need for English at university
- English compulsory until *Abitur*
- often, second foreign language dropped early

Disagree:
- no elite status in Germany (English first foreign language at school, no alternative)
- no pressure from parents
- no extra courses

ISBN 978-3-425-73646-4

Erwartungshorizont für eine gute sprachliche Leistung

Für die Einschätzung der sprachlichen Leistung schriftlicher Arbeiten kann folgende Tabelle eine Orientierung bieten.

Die Bewertung der sprachlichen Leistung erfolgt auf der Grundlage der in der Tabelle genannten Kriterien ganzheitlich über die in der linken Spalte genannten Teilaspekte hinweg; es werden also keine Einzelnoten zu diesen Teilaspekten gebildet. Die Gewichtung der einzelnen Kriterien innerhalb der Kategorien hängt von den Anforderungen der jeweiligen Aufgabenstellung ab.

	Der Schüler/Die Schülerin ...
Kommunikative Textgestaltung Textaufbau Textsortenspezifik Situationsangemessenheit und Adressatenbezug (Register)	• verfasst einen weitgehend zielgerichteten, strukturierten und kohärenten Text. • setzt die geforderten Textsortenmerkmale weitgehend überzeugend um. • schreibt weitgehend situationsangemessen und mit gelungenem Adressatenbezug.
Ausdrucksvermögen, Verwendung sprachlicher Mittel Eigenständigkeit Wortschatz Idiomatik Satzbau Umgang mit Materialien/ Belegtechnik	• verfasst eine eigenständige Darstellung. • verwendet sowohl allgemeinen als auch themenspezifischen Wortschatz weitgehend treffsicher und variabel. • verwendet weitgehend angemessene idiomatische Strukturen. • formuliert mit weitgehend variablem und funktionalem Satzbau unter Verwendung angemessen komplexer Strukturen. • verwendet Zitate weitgehend funktional und bettet diese weitgehend korrekt in den Textfluss ein. • kennzeichnet Zitate/Textverweise weitgehend korrekt.
Sprachrichtigkeit Lexik Grammatik/Syntax Orthografie Verständlichkeit	• drückt sich lexikalisch, grammatisch, syntaktisch und orthografisch weitgehend korrekt aus. • drückt sich verständlich aus: Sprachliche Verstöße beeinträchtigen die Verständlichkeit nicht.

Gesamteindruck	Die sprachliche Leistung entspricht in vollem Maße den Anforderungen der Aufgabe.

Lösungen und Erwartungshorizont für eine gute inhaltliche Leistung

Listening 1: Globalization and regionalization Webcode: WES-73646-14

1. a) technological development, b) deregulation
2. removal of historic barriers (tariff and non-tariff)
3. free movement of a) goods, b) capital, c) labour (within the EU)
4. a) time, b) costs, c) administrative complexity
5. a) reproduces trade barriers, b) creates "insider" and "outsider" countries

Listening/Viewing 2: The impact of globalization Webcode: WES-73646-15 (Ausschnitt: 01:22–05:39)

1 b+c, 2b+d, 3a+d, 4c, 5b

Listening 3: The future of work in a globalized world Webcode: WES-73646-16

1. a) automation (robots/AI) leading to the loss of jobs/jobs disappearing, b) precarious employment/low job quality
2. 14 per cent
3. robots being used a) in the military, b) for space exploration
4. robots a) looking after the elderly, b) being used in child care
5. *three of these aspects:* creates new kinds of jobs (that did not exist ten years ago)/makes goods and services cheaper to produce/raises the quality/increases demand and therefore employment
6. less than one per cent
7. a) providers of rides, b) providers of accommodation

Mediation: Withdrawal from globalization

Your friend from the US supports the "America First" movement in her country. She believes America could become independent, given the country's size, its geological diversity, its available natural resources and its economic power. In her last email she wondered whether Germany would also be able to cut itself off from globalization. You decide to write a reply to your friend's question, in which you summarize a corresponding article you have found online.

	Der Schüler/Die Schülerin ...
Umsetzung der Aufgabenstellung	erfüllt weitgehend die Erfordernisse einer *Mediation*-Aufgabe: • Verzicht auf wortwörtliche Übersetzungen • Entnahme der nötigen Informationen aus dem deutschen Text (Textsorte: Zeitungsartikel) zum Verfassen eines eigenen Textes (Textsorte: E-Mail)
Textsortenspezifik	setzt die textsortenspezifischen Merkmale für *email* weitgehend um: • Betreff • Anrede • Einleitung, die in das Thema und die Situation ein-/hinführt (möglicher Reiz, sich von der Globalisierung unabhängig zu machen) • inhaltlich aspektorientierte Strukturierung (Machbarkeit, Konsequenzen) • zusammenfassender Schluss, der die Situation (Frage der Freundin) aufgreift und adäquat persönlich endet • Schlussgrußformel
Situationsangemessenheit und Adressatenbezug	schreibt weitgehend situationsangemessen und adressatenbezogen: • Freundin in den USA • Register: informell, informativ-kritisch
Text- und Problemverständnis	kann das Thema des Artikels ggfs. in größere Zusammenhänge (*fears related to globalization*) einordnen.

	Der Schüler/Die Schülerin ...
Darstellung und Gliederung	kann die Problematik einer selbst gewählten Isolation differenziert und überwiegend klar und logisch darstellen.
Gesamteindruck	Die inhaltliche Leistung entspricht in vollem Maße den Anforderungen der Aufgabe.

Mögliche inhaltliche Aspekte:

- *so far, no industrial country has dared to cut itself off from the global economy; this would require producing their own goods without engaging in international trade*
- *although it might be tempting to close Germany's borders to avoid trade disputes, this would not be easy to do*
- *given the amount of money Germany gains through its export industry (1.279 billion euros last year), it can be estimated that every second job in the industrial field is dependent on export*
- *hypothetically, imported goods in Germany could provide the economy with 1.034 billion euros; although this would mean a decrease of 245 billion euros from the current situation, in the grand scheme of things this is not very much money, as Germany's economic output is 3.263 billion euros*
- *however, Germany cannot implement a break from globalization quickly or easily, as companies rely on global supply chains and therefore Germany would need to radically change its production processes*
- *globalization has resulted in a lack of particular types of skilled workers in Germany, meaning training programmes would need to be implemented for computer programmers, textile engineers and toy inventors*
- *furthermore, Germany does not have any natural resources, meaning they would have to continue to import them*
- *largely withdrawing from globalization is possible for Germany, at least in theory; however, due to basic human needs, new jobs would have to be created*
- *as international competitiveness would no longer be a factor, the redistribution of wealth would be easier*
- *however, isolation would bring about two drawbacks: 1. life would become much more boring, as many interesting products from abroad would no longer be available, 2. economic and social stagnation, as innovations and ultimately wealth depend on trade*

Writing: The global "flip-flop trail"

1. Comprehension: Outline the global production of flip-flops that Caroline Knowles refers to as the "flip-flop trail" in her article.

	Der Schüler/Die Schülerin ...
Umsetzung der Aufgabenstellung	führt die im Sinne der Aufgabenstellung relevanten Informationen weitgehend präzise aus.
Text- und Problemverständnis	durchdringt die Textvorlage weitgehend.
Darstellung und Gliederung	verfasst einen strukturierten und kohärenten Text, der überwiegend den Erfordernissen des Operators *outline* entspricht: • knappe Darstellung • keine Zusatzinformationen zum Text • present tense • keine Zitate und Textverweise • keine Kommentare
Gesamteindruck	Die inhaltliche Leistung entspricht in vollem Maße den Anforderungen der Aufgabe.

Mögliche inhaltliche Aspekte:
- *hydrocarbon is the raw material for plastic; it is obtained in the form of crude oil on drilling rigs in the Middle East, where Syrian and southern Indian migrants work under sweatshop conditions*

ISBN 978-3-425-73646-4

- *crude oil is then transported to a South Korean city where it is made into plastic pellets by human-monitored, computerized machinery in giant factories*
- *the plastic pellets are sold to flip-flop factories in countries where wages are low*
- *the production of flip-flops creates large amounts of plastic waste*
- *after their production, flip-flops are sold to destinations like Ethiopia, but direct routes are avoided to evade taxes*
- *the flip-flop trail often ends at landfill sites, as the non-recyclable parts of a flip-flop end up as garbage*

2. Analysis: Examine the given cartoon and contrast it with Knowles' article.

	Der Schüler/Die Schülerin ...
Umsetzung der Aufgabenstellung	kann den Cartoon als diskontinuierlichen Text im Sinne der Aufgabenstellung prägnant beschreiben und wesentliche Bildelemente kontrastiv zum Artikel analysieren.
Text- und Problemverständnis	weist eine weitgehend treffende Beschreibung und kontrastive Auswertung des Cartoons im Vergleich zum Artikel nach und zeigt so ein differenziertes Text- und Problemverständnis.
Darstellung und Gliederung	verfasst einen eigenständigen, strukturierten, kohärenten und durchgängig lesbaren Text, der den Erfordernissen der Operatoren *examine* und *contrast* überwiegend entspricht: • Beschreibung des Cartoons (dabei Verwendung von Lokalisierungsphrasen) • Interpretation des Cartoons unter Beachtung von bildlichen und textlichen Elementen • Benennung der inhaltlichen Unterschiede zwischen Cartoon und Zeitungsartikel (dabei Hinzuziehen von relevanten Verweisen auf den Cartoon und den Artikel)

Gesamteindruck	Die inhaltliche Leistung entspricht in vollem Maße den Anforderungen der Aufgabe.

Mögliche inhaltliche Aspekte:

Description:
- *the cartoon by Jeff Danziger is split in half: on the left-hand side, entitled "USA", there is an American teenager leaning with his back against a wall in a rather relaxed way; apart from wearing baggy clothes and a cap, he is wearing shoes which are labelled as having cost $150; the writing in the top left-hand corner states that the teenager has "no work"*
- *on the right-hand side, entitled "Indonesia", there is a young Indonesian girl working on a sewing machine sewing shoes; she herself is not wearing any shoes, which is also underlined by the writing in the bottom right-hand corner*
- *another piece of writing in the top right-hand corner states that the girl has lots of work to do, and this is also illustrated by the large number of shoe boxes behind her (sporting the Nike logo)*
- *both sides of the cartoon use similar layouts yet reflect two opposing stories*
- *the written comment "The World According to Nike" refers to the big American sports company Nike and the way they produce and sell their goods*

Interpretation:
- *the topic addressed by the cartoon is global inequality with regards to work and consumption*
- *an unemployed teenager/young man in the USA can still afford a rather expensive pair of trainers whereas a young woman of the same age in Indonesia cannot afford a pair of shoes, despite working long hours producing shoes (for people on the other side of the world)*
- *the written comment can be seen as a critique of the big sports companies, such as Nike, which produce their goods cheaply in poor countries, then sell them at a high price in the US and other industrialized countries; in this way, they make a lot of money whilst exploiting the producers of their products and ensuring they remain poor*

Contrast:
Both the article and cartoon are a critique of shoe production in a globalized world; however, there are differences:
- *location of production: Indonesia ←→ Asia/Africa*
- *sales market: Ethiopia ←→ USA*

ISBN 978-3-425-73646-4

- *worker: teenage girl ←→ migrant workers from Syria/southern India*
- *labour conditions: sweatshop conditions in a factory ←→ sweatshop conditions on drilling rigs ("searing heat"/12-hour shifts/"living in desert camps")*
- *manufacturing: production process of plastic ←→ production of the final product (shoes)*
- *problem: exploitation of worker ←→ exploitation of workers + disastrous effects on the environment (extraction of crude oil, landfill)*

3. Writing a blog post: After having read Knowles' article on the "flip-flop trail", you are wondering whether boycotting flip-flops is a good way of helping to end one of "globalisation's darker stories". Based on this article and materials dealt with in class, you decide to discuss boycotting flip-flops in a blog post on a website called "Globalization – a Blessing or a Curse".

	Der Schüler/Die Schülerin ...
Umsetzung der Aufgabenstellung	kann sich in Form eines Blogeintrags mit dem Für und Wider eines Boykotts von Flip-Flops differenziert auseinandersetzen.
Textsortenspezifik	setzt die textsortenspezifischen Merkmale für *blog post* weitgehend um: • Titel • Einleitung, die auf das Thema hinführt • Gliederung in Absätzen • zusammenfassender Schluss, der eine Frage aufwirft und die Leserschaft auffordert, den Beitrag zu kommentieren bzw. ihre Meinung kundzutun
Text- und Problemverständnis	• kann das Thema ggfs. in größere Zusammenhänge *(benefits and drawbacks of globalization, environmentalism, conscious consumption)* einordnen.
Darstellung und Gliederung	• erfüllt mit seinen/ihren klaren und logischen Ausführungen die überwiegend Erfordernisse des Operators *discuss*: Ausgewogene Behandlung der Pro/Contra-Argumente mit Fazit
Gesamteindruck	Die inhaltliche Leistung entspricht in vollem Maße den Anforderungen der Aufgabe.

Mögliche inhaltliche Aspekte:

Arguments in favour of boycotting flip-flops:
- *consumer power can draw attention to issues (e.g. sweatshop working conditions, pollution, the "darker stories of globalisation" ...)*
- *might lead to improvements for workers and the environment*
- *if companies are losing customers, they may be encouraged to seek more environmentally friendly and fairer ways to produce flip-flops*

Arguments against a boycott:
- *people within the production chain of flip-flops might lose their jobs*
- *flip-flops might become more expensive, which has the largest effect on people in low-income countries, where they need cheap footwear the most*
- *may not be very effective at all because the biggest market for flip-flops is in low-income countries*
- *better alternative: get politicians and governments to change regulations*

ISBN 978-3-425-73646-4

Erwartungshorizont für eine gute sprachliche Leistung

Für die Einschätzung der sprachlichen Leistung schriftlicher Arbeiten kann folgende Tabelle eine Orientierung bieten.

Die Bewertung der sprachlichen Leistung erfolgt auf der Grundlage der in der Tabelle genannten Kriterien ganzheitlich über die in der linken Spalte genannten Teilaspekte hinweg; es werden also keine Einzelnoten zu diesen Teilaspekten gebildet. Die Gewichtung der einzelnen Kriterien innerhalb der Kategorien hängt von den Anforderungen der jeweiligen Aufgabenstellung ab.

	Der Schüler/Die Schülerin ...
Kommunikative Textgestaltung Textaufbau Textsortenspezifik Situationsangemessenheit und Adressatenbezug (Register)	• verfasst einen weitgehend zielgerichteten, strukturierten und kohärenten Text. • setzt die geforderten Textsortenmerkmale weitgehend überzeugend um. • schreibt weitgehend situationsangemessen und mit gelungenem Adressatenbezug.
Ausdrucksvermögen, Verwendung sprachlicher Mittel Eigenständigkeit Wortschatz Idiomatik Satzbau Umgang mit Materialien/ Belegtechnik	• verfasst eine eigenständige Darstellung. • verwendet sowohl allgemeinen als auch themenspezifischen Wortschatz weitgehend treffsicher und variabel. • verwendet weitgehend angemessene idiomatische Strukturen. • formuliert mit weitgehend variablem und funktionalem Satzbau unter Verwendung angemessen komplexer Strukturen. • verwendet Zitate weitgehend funktional und bettet diese weitgehend korrekt in den Textfluss ein. • kennzeichnet Zitate/Textverweise weitgehend korrekt.
Sprachrichtigkeit Lexik Grammatik/Syntax Orthografie Verständlichkeit	• drückt sich lexikalisch, grammatisch, syntaktisch und orthografisch weitgehend korrekt aus. • drückt sich verständlich aus: Sprachliche Verstöße beeinträchtigen die Verständlichkeit nicht.

Gesamteindruck	Die sprachliche Leistung entspricht in vollem Maße den Anforderungen der Aufgabe.

 ISBN 978-3-425-73646-4

Lösungen und Erwartungshorizont für eine gute inhaltliche Leistung

Listening 1: Globalization at the World Economic Forum Webcode: WES-73646-17

1. exchange notes on global business
2. anxiety
3. series of political earthquakes
4. increase free trade
5. unexpected victory
6. garnering better results
7. forthrightly asked
8. International Monetary Fund
9. hedging or miscounting
10. job losses and depressed
11. political consequences
12. backlash
13. relentlessly attacked
14. tilt the terms
15. the flight of manufacturing
16. inherited wealth
17. free movement of people
18. endangering our civilization

Listening 2: Facebook and the global community Webcode: WES-73646-18

1. a) his company, b) its value in the world
2. connect to each other quickly (in local communities, across countries)
3. a) the biggest Yellow Pages on earth, b) phone, email, direct message/a group announcement tool all in one
4. people who want global citizenship/a borderless world
5. *two of these aspects:* Facebook is convenient/(we should) step into the "walled garden"/live your social, economic and religious lives inside Facebook/people should trust Facebook
6. a) the news industry, b) small advertisers
7. news sources cannot be distinguished/everything is visually blurred
8. people say that Zuckerberg is a politician (for his digital state)/praise him for being a leader/praise him for spelling out a positive vision for breaking down barriers

Mediation: Jobs of the future

With your social studies class you are taking part in an international school project about the future of work. Using the information from the article below, write a blog post for the project website. In your post, outline the changes in the world of work that are to be expected and introduce the jobs that are likely to be in demand in Germany ten years from now. End your blog post with a general recommendation for your fellow students and invite them to share pieces of information they have also found about the subject.

	Der Schüler/Die Schülerin ...
Umsetzung der Aufgabenstellung	erfüllt weitgehend die Erfordernisse einer *Mediation*-Aufgabe: • Verzicht auf wortwörtliche Übersetzungen der zum Teil anspruchsvollen Begrifflichkeiten • Entnahme der nötigen Informationen aus dem deutschen Text (Textsorte: Zeitungsartikel) zum Verfassen eines eigenen Textes (Textsorte: Blogeintrag)
Textsortenspezifik	setzt die textsortenspezifischen Merkmale für *blog post* weitgehend um: • Titel • Einleitung, die auf das Thema hinführt • Gliederung in Absätzen • zusammenfassender Schluss, in der eine allgemeine Empfehlung für die Ausbildungs- und Berufswahl ausgesprochen und die Leserschaft aufgefordert wird, ihre Informationen zu dem Thema zu teilen.
Situationsangemessenheit und Adressatenbezug	schreibt weitgehend situationsangemessen und adressatenbezogen: • breite Schulöffentlichkeit • eher neutrales/sachliches Register

	Der Schüler/Die Schülerin ...
Kulturspezifik	kann ggfs. kulturspezifische Aspekte und Begriffe (NC, Bundesbildungsministerium) weitgehend nachvollziehbar erläutern bzw. verständlich umschreiben.
Text- und Problemverständnis	kann das Thema des Artikels ggfs. in größere Zusammenhänge (*life after school, work in a globalized world, the future of work*) einordnen.
Darstellung und Gliederung	kann den Wandel der Arbeitswelt sowie die empfohlenen Arbeitsbereiche weitgehend logisch, gegliedert und zusammenhängend darstellen.

Gesamteindruck	Die inhaltliche Leistung entspricht in vollem Maße den Anforderungen der Aufgabe.

Mögliche inhaltliche Aspekte:

Changes in the world of work: *old traditional occupations will vanish and completely new ones will appear, e.g. manual labour may cease to exist due to automation processes*

Potentially future-proof professions:
- *software engineers who design the digital world of tomorrow*
- *IT security experts who help design and secure any kind of existing and newly developed software*
- *data analysts who collect and evaluate data to come up with predictions for the future*
- *engineers are still highly in demand*
- *medical occupations (e.g. doctors, nurses, health management) will be in high demand due to the change in demographic*
- *there will be new professions that we can only speculate about, e.g. cyber city analysts or carers who provide company for elderly people*

Recommendation: *jobs in the IT sector or medical field are reliable*

Writing: Saeed and Nadia

Read the following extract from the novel *Exit West* (2017) by Mohsin Hamid. The novel is set in an unnamed city increasingly afflicted by terrorism and unrest. There, two people meet and fall in love: Saeed, a young man from an educated, liberal background and Nadia, who broke away from her traditional family but nevertheless chooses to wear a black robe in public.

1. Comprehension: Outline what the extract is about.

	Der Schüler/Die Schülerin ...
Umsetzung der Aufgabenstellung	kann die inhaltlichen Hauptlinien des Romanauszugs weitgehend überzeugend darstellen
Text- und Problemverständnis	durchdringt die Textvorlage weitgehend.
Darstellung und Gliederung	verfasst einen strukturierten und kohärenten Text, der überwiegend den Erfordernissen des Operators *outline* entspricht: • prägnante Darstellung • keine Zitate oder Textverweise

Gesamteindruck	Die inhaltliche Leistung entspricht in vollem Maße den Anforderungen der Aufgabe.

ISBN 978-3-425-73646-4

Mögliche inhaltliche Aspekte:

- *the first paragraph depicts the changes smartphones have brought to the city Saeed and Nadia live in; before the arrival of smartphones, it was difficult even to get a normal telephone line*
- *the second paragraph deals with the cautious way Saeed uses his smartphone*
- *the third paragraph then depicts the way Nadia uses her phone; she orders magic mushrooms for her date with Saeed through social media*
- *the fourth paragraph hints at the violent future the city faces by mentioning the mushroom dealer's death, whereas the last paragraph is about the hardships of their social reality in contrast to the world presented through the Internet*

2. Analysis: Compare Saaed und Nadia's character traits.

	Der Schüler/Die Schülerin ...
Umsetzung der Aufgabenstellung	kann die beiden Protagonisten anhand ihres im Romanauszug geschilderten Verhaltens weitgehend überzeugend miteinander vergleichen.
Text- und Problemverständnis	durchdringt die Textvorlage weitgehend.
Darstellung und Gliederung	verfasst einen strukturierten und kohärenten Text, der überwiegend den Erfordernissen des Operators *compare* entspricht: • Darstellung der Gemeinsamkeiten und Unterschiede zwischen den beiden Charakteren • Untermauerung durch relevante Zitate und Textverweise • Einteilung in Einleitung, Hauptteil und Schluss
Gesamteindruck	Die inhaltliche Leistung entspricht in vollem Maße den Anforderungen der Aufgabe.

Mögliche inhaltliche Aspekte:

Similarities:

- *Saeed and Nadia both enjoy having access to the Internet through their phones*
- *they both appear to be modern and not very traditional; this is also illustrated by the fact that they consume drugs together and become intimate with each other*

Differences:

- *the way they use their phones shows differences in character*
- *Saeed seems to be a cautious or even anxious person; he is afraid that too much Internet can make him "dazed and sick" (l. 19)*
- *he is also a controlled person as he voluntarily limits surfing the Internet to one hour a day; he even has an alarm installed that reminds him when the time is up ("But this hour was tightly regulated, and when it ended, a timer would set off an alarm", ll. 26f.); furthermore, Saeed seems to be interested in astronomy as he has an app that can identify celestial bodies (l. 22)*
- *Nadia, on the other hand, is far more free-spirited and daring than Saeed: she sees "no need to limit her phone" (ll. 32f.), uses social media and even orders psychedelic mushrooms through social media*
- *however, she is also cautious, but in a more secretive way than Saeed: she does not reveal her true identity on the Internet and wears black robes in public (ll. 39f.)*

3. Writing an assessment: The Internet brings the global to the local. Asses its value for the society Saeed and Nadia live in. Refer to the extract as well as to materials dealt with in class.

	Der Schüler/Die Schülerin ...
Umsetzung der Aufgabenstellung	kann den Wert des Internets für die in dem Romanauszug geschilderte Gesellschaft weitgehend überzeugend beurteilen.

 ISBN 978-3-425-73646-4

	Der Schüler/Die Schülerin ...
Text- und Problemverständnis	weist ein weitgehend sicheres Textverständnis nach. kann das Thema ggfs. in größere Zusammenhänge (*tradition and modernity*) einordnen.
Darstellung und Gliederung	verfasst einen strukturierten und kohärenten Text, der überwiegend den Erfordernissen des Operators *assess* entspricht: • ausgewogene Darstellung der Vor- und Nachteile • fundiertes Fazit • Einteilung in Einleitung, Hauptteil und Schluss • Bezugnahme auf den Text und im Unterricht bearbeitete Materialien
Gesamteindruck	Die inhaltliche Leistung entspricht in vollem Maße den Anforderungen der Aufgabe.

Mögliche inhaltliche Aspekte:

Pros:
- *liberating: women like Nadia can live more freely than would be otherwise possible*
- *democratic, as „millions" (ll. 12f.) can access the Internet cheaply*
- *a way to escape, especially for young people who cannot leave home (possibly due to unrest in the city)*

Cons:
- *danger of overconsumption and possible addiction to surfing the Internet (see Saeed's fears)*
- *these fears are universal, not just limited to Saeed and Nadia's society*
- *cruelty that springs from the contrast between the real life of poverty and hunger and the opulence presented online (ll. 52–59)*

ISBN 978-3-425-73646-4

Erwartungshorizont für eine gute sprachliche Leistung

Für die Einschätzung der sprachlichen Leistung schriftlicher Arbeiten kann folgende Tabelle eine Orientierung bieten.

Die Bewertung der sprachlichen Leistung erfolgt auf der Grundlage der in der Tabelle genannten Kriterien ganzheitlich über die in der linken Spalte genannten Teilaspekte hinweg; es werden also keine Einzelnoten zu diesen Teilaspekten gebildet. Die Gewichtung der einzelnen Kriterien innerhalb der Kategorien hängt von den Anforderungen der jeweiligen Aufgabenstellung ab.

	Der Schüler/Die Schülerin …
Kommunikative Textgestaltung Textaufbau Textsortenspezifik Situationsangemessenheit und Adressatenbezug (Register)	• verfasst einen weitgehend zielgerichteten, strukturierten und kohärenten Text. • setzt die geforderten Textsortenmerkmale weitgehend überzeugend um. • schreibt weitgehend situationsangemessen und mit gelungenem Adressatenbezug.
Ausdrucksvermögen, Verwendung sprachlicher Mittel Eigenständigkeit Wortschatz Idiomatik Satzbau Umgang mit Materialien/ Belegtechnik	• verfasst eine eigenständige Darstellung. • verwendet sowohl allgemeinen als auch themenspezifischen Wortschatz weitgehend treffsicher und variabel. • verwendet weitgehend angemessene idiomatische Strukturen. • formuliert mit weitgehend variablem und funktionalem Satzbau unter Verwendung angemessen komplexer Strukturen. • verwendet Zitate weitgehend funktional und bettet diese weitgehend korrekt in den Textfluss ein. • kennzeichnet Zitate/Textverweise weitgehend korrekt.
Sprachrichtigkeit Lexik Grammatik/Syntax Orthografie Verständlichkeit	• drückt sich lexikalisch, grammatisch, syntaktisch und orthografisch weitgehend korrekt aus. • drückt sich verständlich aus: Sprachliche Verstöße beeinträchtigen die Verständlichkeit nicht.

Gesamteindruck	Die sprachliche Leistung entspricht in vollem Maße den Anforderungen der Aufgabe.

ISBN 978-3-425-73646-4

Lösungen und Erwartungshorizont für eine gute inhaltliche Leistung

Listening: A historic anti-immigration speech

a) Webcode: WES-73646-19 (Ausschnitt: 00:00–04:13)

1. 50 years ago/1968
2. the dangers of mass immigration
3. the (fiery) rhetoric
4. it made it illegal to deny a) employment, b) housing, c) public services based on race or national origin
5. they were called over/labour shortage in Britain
6. mass immigration
7. a) (to) shave his beard, b) (to) take the turban off
8. protests from the Sikh community
9. "the black man will have the whip hand over the white man"
10. would cause great racial tension
11. a translated verse (from Virgil's "Aeneid") about the River Tiber

b) Webcode: WES-73646-20 (Ausschnitt: 04:17–07:01)
1F, 2E, 3A+G, 4I, 5H, 6B

Mediation: National identity

Having discussed the question of British identity in their social studies class, your English friend wonders what it means to be German. In order to provide them with some information, you decide to write an email in which you outline the problems with defining a shared sense of nationality as presented in the article.

	Der Schüler/Die Schülerin ...
Umsetzung der Aufgabenstellung	erfüllt weitgehend die Erfordernisse einer *Mediation*-Aufgabe: • Verzicht auf wortwörtliche Übersetzungen • Entnahme der nötigen Informationen aus dem deutschen Text (Textsorte: Zeitungsbericht über eine Podiumsdiskussion) zum Verfassen eines eigenen Textes (Textsorte: E-Mail)
Textsortenspezifik	setzt die textsortenspezifischen Merkmale für *email* weitgehend um: • Betreff • Anrede • Einleitung, die in das Thema und die Situation ein-/hinführt (Frage, was eigentlich deutsche Identität ausmacht) • inhaltlich aspektorientierte Strukturierung • zusammenfassender Schluss, der die Frage des Freundes/der Freundin aufgreift • Schlussgrußformel
Situationsangemessenheit und Adressatenbezug	schreibt weitgehend situationsangemessen und adressatenbezogen: • Freund/in in England • Register: informell, neutral-sachlich
Text- und Problemverständnis	kann das Thema des Artikels ggfs. in größere Zusammenhänge (*national identity*) einordnen.
Darstellung und Gliederung	kann die verschiedenen Gedanken zur Definition einer deutschen Identität in der heutigen Zeit und Gesellschaft differenziert und überwiegend klar und logisch darstellen.

Gesamteindruck	Die inhaltliche Leistung entspricht in vollem Maße den Anforderungen der Aufgabe.

Mögliche inhaltliche Aspekte:

- *what it means to be German is a question everyone has to deal with/answer for themselves*
- *as Germans themselves cannot really define what it means to be German, migrants also suffer from an inability to identify as German*
- *rules and laws are not a suitable basis for personal identification*
- *if integration is going to work, there needs to be something more profound than just laws*
- *the participants of the debate offer different solutions to finding a common national identity, ranging from solidarity to collectively coming to terms with Germany's Nazi past*
- *one quarter of all Germans have an immigrant background, hence the inadequacy of defining what it means to be German solely by descent or religion*
- *according to one speaker, the ongoing radicalization of some Germans on the one hand and that of a minority of migrants on the other hand poses a great risk – this could end up in a civil war scenario*
- *as migration is something that has always happened, the same speaker suggests that it is time to step away from the search for a common national identity; instead, we should admit that it might be better to consider simply living side by side in a civilized manner*

Writing: What is "British"?

1. Comprehension: Briefly summarize the poem *We're British and We Know It* by Josie Whitehead (A) and the introduction to the book *The How To Be British Collection* by Martyn Ford and Peter Legon (B).

	Der Schüler/Die Schülerin ...
Umsetzung der Aufgabenstellung	kann aus dem Gedicht und der Bucheinleitung wesentliche Hauptaussagen in einer kohärenten, präzisen Darstellung unter Beachtung der Textsortenmerkmale für *summary* zusammenfassen.
Textsortenspezifik	setzt die textsortenspezifischen Merkmale für *summary* weitgehend um: • Einleitungssätze zu beiden Texten (Genre, Titel, Autor/inQuelle, Publikationsjahr, Thema) • *present tense* • eigene Worte, keine Zitate, keine Verweise • keine Nacherzählung • keine Wertung • pointierte, straffe, knappe Darstellung
Text- und Problemverständnis	durchdringt die Textvorlage weitgehend.
Darstellung und Gliederung	verfasst einen eigenständigen, strukturierten, kohärenten und durchgängig lesbaren Text, der überwiegend den Erfordernissen des Operators *summarize* entspricht.

Gesamteindruck	Die inhaltliche Leistung entspricht in vollem Maße den Anforderungen der Aufgabe.

Mögliche inhaltliche Aspekte:

Poem:

- *the speaker points out her/his pride in being British*
- *the speaker outlines his/her reasons for that, thereby mentioning typical British characteristics and habits, e.g. common drinking and eating habits, Britain's historical nationalism, its love for certain sports, and taking queuing very seriously*
- *the speaker also mentions the stereotype that British men have "stiff upper lips", which means that they are reserved and don't reveal their emotions*
- *the speaker ends the poem by stating that they would like to live in Britain forever, and grow old with the same grace as the Queen*

ISBN 978-3-425-73646-4

Book introduction:
- *the authors explain why they each believe that Britain is so great by enumerating several aspects of Britain such as its outstanding past, the untouched countryside, the variety of the climate, and success in sport competitions like football and cricket*
- *furthermore, they present common British customs with regard to meal times and the British mindset, which is to be polite, respectful and humorous*
- *they mention that Britain still partially uses the Imperial measurement system, meaning e.g. height is usually measured in "feet" and "inches", and that Britain's currency is pounds sterling*
- *additionally, the authors point out that many Britons live in expensive houses, the mortgage on which they may never pay off*
- *the authors end by stating the importance of one's home including a garden for recreation and relaxation*

2. Analysis: Analyse how both texts define Britishness in terms of structure, style and content.

	Der Schüler/Die Schülerin ...
Umsetzung der Aufgabenstellung	kann das Gedicht sowie die Bucheinleitung zieltreffend analysieren und explizit und implizit dargestellte Aussagen aufgabenbezogen bezüglich *Britishness* deuten.
Text- und Problemverständnis	weist ein analytisches Textverständnis durch einen weitgehend hohen Grad der Durchdringung der Textvorlagen nach.
Darstellung und Gliederung	verfasst einen eigenständigen, strukturierten, kohärenten und durchgängig lesbaren Text, der überwiegend den Erfordernissen des Operators *analyse* entspricht: • eingehende Untersuchung, wie in beiden Texten *Britishness* durch Aufbau, Stil und Inhalt definiert wird • Untermauerung durch sinnvolle und aussagekräftige Beispiele aus den Texten • Zitate und Textverweise
Gesamteindruck	Die inhaltliche Leistung entspricht in vollem Maße den Anforderungen der Aufgabe.

Mögliche inhaltliche Aspekte:

Poem:
Structure:
- *the poem begins with six stanzas outlining different ways in which Brits know that they are British, before the narrative voice switches perspective and explains to the reader how they can also identify with the British*
- *in the last stanza, the poem switches narrative perspective again, and reflects on the speaker's own pride in being British, concluding that he/she would like to age gracefully in Britain*

Style:
- *the poem has a straightforward, clear style, with a simplistic choice of words and lack of rhetoric complexities*
- *the* ***repetition*** *of the phrase "We're British and we know it" (l. 1, l. 9, l. 17) at the start of three of the stanzas makes it memorable to the reader*
- *the repetition of the word "British" itself emphasizes the theme of the poem, and creates a strong link between British customs and Britons as people*
- *the use of the* ***first-person plural pronoun*** *("we) and its corresponding possessive ("our") creates a group identity and sense of belonging, portraying the British as one united group of people*
- *this is contrasted with the direct address to the reader in the second half of the poem, beginning with "You can say that you are British" (l. 25), which involves the reader in the poem's message*
- *the poem uses an alternate* ***rhyme scheme****, rhyming the second and fourth line of each stanza, and most of the rhymes are masculine (i.e. rhymes between stressed syllables)*
- *the use of* ***alliterations*** *such as "serving scones" (l. 12), "china cups" (l. 13), and "bound to be the British" (l. 31) creates a sense of rhythm and flow in the poem*
- *the continuous* ***enumeration*** *of different aspects of Britain (e.g. common British habits, Britain's pride in historic combats, sports, queuing) gradually builds up the general picture of a stereotypically British identity and way of life*

ISBN 978-3-425-73646-4

- *the claim that "British men don't show emotions – They just keep stiff upper lips" (ll. 27f.) is* ***juxtaposed*** *with the emotion that British men show when watching sports whilst drinking beer, at which time "stiff upper lips are out" (l. 36); this reveals the contrasting aspects of a British male identity*
- *additionally, the speaker considers the Brits "to be tolerant and fair", yet* ***contrasts*** *this with the threat that "foreigners" should "take care" (l. 44), which also emphasizes the ambiguity of a British identity*
- *in the last lines, the speaker uses the* ***simile*** *that she/he intends to age gracefully in Great Britain "just like our Queen" (l. 48), which suggests that the speaker looks up to the Queen as a role model of how to be graceful as an older person, and also implies that the monarchy is another important aspect of British identity*

Content:
- *the poem lists many different British foods ("roast beef", "Yorkshire pudding", "apple pies", "rhubarb crumble", "custard sauce", "scones with jam and cream", "fish and chips") to give the reader a sense of typical British cuisine, and focuses particularly on "tea" as the epitome of "Britishness"; this suggests that Britishness is tied to an enjoyment of idiosyncratic foods and drinks*
- *the country's location and idyllic nature are also heavily linked to British pride ("surrounded by the sea", "countryside's a dream", "love our country villages", "on the green", "British gardens")*
- *the poem also describes the British attitude as "tolerant and fair" (l. 42), and in particular British men are exemplified as being constantly emotionless, except when watching football matches and under the influence of alcohol*
- *British patriotism seems to come out most strongly during football games, when they show their pride by waving their flags (l. 40)*
- *"queuing" is also described as a typically British pastime*
- *however, as understanding irony and sarcasm is also known to be something typically British, the reader cannot be sure if the poem is meant seriously or should be taken with a pinch of salt*

Book introduction:
Structure:
- *the first paragraph provides insight into what is generally believed to be "Britishness", e.g. the landscape, weather, and attitudes*
- *the second paragraph offers a personal account on British idiosyncrasies, such as the use of Imperial measurements and the love of gardens as a place of relaxation*

Style:
- *the text is short and* ***humorous*** *containing many positive adjectives linked to aspects of Britishness, e.g. "glorious history" (l. 3), "unspoilt beauty of our landscape" (ll. 3f.), "rich variety of our weather" (l. 4), "unrivalled achievements" (l. 5), "cherished traditions" (l. 6)*
- *the text (indirectly) claims that the "Great" in "Great Britain" is an accurate description of the country, and the* ***use of a bold font*** *(l. 2) emphasizes this*
- *the* ***use of italics*** *in "we do like a good laugh" (l. 10) and "pounds sterling" (l. 14) also highlights these phrases*
- *the* ***direct address*** *to the reader at the start of the text in "If you are …" makes the reader feel involved*
- *the use of the* ***first-person plural pronoun*** *("we") and its corresponding possessive ("our") evokes the feeling of unity and the use of the idiom "My home is my castle" underlines the involvement of a broader unified audience*
- *the second paragraph allows insight into the British author's life; the phrase "As for me" … (l. 11) at the start of the paragraph focuses the theme of the paragraph on the author's life, and the use of* ***the first-person singular pronoun*** *("I") reveals it is a personal account, making the account more credible and relatable*
- *the British "sense of humour" (l. 9) is also revealed through the phrase "variety of weather" (l. X) to describe Britain's climate; the author's description of his garden as "recreation and sanctuary to many endangered species, not least of all me!" (ll. 16–18) is a further example of* ***irony***
- *this suggests that the author's stereotypical description of Britain and the British is meant ironically, suggesting that irony is another aspect of Britishness*

Content:
- *the first paragraph enumerates stereotypical beliefs about Britishness: "glorious history", beautiful countryside, diverse weather, achievements in sports competitions, valued drink and food traditions, politeness and humour*
- *the second paragraph uses British measurement parameters ("feet"/"inches"/"pounds"/"ounces"/"pints") to describe the author himself and his life, highlighting how important Britons believe it is to have one's own house including a garden*

ISBN 978-3-425-73646-4

3. Writing a blog post: You have dealt with the question of Britishness in class. While browsing the Internet you have come across a blog with posts and comments on Britishness in the wake of the Brexit referendum. This blog is contributed to and read by people from all over the world. You decide to write a blog post in which you compare Whitehead's poem with Ford and Legon's introduction and critically comment on their depiction of Britishness.

	Der Schüler/Die Schülerin ...
Umsetzung der Aufgabenstellung	kann sich in Form eines Blogeintrags kritisch mit den gegebenen Darstellungen zu *Britishness* auseinandersetzen.
Textsortenspezifik	setzt die textsortenspezifischen Merkmale für *blog post* weitgehend um: • Titel • Einleitung • Hauptteil mit nachvollziehbarer Darstellung der Kritik • zusammenfassender resümierender und klar positionierender Schluss
Situationsangemessenheit und Adressatenbezug	wendet sich mit seinem/ihrem Beitrag an ein breites Publikum.
Text- und Problemverständnis	weist ein weitgehend sicheres Verständnis beider Texte nach.
Darstellung und Gliederung	erfüllt mit seinen/ihren klaren und logischen Ausführungen überwiegend die Erfordernisse der Operatoren *compare* und *comment*: • Darstellung der Gemeinsamkeiten und Unterschiede zwischen Gedicht und Einleitung • Darstellung und nachvollziehbare Begründung der eigenen Meinung durch Beispiele • ggfs. Verknüpfung mit im Unterricht bearbeitetem Material

Gesamteindruck	Die inhaltliche Leistung entspricht in vollem Maße den Anforderungen der Aufgabe.

Mögliche inhaltliche Aspekte:

Comparison:

- *the content of both texts is nearly the same; both express the pride of being British using nearly the same stereotypical ideas, namely landscape, habits/traditions, idiosyncratic foods and drinks, historical and sports achievements, and behaviour*
- *contrary to the poem, the book introduction depicts the peculiarity of British weather (l. 4) and puts great emphasis on British humour (l. 9) which is also used within the text (see above)*
- *furthermore, the book introduction does not express anything about relationships between Britain and other countries or the common stereotype of queuing*
- *the book introduction also does not reveal any differences between Britons, whereas the poem gives stereotypes about British males in particular*
- *the irony of the stereotypical depiction of Britishness is apparent in the book introduction, whereas it is not quite clear whether the poem is also meant ironically*

Comment:

- *both texts perpetuate common and well-known stereotypes about Britain and the British; and so are not very original in terms of content*
- *they do not offer any new or surprising insights into Britishness; the image of Britain that they project seems quite old-fashioned and traditional (even if it is meant ironically)*
- *additionally, British women are strangely absent in the poem, apart from the Queen – it therefore prompts the question of how British women behave – are they also emotionless and only unwind when drinking alcohol and watching sports?*
- *the poem in particular shows some tendencies towards militancy and xenophobia ("we drive our foes all back", l. 20, "So you foreigners, take care!!", l. 44)*
- *neither of the texts expresses anything about multiculturalism or hybrid identities as a part of Britishness*

ISBN 978-3-425-73646-4

Erwartungshorizont für eine gute sprachliche Leistung

Für die Einschätzung der sprachlichen Leistung schriftlicher Arbeiten kann folgende Tabelle eine Orientierung bieten.

Die Bewertung der sprachlichen Leistung erfolgt auf der Grundlage der in der Tabelle genannten Kriterien ganzheitlich über die in der linken Spalte genannten Teilaspekte hinweg; es werden also keine Einzelnoten zu diesen Teilaspekten gebildet. Die Gewichtung der einzelnen Kriterien innerhalb der Kategorien hängt von den Anforderungen der jeweiligen Aufgabenstellung ab.

	Der Schüler/Die Schülerin ...
Kommunikative Textgestaltung Textaufbau Textsortenspezifik Situationsangemessenheit und Adressatenbezug (Register)	• verfasst einen weitgehend zielgerichteten, strukturierten und kohärenten Text. • setzt die geforderten Textsortenmerkmale weitgehend überzeugend um. • schreibt weitgehend situationsangemessen und mit gelungenem Adressatenbezug.
Ausdrucksvermögen, Verwendung sprachlicher Mittel Eigenständigkeit Wortschatz Idiomatik Satzbau Umgang mit Materialien/ Belegtechnik	• verfasst eine eigenständige Darstellung. • verwendet sowohl allgemeinen als auch themenspezifischen Wortschatz weitgehend treffsicher und variabel. • verwendet weitgehend angemessene idiomatische Strukturen. • formuliert mit weitgehend variablem und funktionalem Satzbau unter Verwendung angemessen komplexer Strukturen. • verwendet Zitate weitgehend funktional und bettet diese weitgehend korrekt in den Textfluss ein. • kennzeichnet Zitate/Textverweise weitgehend korrekt.
Sprachrichtigkeit Lexik Grammatik/Syntax Orthografie Verständlichkeit	• drückt sich lexikalisch, grammatisch, syntaktisch und orthografisch weitgehend korrekt aus. • drückt sich verständlich aus: Sprachliche Verstöße beeinträchtigen die Verständlichkeit nicht.

Gesamteindruck	Die sprachliche Leistung entspricht in vollem Maße den Anforderungen der Aufgabe.

ISBN 978-3-425-73646-4

Lösungen und Erwartungshorizont für eine gute inhaltliche Leistung

Listening 1: A royal wedding Webcode: WES-73646-21

1D, 2E, 3H, 4A, 5B, 6G, 7I

Listening/Viewing 2: Millennials on Britishness Webcode: WES-73646-22 (Ausschnitt: 00:00–02:16)

1. group of people
2. independent
3. work well together
4. identity
5. particularly patriotic
6. collective
7. individual
8. embraces
9. accepting of people
10. respect
11. Multicultural
12. to keep business
123. London Eye, Big Ben
14. countryside
15. dog walk
16. no discrimination
17. class
18. standards
19. cup of tea
20. sarcasm
21. freedom and new ideas
22. proud to be

Mediation: Brexit

Your pen pal from Liverpool wonders how Brexit has affected Britons living in Germany. You have found this article about one of the many Britons who have decided to apply for German citizenship since the referendum in 2016. In an email to your friend, summarize the article and state the reason Ian Bennett from Hamburg decided to become a German citizen.

	Der Schüler/Die Schülerin ...
Umsetzung der Aufgabenstellung	erfüllt weitgehend die Erfordernisse einer *Mediation*-Aufgabe: • Verzicht auf wortwörtliche Übersetzungen • Entnahme der nötigen Informationen aus dem deutschen Text (Textsorte: Bericht) zum Verfassen eines eigenen Textes (Textsorte: E-Mail)
Textsortenspezifik	setzt die textsortenspezifischen Merkmale für *email* weitgehend um: • Betreff • Anrede • Einleitung, die in das Thema und die Situation ein-/hinführt (Briten in Deutschland und der Brexit; Annahme der deutschen Staatsbürgerschaft) • inhaltlich aspektorientierte Strukturierung • zusammenfassender Schluss, der die Frage des Freundes/der Freundin aufgreift • Schlussgrußformel
Situationsangemessenheit und Adressatenbezug	schreibt weitgehend situationsangemessen und adressatenbezogen: • Freund/Freundin in England • Register: informell, neutral-sachlich
Text- und Problemverständnis	kann das Thema des Artikels ggfs. in größere Zusammenhänge (*identity, British politics*) einordnen.
Darstellung und Gliederung	kann den Bericht über ein Einzelschicksal in Hamburg weitgehend treffend in der Zielsprache zusammenfassen.

Gesamteindruck	Die inhaltliche Leistung entspricht in vollem Maße den Anforderungen der Aufgabe.

ISBN 978-3-425-73646-4

Mögliche inhaltliche Aspekte:

- *the article features the British teacher and translator Ian Bennett living in Hamburg who is applying for German citizenship*
- *generally speaking, there has been a surge in applications for German citizenship by many of the 4,000 Britons living in Hamburg due to the uncertainty around Brexit*
- *Brexit has affected Ian Bennett in various ways:*
  - *he is tired of being asked about Brexit every day*
  - *he is applying for German citizenship for practical reasons so that he can continue living his life with his German wife (Britons do not have to give up their British citizenship)*
  - *many of his British friends despise the Brexit decision, but Ian Bennett does not consider this to be very helpful as it only deepens the rift*
- *he feels rather sad for future generations in England*
- *all in all, he tries to look at the positive side of having two citizenships*

Writing: Scottish novels

1. Comprehension: Outline the two contrary positions presented in the article.

	Der Schüler/Die Schülerin ...
Umsetzung der Aufgabenstellung	kann die Hauptaussagen beider Autoren weitgehend präzise wiedergeben.
Text- und Problemverständnis	durchdringt die Textvorlage weitgehend.
Darstellung und Gliederung	verfasst einen strukturierten und kohärenten Text, der überwiegend den Erfordernissen des Operators *outline* entspricht: • knappe Darstellung • keine Zusatzinformation zum Text • *present tense* • keine Zitate und Textverweise • keine Kommentare

Gesamteindruck	Die inhaltliche Leistung entspricht in vollem Maße den Anforderungen der Aufgabe.

Mögliche inhaltliche Aspekte:

Ron Butlin:
- *agrees that you can tell a Scottish novelist from an English one*
- *for him, a good novel springs from its native culture, because this gives the novel depth*
- *writers deal with important cultural issues such as devolution, and that makes these novels uniquely Scottish*

Andrew Crumey:
- *disagrees with the statement that you can tell a Scottish novelist from an English one because readers have been repeatedly mistaken about an author's identity*
- *claims that the statement rests on the false premise that an author only has one (national) identity; Crumey disagrees with this because there are authors who were born in Scotland but lived in England*
- *Crumey concludes that it doesn't matter where an author comes from; it is more important to focus on whether their work is any good*

2. Analysis: Contrast Butlin and Crumey's views on whether it is possible to distinguish Scottish from English writing and analyse how they try to convince the readers of their respective positions.

 ISBN 978-3-425-73646-4

	Der Schüler/Die Schülerin ...
Umsetzung der Aufgabenstellung	kann die beiden Standpunkte einander gegenüberstellen und diese weitgehend treffend analysieren.
Text- und Problemverständnis	weist ein analytisches Textverständnis durch einen weitgehend hohen Grad der Durchdringung der Textvorlagen nach.
Darstellung und Gliederung	verfasst einen eigenständigen, strukturierten, kohärenten und durchgängig lesbaren Text, der überwiegend den Erfordernissen der Operatoren *contrast* und *analyse* entspricht: • Herausarbeiten der Unterschiede zwischen beiden Standpunkten • Analyse der Art und Weise, wie beide Autoren argumentieren • Untermauerung durch sinnvolle und aussagekräftige Beispiele aus den Texten • Zitate und Textverweise

Gesamteindruck	Die inhaltliche Leistung entspricht in vollem Maße den Anforderungen der Aufgabe.

Mögliche inhaltliche Aspekte:

Contrast:

- *Butlin emphasizes that writers/novelists have a task to fulfil, namely examining and portraying a particular society and culture; according to him, the best writing brings a particular place to life for its readers, and for this writers need to be deeply rooted in that place, e.g. as Dickens was in London or Balzac was in Paris (ll. 38f.)*
- *Crumey, on the other hand, claims that no nation has "exclusive ownership" (l. 109) over its cultural products; there are many authors who cannot be assigned to one nationality, e.g. Kafka who was Jewish and Czech but whose mother tongue was German (ll. 100–104); for Crumey, it does not matter where an author comes from as long as their writing is good; he even claims that it is a sign of low quality if you can easily detect where a writer comes from*

Analysis:

- *despite their differing viewpoints, both authors **refer to famous novelists** to prove their point; Butlin refers to Dickens and Balzac (ll. 38f.), for example, in order to show that novelists are connected to a particular place and culture whereas Crumey uses Conan Doyle (the inventor of Sherlock Holmes) (l. 86) and Kafka (l. 100) to make his point that good authors do not belong to one place or nationality*
- *both authors also use **inclusive language** (use of first-person pronouns, directly addressing the reader) to show that the question is a matter that concerns everybody and to engage the reader with their line of thinking*
- *Butlin: uses **emotional references** to Scottish history and identity ("lack of self-belief was branded onto the Scottish heart at birth", ll. 48f.), which appeals to the readers' national sentiment and shows the urgency which is common in "Scottish" writing; **contrasts** the emotional depths of Scottish novels to the coldness and emptiness of a world without such novels ("Google-speak that could mean anything or nothing", ll. 30f., "entrusted ... to mouse-click bureaucrats", l. 58)*
- *Crumey: **refers to a personal experience** of not knowing where an author originally came from (Conan Doyle); **refers to a list** of the 100 best Scottish books that includes writers who were not Scottish – this lends credibility to his argument; **broadens the discussion** about Scottish books to include the issue of national and political boundaries– this adds weight to his argument, giving it a sense of moral superiority*

3. Writing a comment: Ron Butlin claims that "all good novels emerge from their native culture". Comment on this view. Refer to materials studied in class.

	Der Schüler/Die Schülerin ...
Umsetzung der Aufgabenstellung	kann einen selbstständig formulierten und strukturierten Kommentar verfassen, in dem wichtige Aspekte argumentativ sowie ausführlich dargestellt und mit relevanten Beispielen gestützt werden.
Text- und Problemverständnis	• weist ein weitgehend sicheres Textverständnis nach. • kann das Thema ggfs. in größere Zusammenhänge (*purpose of literature*) exemplarisch einordnen und kritisch kommentieren.

ISBN 978-3-425-73646-4

	Der Schüler/Die Schülerin ...
Darstellung und Gliederung	verfasst einen eigenständigen, strukturierten, kohärenten und durchgängig lesbaren Text, der überwiegend den Erfordernissen des Operators *comment* entspricht: • Gliederung: Einleitung, Hauptteil, Schluss • Darstellung und nachvollziehbare Begründung der eigenen Meinung durch Beispiele; ggfs eigene Meinung mit einem Gegenargument kontrastieren und dieses dann entkräften • schlüssige, nachvollziehbare sowie widerspruchsfreie Gestaltung des Kommentars, frei von Redundanzen • Verknüpfung mit im Unterricht behandeltem Material • eigener Standpunkt insgesamt überzeugend präsentiert
Gesamteindruck	Die inhaltliche Leistung entspricht in vollem Maße den Anforderungen der Aufgabe.

Pros:

- *the most authentic and credible writing is created when authors write about the things they are familiar with*
- *novels that deal with cultural issues are more meaningful to the readers than novels that could take place anywhere*

Cons:

- *good authors have the ability to make other cultures come alive; they don't necessarily have to be from that culture*
- *there are many good novels that do not deal with a particular culture but with universal human emotions and sensitivities*

Erwartungshorizont für eine gute sprachliche Leistung

Für die Einschätzung der sprachlichen Leistung schriftlicher Arbeiten kann folgende Tabelle eine Orientierung bieten.

Die Bewertung der sprachlichen Leistung erfolgt auf der Grundlage der in der Tabelle genannten Kriterien ganzheitlich über die in der linken Spalte genannten Teilaspekte hinweg; es werden also keine Einzelnoten zu diesen Teilaspekten gebildet. Die Gewichtung der einzelnen Kriterien innerhalb der Kategorien hängt von den Anforderungen der jeweiligen Aufgabenstellung ab.

	Der Schüler/Die Schülerin ...
Kommunikative Textgestaltung Textaufbau Textsortenspezifik Situationsangemessenheit und Adressatenbezug (Register)	• verfasst einen weitgehend zielgerichteten, strukturierten und kohärenten Text. • setzt die geforderten Textsortenmerkmale weitgehend überzeugend um. • schreibt weitgehend situationsangemessen und mit gelungenem Adressatenbezug.
Ausdrucksvermögen, Verwendung sprachlicher Mittel Eigenständigkeit Wortschatz Idiomatik Satzbau Umgang mit Materialien/ Belegtechnik	• verfasst eine eigenständige Darstellung. • verwendet sowohl allgemeinen als auch themenspezifischen Wortschatz weitgehend treffsicher und variabel. • verwendet weitgehend angemessene idiomatische Strukturen. • formuliert mit weitgehend variablem und funktionalem Satzbau unter Verwendung angemessen komplexer Strukturen. • verwendet Zitate weitgehend funktional und bettet diese weitgehend korrekt in den Textfluss ein. • kennzeichnet Zitate/Textverweise weitgehend korrekt.
Sprachrichtigkeit Lexik Grammatik/Syntax Orthografie Verständlichkeit	• drückt sich lexikalisch, grammatisch, syntaktisch und orthografisch weitgehend korrekt aus. • drückt sich verständlich aus: Sprachliche Verstöße beeinträchtigen die Verständlichkeit nicht.

Gesamteindruck	Die sprachliche Leistung entspricht in vollem Maße den Anforderungen der Aufgabe.

Lösungen und Erwartungshorizont für eine gute inhaltliche Leistung

Listening/Viewing 1: The American Dream Webcode: WES-73646-23

1D, 2E, 3C, 4A

Listening 2: Being black in Princeton Webcode: WES-73646-24

1. a) black students, b) Latino students
2. a) threw parties/partied/stayed up late dancing, b) had long dinners (with her friends)
3. to mingle in heterogeneous harmony/ to socialize in ethnically blended groups
4. minority students
5. a) realizing their disadvantages, b) always being in the minority
6. two
7. cautious/she stuck to what she knew
8. she asked the university to separate Cathy and Michelle
9. she was appalled that her daughter had been given a black roommate
10. *two of these aspects:* mother was a school teacher from New Orleans/grandfather was a sheriff/the 'N-word' was used in her home
11. she moved out of the (shared) room

Mediation: A German entrepreneur

Your American friend is taking part in a school project about the American Dream. You have found an article about the German entrepreneur Dirk Roßmann. You want to persuade your friend that Germany can also be a land of opportunity. In an email to your friend, summarize the article, focusing on the advice Dirk Roßmann gives to the pupils of his former school.

	Der Schüler/Die Schülerin ...
Umsetzung der Aufgabenstellung	erfüllt weitgehend die Erfordernisse einer *Mediation*-Aufgabe: • Verzicht auf wortwörtliche Übersetzungen • Entnahme der nötigen Informationen aus dem deutschen Text (Textsorte: Zeitungsartikel) zum Verfassen eines eigenen Textes (Textsorte: E-Mail)
Textsortenspezifik	setzt die textsortenspezifischen Merkmale für *email* weitgehend um: • Kopfzeile • Anrede • Einleitung, die in das Thema und die Situation ein-/hinführt (Erfolg und Reichtum durch gute Ideen und Fleiß) • aspektorientierte Zusammenfassung des Zeitungsartikels • Schlussgrußformel
Situationsangemessenheit und Adressatenbezug	schreibt weitgehend situationsangemessen und adressatenbezogen: • Freund/in in den USA • Register: informell, neutral-sachlich
Text- und Problemverständnis	kann das Thema des Artikels ggfs. in größere Zusammenhänge (*American Dream, "from rags to riches", land of opportunity*) einordnen.
Darstellung und Gliederung	kann die den Artikel und insbesondere die Ratschläge Dirk Roßmanns an die Schüler/innen zusammenfassend darstellen.

Gesamteindruck	Die inhaltliche Leistung entspricht in vollem Maße den Anforderungen der Aufgabe.

Mögliche inhaltliche Aspekte:

- *the successful entrepreneur Dirk Roßmann visits his old school and reads from his book*
- *he tells the audience that he didn't like school very much, not least because he was discouraged by his teacher*
- *his family didn't have much money but he nevertheless managed to become "drugstore king" and now heads a company that employs 56,000 people and that makes ten billion euros a year*
- *his advice to the pupils of his former school: learn English, a bit of arithmetics, but more importantly: don't give up early*

Writing: Upward mobility

You are an intern at the *Pacific Standard* magazine and have to decide on a suitable cartoon to accompany Tom Jacobs' article, which will be published on the magazine's website.

1. Comprehension: Briefly summarize Tom Jacobs' article below.

	Der Schüler/Die Schülerin ...
Umsetzung der Aufgabenstellung	kann aus dem Artikel wesentliche Hauptaussagen in einer kohärenten, präzisen Darstellung unter Beachtung der Textsortenmerkmale für *summary* zusammenfassen.
Textsortenspezifik	setzt die textsortenspezifischen Merkmale für *summary* weitgehend um: • Einleitungssatz zu beiden Texten (Genre, Titel, Autor/in, Quelle, Publikationsjahr, Thema) • *present tense* • eigene Worte, keine Zitate, keine Verweise • keine Nacherzählung • keine Wertung • pointierte, straffe, knappe Darstellung
Text- und Problemverständnis	durchdringt die Textvorlage weitgehend.
Darstellung und Gliederung	verfasst einen eigenständigen, strukturierten, kohärenten und durchgängig lesbaren Text, der überwiegend den Erfordernissen des Operators *summarize* entspricht.

Gesamteindruck	Die inhaltliche Leistung entspricht in vollem Maße den Anforderungen der Aufgabe.

Mögliche inhaltliche Aspekte:

- *according to research carried out by sociologist Michael Hout, upward social mobility is far less common in the USA than is often thought: a person's social standing is closely linked to their parents' occupations and social status*
- *Hout used a socioeconomic index to compare the careers of parents and their children over a large time span (1994–2016), and consistently got the same result: if the parents had a high-status profession and earned a lot of money, their children were highly likely to achieve a similar status; however, if the parents didn't have a high-status profession and earned little, their children wouldn't get ahead, but would instead remain within the same social class*
- *the profession a person's father seems to have a greater impact than that of their mother*
- *yet there is a common belief that children will always be more successful in their careers than their parents; this myth has its origins in the aftermath of WWII, when the Baby Boomer generation earned (much) more money than their parents had; this generation benefitted from the steep economic growth of those years*
- *the research clearly draws the conclusion that people from disadvantaged backgrounds struggle to climb up the socioeconomic ladder and that this prevailing social immobility worsens issues for blue-collar workers whose wages are continuously decreasing*

ISBN 978-3-425-73646-4

2. Analysis: Analyse cartoons A and B.

	Der Schüler/Die Schülerin ...
Umsetzung der Aufgabenstellung	kann die Cartoons als diskontinuierliche Texte differenziert im Sinne der Aufgabenstellung beschreiben und wesentliche Bildelemente themenbezogen analysieren.
Text- und Problemverständnis	weist eine weitgehend treffende Beschreibung und Auswertung der Cartoons nach und zeigt so ein überwiegend differenziertes Text- und Problemverständnis.
Darstellung und Gliederung	verfasst einen eigenständigen, strukturierten, kohärenten und durchgängig lesbaren Text, der den Erfordernissen des Operators *analyse* überwiegend entspricht: • präzise, nachvollziehbare Beschreibung, die Lokalisierungsphrasen beinhaltet • bildliche Elemente und deren Funktion/Bedeutung werden im Kontext der Cartoons erläuternd benannt

Gesamteindruck	Die inhaltliche Leistung entspricht in vollem Maße den Anforderungen der Aufgabe.

Mögliche inhaltliche Aspekte:

	Cartoon A	Cartoon B
Description	• *the cartoon shows a father and son sat together on the street; next to them is a sign saying "PLEASE GIVE", which indicates that they are homeless and begging for money on the streets* • *both of them are wearing shabby clothes and pessimistic expressions, with the empty cans and water puddles around them implying that the conditions in which they are living are miserable and bleak* • *the caption of the cartoon is spoken by the son, as is indicated by the son's open mouth and the reference to his "dad": "Remind me again, Dad. Why did you want me to get that college degree?"*	• *the cartoon shows a (married) couple sitting in front of the TV* • *the TV is on the left and the couple is on the right* • *the man and the woman both have a rather sullen/unhappy look on their face; the woman has her arms folded in front of her chest* • *the reader cannot see what is on the TV screen but there is a speech bubble coming out of the TV asking: "Are you living with limited mobility?"* • *while looking at the TV, the husband asks: "Does limited upward mobility count?"*
Analysis	*The cartoon suggests that education does not help people achieve upward social mobility. The son reveals in his statement that he has a college degree, and yet he is begging on the streets with his father. This implies that his father had wanted him to go to college to escape the poorer lower class he was born into, and yet after completing his education, the son is back in the same position as his father. Evidently this cartoon is criticizing the American Dream, which states that it is possible to move up to a higher social class if you work hard and get a good education, as it is clear that the man's situation has not at all improved after finishing his degree. It may also relate to the high costs of college education in America, and suggest that the debt caused by education leads to people becoming homeless.*	*The joke lies in the different meanings of mobility. The voice on TV is talking about limited physical mobility, whereas the man watching TV means limited social mobility. He believes he and his wife are not able to move up the socioeconomic ladder and implies with his question that their issue of limited social mobility should also be addressed.*

3. Writing an evaluation: Write an email to the editors in which you evaluate if either of the cartoons goes well with the article.

	Der Schüler/Die Schülerin ...
Umsetzung der Aufgabenstellung	kann einen selbstständig formulierten, adressatengerechten und strukturierten, zusammenhängenden Text gemäß der Aufgabenstellung unter Beachtung der Textkonvention E-Mail verfassen, indem das das Für und Wider von Cartoon A und B zur bildlichen Repräsentation des Artikels ausgangstextbasiert argumentativ sowie differenziert evaluiert wird.
Textsortenspezifik	setzt die textsortenspezifischen Merkmale für *email* um: • Betreff • Anrede • Einleitung, die die Situation und den Anlass der Email aufgreift • inhaltlich aspektorientierte Abwägung des Für und Wider beider Cartoons (A/B) • zusammenfassender Schluss, der sich begründet für einen Cartoon oder keinen ausspricht • Schlussgrußformel
Situationsangemessenheit und Adressatenbezug	schreibt situationsangemessen (Arbeitskontext, Rolle als Praktikant/in) und adressatenbezogen (Vorgesetzte, Herausgeber eines Magazins) → neutrales/sachliches Register
Text- und Problemverständnis	weist ein weitgehend differenziert umfassendes Textverständnis (Cartoon) im Sinne der Aufgabenstellung nach.
Darstellung und Gliederung	erfüllt mit seinen/ihren klaren und logischen Ausführungen überwiegend die Erfordernisse des Operators *evaluate*: • ausgewogene Beurteilung der beiden Cartoons im Hinblick auf die Frage, welcher besser zum Artikel passt (oder ob keiner zum Artikel passt) • Fazit

Gesamteindruck	Die inhaltliche Leistung entspricht in vollem Maße den Anforderungen der Aufgabe.

Mögliche inhaltliche Aspekte:

Cartoon A
Pros:
- *is more complex than cartoon B as it provides more specific details about limited upward mobility, namely that education is meant to improve the situation of those in the lower classes, but that it often fails to do so*
- *as in the article, the cartoon implies that social progression in America remains stagnant for anyone born into the lower classes*
- *the link specifically between the position of father and son in the cartoon relates directly to the article, as the article states that the occupation of a father has a big impact on the occupation of their children; when the article is put together with the cartoon, this statistic becomes humorous, as the "occupation" shared between father and son in the cartoon is that of a beggar*

Cons:
- *this cartoon exaggerates the stagnation in American society, as it seems unlikely that a person with a college degree would be unable to find any job*
- *this cartoon could also be expressing the level of debt caused by gaining a college degree, so its meaning isn't as clear as that of cartoon B*

ISBN 978-3-425-73646-4

Cartoon B:
Pros:
- *addresses limited upward mobility just like the article does*
- *the meaning of the cartoon is easy to understand and might therefore appeal to a broader readership*

Cons:
- *doesn't address the reasons for limited upward mobility*
- *despite dealing with the same overall topic as the article, it doesn't share its central message*

Conclusion: Cartoon A goes better with the article than cartoon B.
(other conclusions possible!)

Erwartungshorizont für eine gute sprachliche Leistung

Für die Einschätzung der sprachlichen Leistung schriftlicher Arbeiten kann folgende Tabelle eine Orientierung bieten.

Die Bewertung der sprachlichen Leistung erfolgt auf der Grundlage der in der Tabelle genannten Kriterien ganzheitlich über die in der linken Spalte genannten Teilaspekte hinweg; es werden also keine Einzelnoten zu diesen Teilaspekten gebildet. Die Gewichtung der einzelnen Kriterien innerhalb der Kategorien hängt von den Anforderungen der jeweiligen Aufgabenstellung ab.

	Der Schüler/Die Schülerin ...
Kommunikative Textgestaltung Textaufbau Textsortenspezifik Situationsangemessenheit und Adressatenbezug (Register)	• verfasst einen weitgehend zielgerichteten, strukturierten und kohärenten Text. • setzt die geforderten Textsortenmerkmale weitgehend überzeugend um. • schreibt weitgehend situationsangemessen und mit gelungenem Adressatenbezug.
Ausdrucksvermögen, Verwendung sprachlicher Mittel Eigenständigkeit Wortschatz Idiomatik Satzbau Umgang mit Materialien/ Belegtechnik	• verfasst eine eigenständige Darstellung. • verwendet sowohl allgemeinen als auch themenspezifischen Wortschatz weitgehend treffsicher und variabel. • verwendet weitgehend angemessene idiomatische Strukturen. • formuliert mit weitgehend variablem und funktionalem Satzbau unter Verwendung angemessen komplexer Strukturen. • verwendet Zitate weitgehend funktional und bettet diese weitgehend korrekt in den Textfluss ein. • kennzeichnet Zitate/Textverweise weitgehend korrekt.
Sprachrichtigkeit Lexik Grammatik/Syntax Orthografie Verständlichkeit	• drückt sich lexikalisch, grammatisch, syntaktisch und orthografisch weitgehend korrekt aus. • drückt sich verständlich aus: Sprachliche Verstöße beeinträchtigen die Verständlichkeit nicht.

Gesamteindruck	Die sprachliche Leistung entspricht in vollem Maße den Anforderungen der Aufgabe.

ISBN 978-3-425-73646-4

Lösungen und Erwartungshorizont für eine gute inhaltliche Leistung

Listening 1: No miracles Webcode: WES-73646-25

1d, 2b+d, 3c, 4b, 5a+c, 6b, 7d, 8a+c

Listening 2: White supremacy and terrorism Webcode: WES-73646-26

1. focus on white power groups.
2. former FBI counterterrorism special agent.
3. a) the USS Cole bombing and, b) the events of 9/11.
4. Islamic extremism and white power.
5. a) ideology, b) strategy and, c) recruitment tactics.
6. a global network.
7. a priority (in the US).
8. an increasing threat emerging in the United States and Europe.
9. about the impact of Moscow on white power movements.
10. left-wing extremists to right-wing extremists.
11. a horrible act.
12. in a place or at a place of worship (like a mosque in Quebec or a mosque in London or a mosque in New Zealand or a synagogue in Pittsburgh).

Mediation: Black Lives Matter in Germany

At his college, your former American exchange partner attends a course dealing with the Black Lives Matter movement in the US. In his course, he has learned that there is also a German branch of this movement fighting racism towards people of colour. He has asked you to give him some insight into the movement in Germany.
On the basis of an article you have found, you decide to write an email to your friend. This email should explain the reasons a German branch of the Black Lives Matter movement was set up, including why the branch is necessary, historical aspects and the present-day situation with regard to racism in Germany, and how to fight this racism.

	Der Schüler/Die Schülerin ...
Umsetzung der Aufgabenstellung	erfüllt weitgehend die Erfordernisse einer *Mediation*-Aufgabe: • Verzicht auf wortwörtliche Übersetzungen • Entnahme der nötigen Informationen aus dem deutschen Text (Textsorte: Zeitungsinterview) zum Verfassen eines eigenen Textes (Textsorte: E-Mail)
Textsortenspezifik	setzt die textsortenspezifischen Merkmale für *email* weitgehend um: • Betreff • Anrede • Einleitung, die in das Thema und die Situation ein-/hinführt (Black-Lives-Matter-Bewegung, Alltagsrassismus gegenüber Schwarzen in Deutschland) • inhaltlich aspektorientierte Strukturierung • zusammenfassender Schluss, der die Frage des Freundes/der Freundin aufgreift • Schlussgrußformel
Situationsangemessenheit und Adressatenbezug	schreibt weitgehend situationsangemessen und adressatenbezogen: • Student in the USA • Register: informell, neutral-sachlich
Kulturspezifik	kann relevante kulturspezifische Aspekte weitgehend nachvollziehbar erläutern (ggfs. deutsche Kolonialzeit)
Text- und Problemverständnis	kann das Thema des Artikels ggfs. in größere Zusammenhänge *(discrimination, racism, minorities)* einordnen.

ISBN 978-3-425-73646-4

Darstellung und Gliederung	kann auf Grundlage des Zeitungsinterviews die Hintergründe der Black-Lives-Matter-Bewegung in Deutschland erklären.

Gesamteindruck	Die inhaltliche Leistung entspricht in vollem Maße den Anforderungen der Aufgabe.

Mögliche inhaltliche Aspekte:

Reasons for a German branch of the Black Lives Matter movement:
- *black people experience racism on a daily basis: they don't have equal access to education, the workplace or housing, they experience more violence and are disproportionally targeted by the police*
- *they are not accepted as being German → people are either seen as black or German, not both at the same time*

Why the movement is necessary: *when dealing with racism, people usually come up with a hierarchy of violence; it is always worth fighting for equality, not just when lives are in danger*

History of racism (towards people of colour) in Germany:
- *Germany has a different history of racism to that of the US*
- *examples of historical racism in Germany include: Prussian involvement in the slave trade, German behaviour in colonial times and during National Socialism, as well as the genocides of different peoples in Africa*
- *black people still experience the aftermath of colonial times → German society does not critically reflect on its past and there are still places or streets named after colonialists who were known racists*

Present-day racism and how to fight it:
- *societal privileges are often not recognized, meaning people do not responsibly reflect upon their favoured social position*
- *many people simplify complex social realities, meaning, for example, that they regard all people of colour as criminals*
- *every single person has to reflect on their role and involvement in society, acknowledge that they may have an advantage over others, and take responsibility for helping to make society fairer*
- *it is not enough to be a decent person; it is about making a difference and changing established power structures*

Writing: Oprah Winfrey for president?

You are an intern at the *The Guardian* newspaper and have to decide on a suitable cartoon to accompany Emine Saner's article on Oprah Winfrey.

1. Comprehension: Briefly summarize Emine Saner's article below.

	Der Schüler/Die Schülerin ...
Umsetzung der Aufgabenstellung	kann aus dem Artikel wesentliche Hauptaussagen in einer kohärenten, präzisen Darstellung unter Beachtung der Textsortenmerkmale für *summary* zusammenfassen.
Textsortenspezifik	setzt die textsortenspezifischen Merkmale für *summary* weitgehend um: • Einleitungssatz (Genre, Titel, Autor/in, Quelle, Publikationsjahr, Thema) • *present tense* • eigene Worte, keine Zitate, keine Verweise • keine Nacherzählung • keine Wertung • pointierte, straffe, knappe Darstellung
Text- und Problemverständnis	durchdringt die Textvorlage weitgehend.

	Der Schüler/Die Schülerin ...
Darstellung und Gliederung	verfasst einen eigenständigen, strukturierten, kohärenten und durchgängig lesbaren Text, der überwiegend den Erfordernissen des Operators *summarize* entspricht.

Gesamteindruck	Die inhaltliche Leistung entspricht in vollem Maße den Anforderungen der Aufgabe.

Mögliche inhaltliche Aspekte:

- *according to a poll carried out in 2018, more people would vote for Oprah Winfrey to become the next president than would re-elect Trump*
- *this result prompted speculation about Winfrey's possible candidacy in the next presidential election*
- *although Winfrey has always denied wanting to run for president, she might be reconsidering this position, since Trump is also a former TV celebrity with no political experience*
- *Winfrey's story is representative of the American success story, as she had a disadvantaged childhood and still became one of the richest and most powerful (black) women in the world by working hard*
- *the key to her success is said to be her kindness and charitable character*
- *she is respected and regarded as an icon by people of all ethnicities, though some people, including Oprah herself, think that the public desire for her to become president should be investigated – many people support her over other, potentially more qualified, nominees, and pin all their hopes for the future on this one woman*

2. Analysis: Analyse cartoons A and B.

	Der Schüler/Die Schülerin ...
Umsetzung der Aufgabenstellung	kann die Cartoons als diskontinuierliche Texte differenziert im Sinne der Aufgabenstellung beschreiben und wesentliche Bildelemente themenbezogen analysieren.
Text- und Problemverständnis	weist eine weitgehend treffende Beschreibung und Auswertung der Cartoons nach und zeigt so ein überwiegend differenziertes Text- und Problemverständnis.
Darstellung und Gliederung	verfasst einen eigenständigen, strukturierten, kohärenten und durchgängig lesbaren Text, der den Erfordernissen des Operators *analyse* überwiegend entspricht: • präzise, nachvollziehbare Beschreibung, die Lokalisierungsphrasen beinhaltet • bildliche Elemente und deren Funktion/Bedeutung werden im Kontext der Cartoons erläuternd benannt

Gesamteindruck	Die inhaltliche Leistung entspricht in vollem Maße den Anforderungen der Aufgabe.

ISBN 978-3-425-73646-4

Mögliche inhaltliche Aspekte:

	Cartoon A	Cartoon B
Description	• *the cartoon shows Oprah Winfrey holding a long list in her right hand and a pen or pencil in her left hand* • *her facial expression and posture suggest confidence and openness* • *the list is entitled "Oprah" and has six attributes which apply to Oprah Winfrey* • *they are: "billionaire", "TV celeb", "never held public office", "no political experience, "Washington outsider", and "huge fan base"* • *In a speech bubble, Oprah says: "Hey, it worked for Trump …"*	• *the cartoon is split into two halves; on the left, there is a couple sitting in front of the TV; in the top left corner it says "2016" and you can see (a caricature of) Donald Trump on TV* • *in a speech bubble, the man comments: "The last thing we need as president is a celebrity billionaire with zero governing experience …"* • *the right half of the cartoon shows the same couple in front of a stand that says "Oprah 2020"* • *in the top left corner it says "2018"; the stand is staffed by two people who wear "Oprah 2020" T-shirts and behind them are posters bearing the same slogan* • *the suggestion is that this is a political campaign event for Winfrey's presidential candidacy* • *the couple also wear Oprah T-shirts, and the man asks the people at the stand: "Is this where we volunteer?"*
Analysis	*The cartoon plays on the fact that Oprah Winfrey and Donald Trump have a lot in common. The same attributes that apply to Winfrey also apply to Trump, e.g. TV celeb with no political experience. The cartoon is meant to be ironic, since most of the attributes do not usually recommend a person for the office of US president. However, since Trump won, Winfrey is confident that she can benefit from the same (non-presidential) qualities.*	*The cartoon plays on the fact that before Trump's election, it was almost unthinkable that someone with his (lack of) credentials would become president of the United States. This is underlined by the man's statement that this was the last thing the American people needed. Two years later, however, the same man and his wife are prepared to vote for and even support another billionaire with no political experience, namely Oprah Winfrey. The cartoon is a comment on the shift that has occurred since Trump's election with regard to the suitability of a candidate.*

3. Writing an evaluation: Write an email to the editors in which you evaluate if either of the cartoons goes well with the article.

	Der Schüler/Die Schülerin …
Umsetzung der Aufgabenstellung	kann einen selbstständig formulierten, adressatengerechten und strukturierten, zusammenhängenden Text gemäß der Aufgabenstellung unter Beachtung der Textkonvention E-Mail verfassen, indem das das Für und Wider von Cartoon A und B zur bildlichen Repräsentation des Artikels ausgangstextbasiert argumentativ sowie differenziert evaluiert wird.

ISBN 978-3-425-73646-4

	Der Schüler/Die Schülerin ...
Textsortenspezifik	setzt die textsortenspezifischen Merkmale für *email* um: • Betreff • Anrede • Einleitung, die die Situation und den Anlass der Email aufgreift • inhaltlich aspektorientierte Abwägung des Für und Wider beider Cartoons (A/B) • zusammenfassender Schluss, der sich begründet für einen Cartoon oder keinen ausspricht • Schlussgrußformel
Situationsangemessenheit und Adressatenbezug	schreibt situationsangemessen (Arbeitskontext, Rolle als Praktikant/in) und adressatenbezogen (Vorgesetzte, Herausgeber einer Zeitung) → neutrales/sachliches Register
Text- und Problemverständnis	weist ein weitgehend differenziert umfassendes Textverständnis (Cartoon) im Sinne der Aufgabenstellung nach.
Darstellung und Gliederung	erfüllt mit seinen/ihren klaren und logischen Ausführungen überwiegend die Erfordernisse des Operators *evaluate*: • ausgewogene Beurtielung der beiden Cartoons im Hinblick auf die Frage, welcher besser zum Artikel passt (oder ob keiner zum Artikel passt) • Fazit

Gesamteindruck	Die inhaltliche Leistung entspricht in vollem Maße den Anforderungen der Aufgabe.

Mögliche inhaltliche Aspekte:

Cartoon A
Pros:
- *addresses the question of Oprah Winfrey's suitability as a possible presidential candidate; this is also the topic at the beginning and the end of the article*
- *is straightforward and easy to understand*

Cons:
- *doesn't deal with the bulk of the article, which is about Winfrey's life and success story*

Cartoon B
Pros:
- *refers to the views and hopes of the voters with regard to Winfrey; this is also dealt with at the end of the article*

Cons:
- *the cartoon is as much about the perception of Trump as it is about Winfrey and doesn't match the core of the article*

Conclusion: *Cartoon A goes better with the article than cartoon B.*
(other conclusions possible!)

ISBN 978-3-425-73646-4

Erwartungshorizont für eine gute sprachliche Leistung

Für die Einschätzung der sprachlichen Leistung schriftlicher Arbeiten kann folgende Tabelle eine Orientierung bieten.

Die Bewertung der sprachlichen Leistung erfolgt auf der Grundlage der in der Tabelle genannten Kriterien ganzheitlich über die in der linken Spalte genannten Teilaspekte hinweg; es werden also keine Einzelnoten zu diesen Teilaspekten gebildet. Die Gewichtung der einzelnen Kriterien innerhalb der Kategorien hängt von den Anforderungen der jeweiligen Aufgabenstellung ab.

	Der Schüler/Die Schülerin ...
Kommunikative Textgestaltung Textaufbau Textsortenspezifik Situationsangemessenheit und Adressatenbezug (Register)	• verfasst einen weitgehend zielgerichteten, strukturierten und kohärenten Text. • setzt die geforderten Textsortenmerkmale weitgehend überzeugend um. • schreibt weitgehend situationsangemessen und mit gelungenem Adressatenbezug.
Ausdrucksvermögen, Verwendung sprachlicher Mittel Eigenständigkeit Wortschatz Idiomatik Satzbau Umgang mit Materialien/ Belegtechnik	• verfasst eine eigenständige Darstellung. • verwendet sowohl allgemeinen als auch themenspezifischen Wortschatz weitgehend treffsicher und variabel. • verwendet weitgehend angemessene idiomatische Strukturen. • formuliert mit weitgehend variablem und funktionalem Satzbau unter Verwendung angemessen komplexer Strukturen. • verwendet Zitate weitgehend funktional und bettet diese weitgehend korrekt in den Textfluss ein. • kennzeichnet Zitate/Textverweise weitgehend korrekt.
Sprachrichtigkeit Lexik Grammatik/Syntax Orthografie Verständlichkeit	• drückt sich lexikalisch, grammatisch, syntaktisch und orthografisch weitgehend korrekt aus. • drückt sich verständlich aus: Sprachliche Verstöße beeinträchtigen die Verständlichkeit nicht.

Gesamteindruck	Die sprachliche Leistung entspricht in vollem Maße den Anforderungen der Aufgabe.

ISBN 978-3-425-73646-4

Lösungen und Erwartungshorizont für eine gute inhaltliche Leistung

Listening: Chinua Achebe's legacy

a) **Webcode:** WES-73646-27 (Ausschnitt: 00:00–02:27)

1. told the story of African peoples from an African point of view
2. youngest child
3. what we now know as the genre of African literature
4. the Igbo culture under British colonial rule in Nigeria
5. scholarships to the top schools
6. siding with the "white man" against the "African savage"
7. was not innocent/had the ability to turn you against your own
8. their authors did not speak the language of their creatures
9. the entire philosophy of life, the world view
10. a need/a compulsion to write the story of his people

b) **Webcode:** WES-73646-28 (Ausschnitt: 02:27–06:42)
1c, 2a+b, 3b+c, 4a+d, 5a+b+d

c) **Webcode:** WES-73646-29 (Ausschnitt: 06:42–08:55)

1. *two of these aspects:* Chinua Achebe's books were banned/one (tattered and torn) copy was smuggled by him and his friends/he started memorizing the book
2. reading his work made the prison walls fall down
3. "you are a freedom fighter like me" ("but we fought in different ways. You fought through the word of your story.")
4. *two of these aspects:* we are a people of great civilization/of culture/a dignified people/truly human

Mediation: A road trip through Nigeria

You are part of an international online community that is interested in travelling to Africa after finishing school. You have come across the following blog post about a recent trip to Nigeria. For the online forum, write a summary of the blog post and give a short evaluation as to whether Maxi Brommer's descriptions make you want to travel to Nigeria.

	Der Schüler/Die Schülerin ...
Umsetzung der Aufgabenstellung	erfüllt weitgehend die Erfordernisse einer *Mediation*-Aufgabe: • Verzicht auf wortwörtliche Übersetzungen • Entnahme der nötigen Informationen aus dem deutschen Text (Textsorte: Blogeintrag) zum Verfassen eines eigenen Textes (Textsorte: Zusammenfassung und kurze Einschätzung)
Textsortenspezifik	setzt die textsortenspezifischen Merkmale für *summary* und *evaluation* weitgehend um. *Summary:* • Einleitungssatz (Genre, Titel, Autor, Publikationsjahr, Thema) • *present tense* • eigene Worte, keine Zitate, keine Verweise • keine Nacherzählung • keine Wertung • pointierte, straffe Darstellung *Evaluation:* Schlussfolgerung auf Basis einer ausgewogenen Betrachtung positiver wie negativer Aspekte
Situationsangemessenheit und Adressatenbezug	schreibt weitgehend situationsangemessen und adressatenbezogen: • Online-Community • Register: informell, neutral-sachlich
Text- und Problemverständnis	kann das Thema des Artikels ggfs. in größere Zusammenhänge (*postcolonial world*) einordnen.

ISBN 978-3-425-73646-4

	Der Schüler/Die Schülerin ...
Darstellung und Gliederung	kann die Erfahrungen des Bloggers zusammenfassend darstellen und eine Einschätzung darüber abgeben, inwiefern der Blogeintrag den Leser/die Leserin zu einer Reise nach Nigeria anregen kann.

Gesamteindruck	Die inhaltliche Leistung entspricht in vollem Maße den Anforderungen der Aufgabe.

Mögliche inhaltliche Aspekte:

Summary:
- *if you are travelling through West Africa, you cannot avoid passing through Nigeria; the author calls it a nightmare for anybody travelling to Africa*
- *an estimated 25 million people live in Lagos*
- *on his way there the author is stopped by a street gang demanding money and gets stuck in complete traffic chaos for many hours*
- *there are slums on both sides of the street where children rummage in garbage and where the chance of being robbed is very high*
- *there are more than 200 million people living in Nigeria but the government has lost control over many areas due to the fight against terrorism*
- *in Lagos there are also very rich areas such as Victoria Island*
- *the author and his companion continue their journey through the country and experience a completely different side of Nigeria: the people are very friendly, the landscape is greener and the temperatures cooler*
- *the author considers his time in Nigeria as very intensive; the country is very varied and full of energy; the author thinks that this is how the Wild West in America must have been like*

Evaluation:
- *Pros: energy; positive experiences in the mountainous areas of Nigeria*
- *Cons: dangerous (robberies, terrorism); extreme poverty and pollution; chaotic conditions*
- *Conclusion: the descriptions in the blog post doesn't entice one to travel to Nigeria; especially Lagos seems to be best avoided; a journey to the mountainous areas of the country might be interesting; however, it is questionable if you can get there easily*

Writing: From Nigeria to Britain

Read the following extract from the novel *The Other Hand* (2008) by Chris Cleave. The novel centres around the story of Little Bee, who is a young girl from Nigeria and Sarah O'Rourke, a magazine editor from Surrey. After two years of being held in a British detention centre, Little Bee is illegally released. She travels to Sarah and her husband Andrew, whom she met two years previously on a beach in the Niger Delta. The following extract is taken from the beginning of the novel.

1. Comprehension: Sum up the extract at hand.

	Der Schüler/Die Schülerin ...
Umsetzung der Aufgabenstellung	kann aus dem Romanauszug wesentliche Hauptaussagen zusammenstellen und ich einer kohärenten zusammenfassen.
Textsortenspezifik	setzt die textsortenspezifischen Merkmale für *summary* weitgehend um: • Einleitungssatz (Genre, Titel, Autor, Publikationsjahr, Thema) • *present tense* • eigene Worte, keine Zitate, keine Verweise • keine Nacherzählung • keine Wertung • pointierte, straffe Darstellung

	Der Schüler/Die Schülerin ...
Text- und Problemverständnis	durchdringt die Textvorlage weitgehend.
Darstellung und Gliederung	verfasst einen eigenständigen, strukturierten, kohärenten und durchgängig lesbaren Text, der überwiegend den Erfordernissen des Operators *summarize* entspricht.

Gesamteindruck	Die inhaltliche Leistung entspricht in vollem Maße den Anforderungen der Aufgabe.

Mögliche inhaltliche Aspekte:

- *Little Bee wished she was a British pound coin, which is liked by everyone and can go wherever it wants*
- *globalization makes it possible for the British pound to travel everywhere but not for migrants*
- *Little Bee reflects on the fact that it is the command of proper British English (the Queen's English) that makes one powerful*

2. Analysis: Analyse the way in which Little Bee reflects upon her experiences in the United Kingdom by considering her use of stylistic devices.

	Der Schüler/Die Schülerin ...
Umsetzung der Aufgabenstellung	führt die im Sinne der Aufgabenstellung relevanten Informationen weitgehend präzise aus.
Text- und Problemverständnis	durchdringt die Textvorlage weitgehend.
Darstellung und Gliederung	verfasst einen eigenständigen, strukturierten, kohärenten und durchgängig lesbaren Text, der den Erfordernissen des Operators *analyse* überwiegend entspricht: • Untersuchung der sprachlichen Mittel, um Little Bees Erfahrungen zu analysieren • Untermauerung durch sinnvolle und prägnante Beispiele aus dem Romanauszug

Gesamteindruck	Die inhaltliche Leistung entspricht in vollem Maße den Anforderungen der Aufgabe.

Mögliche inhaltliche Aspekte:

- ***personification*** *of the British pound coin → highlights the discrepancy between the freedom of movement for money and the lack of freedom of movement for people that Little Bee experienced*
- ***comparison:***
  - *"like lovers who met on holiday and forgot each other's names" → shows that freedom of movement is carefree and light in contrast to Little Bee's experience*
  - *"in a voice as clear as the Cullinan diamond" → reference to British colonial rule in Africa; the diamond was found in Africa but became property of the British monarchs; highlights the fact that although the UK has taken from Africa they don't welcome African migrants*
- ***contrast:*** *"cross deserts and oceans" → draws attention to the long distances money and migrants cover*
- ***alliteration:*** *"bitter smell of burning thatch behind" → draws attention to the experience of war that Little Bee and other migrants went through in their home countries*
- ***rhetorical questions:*** *"If the Queen spoke to you in such a voice, do you suppose it would be possible to disobey" → to convince the reader of her point that the way you speak matters*

ISBN 978-3-425-73646-4

3. Writing a discussion: Discuss Little Bee's statement that globalization is a "human triumph" against the backdrop of your knowledge about global challenges in today's postcolonial world.

	Der Schüler/Die Schülerin ...
Umsetzung der Aufgabenstellung	kann einen selbstständig formulierten und zusammenhängenden Text verfassen, in dem Little Bees Aussage ausgewogen diskutiert wird. Dabei wird Hintergrundwissen über die globalen Herausforderungen einbezogen.
Text- und Problemverständnis	weist ein weitgehend differenziert umfassendes Textverständnis im Sinne der Aufgabenstellung nach.
Darstellung und Gliederung	erfüllt mit seinen/ihren klaren und logischen Ausführungen überwiegend die Erfordernisse des Operators *discuss*: • ausgewogene Darstellung des Für und Wider von Little Bees Aussage • Verweise auf den Romanauszug • Einbeziehung von Hintergrundwissen • Fazit

Gesamteindruck	Die inhaltliche Leistung entspricht in vollem Maße den Anforderungen der Aufgabe.

Mögliche inhaltliche Aspekte:

Pros:

- *globalization allows for the freedom of movement of capital → economic progress and greater wealth in many regions of the world*
- *those who can afford it or who are wanted as employees can also travel fairly freely → this can be seen as a "human triumph"*

Cons:

- *globalization favours money over people → poor people are not free to move, yet they are often forced to move due to war or global warming → they are criminalized like Little Bee*
- *globalization spreads wealth unevenly → wealth of richer nations has been amassed on the back of poorer nations (reference to the Cullinan diamond)*

ISBN 978-3-425-73646-4

Erwartungshorizont für eine gute sprachliche Leistung

Für die Einschätzung der sprachlichen Leistung schriftlicher Arbeiten kann folgende Tabelle eine Orientierung bieten.

Die Bewertung der sprachlichen Leistung erfolgt auf der Grundlage der in der Tabelle genannten Kriterien ganzheitlich über die in der linken Spalte genannten Teilaspekte hinweg; es werden also keine Einzelnoten zu diesen Teilaspekten gebildet. Die Gewichtung der einzelnen Kriterien innerhalb der Kategorien hängt von den Anforderungen der jeweiligen Aufgabenstellung ab.

	Der Schüler/Die Schülerin ...
Kommunikative Textgestaltung Textaufbau Textsortenspezifik Situationsangemessenheit und Adressatenbezug (Register)	• verfasst einen weitgehend zielgerichteten, strukturierten und kohärenten Text. • setzt die geforderten Textsortenmerkmale weitgehend überzeugend um. • schreibt weitgehend situationsangemessen und mit gelungenem Adressatenbezug.
Ausdrucksvermögen, Verwendung sprachlicher Mittel Eigenständigkeit Wortschatz Idiomatik Satzbau Umgang mit Materialien/ Belegtechnik	• verfasst eine eigenständige Darstellung. • verwendet sowohl allgemeinen als auch themenspezifischen Wortschatz weitgehend treffsicher und variabel. • verwendet weitgehend angemessene idiomatische Strukturen. • formuliert mit weitgehend variablem und funktionalem Satzbau unter Verwendung angemessen komplexer Strukturen. • verwendet Zitate weitgehend funktional und bettet diese weitgehend korrekt in den Textfluss ein. • kennzeichnet Zitate/Textverweise weitgehend korrekt.
Sprachrichtigkeit Lexik Grammatik/Syntax Orthografie Verständlichkeit	• drückt sich lexikalisch, grammatisch, syntaktisch und orthografisch weitgehend korrekt aus. • drückt sich verständlich aus: Sprachliche Verstöße beeinträchtigen die Verständlichkeit nicht.

Gesamteindruck	Die sprachliche Leistung entspricht in vollem Maße den Anforderungen der Aufgabe.

ISBN 978-3-425-73646-4

Lösungen und Erwartungshorizont für eine gute inhaltliche Leistung

Listening: India's rising middle class

a) **Webcode:** WES-73646-30 (Ausschnitt: 00:40–02:51)

1. *three of the following:* office workers/software engineers/developers/researchers/clerks
2. information technology
3. a sleepy backwater
4. the size of Atlanta
5. a condo/an apartment
6. a) buying bigger homes (made out of steel and concrete), b) driving more cars, c) eating better food
7. a) prices worldwide go up, b) our standard of living goes down

b) **Webcode:** WES-73646-31 (Ausschnitt: 02:50–07:50)

1b+d, 2a, 3b+d, 4a+d, 5a+b

c) **Webcode:** WES-73646-32 (Ausschnitt: 16:14–19:45)

1. people are eating a) more and b) better
2. *two of these aspects:* can now buy what they want/more meat, fish and protein/more variety
3. *two of the following:* steel/concrete/oil/natural gas
4. they want what developed nations already have: a chance at a good life
5. their way of life/their patterns of consumption
6. *two of the following:* (stunning) poverty/not enough good roads/lack of electricity/lack of clean water/history of coruption and inaction

Mediation: Mumbai

Imagine you are an exchange student at an English grammar school. In your geography class, you discuss "mega-cities" in India. You have come across this article about the history of Mumbai with its more than 18 million inhabitants. Write a presentation about Mumbai based on the information from the article.

	Der Schüler/Die Schülerin ...
Umsetzung der Aufgabenstellung	erfüllt weitgehend die Erfordernisse einer *Mediation*-Aufgabe: • Verzicht auf wortwörtliche Übersetzungen • Entnahme der nötigen Informationen aus dem deutschen Text (Textsorte: Sachtext) zum Verfassen eines eigenen Textes (Textsorte: Präsentation)
Textsortenspezifik	setzt die textsortenspezifischen Merkmale für *presentation* weitgehend um: • klare Ansprache der Zuhörer/innen • Einleitung • interessante Hinführung zum Thema • Sinnvoll gegliederter Hauptteil • Schluss
Situationsangemessenheit und Adressatenbezug	schreibt weitgehend situationsangemessen und adressatenbezogen: • breite Schulöffentlichkeit • Bezug zum Thema im Erdkundeunterricht • Register: neutral-sachlich
Text- und Problemverständnis	kann das Thema des Artikels ggfs. in größere Zusammenhänge (*colonial/postcolonial world; India as a country of extremes*) einordnen.
Darstellung und Gliederung	kann die Erfahrungen des Bloggers zusammenfassend stellt das Thema eigenständig und überwiegend klar und logisch dar.

ISBN 978-3-425-73646-4

Gesamteindruck	Die inhaltliche Leistung entspricht in vollem Maße den Anforderungen der Aufgabe.

Mögliche inhaltliche Aspekte:

- *Mumbai is the most diverse city in India*
- *it is still known as Bombay which derives from Bom Bahia, Portuguese for "good bay"*
- *Early history of Mumbai:*
  - *was built on seven islands*
  - *was inhabited by fishermen*
  - *had different rulers: first the sultanate of Gujarat, then the Portuguese and after that it came under British rule*
- *Later history:*
  - *by the late 19th century, Bombay, as it was then called, had become one of the most important trading centres in India and had 800,000 inhabitants*
  - *a railway was built to connect Bombay with the hinterland; from then on, Bombay was also called the "Gateway of India" and it also became an important centre for the cotton industry*
  - *Gandhi turned Bombay into an important centre of resistance to British rule*
  - *In 1947, India became independent and the last British troops left the former colony through the "Gateway of India"*
  - *After independence, Bombay grew continuously, and in 1995 it was renamed Mumbai, after the local Hindu goddess Mumbadevi*

Writing: A new age in Bangalore

Read the following extract from the novel *The White Tiger* (2008) by Aravind Adiga. The novel centres around the story of Balram Halwai, who was born into a poor family in rural India but who manages to work his way up to become a chauffeur in Delhi. He murders his employer, Mr Ashok, steals seven hundred thousand rupees from him and uses the money to establish himself as an entrepreneur in Bangalore, a thriving metropolis whose growth is based on IT companies and call centres. The novel consists of seven emails written by Balram who calls himself "The White Tiger". His emails are addressed to Wen Jiabao, the Chinese premier, who will visit Bangalore to meet Indian business people and to learn the secret behind their economic success.

1. Comprehension: Describe the "New Bangalore" as seen by Balram Halwai.

	Der Schüler/Die Schülerin ...
Umsetzung der Aufgabenstellung	kann das in dem Romanauszug durch den Ich-Erzähler vermittelte „neue" Bangalore weitgehend treffend beschreiben.
Text- und Problemverständnis	durchdringt die Textvorlage weitgehend.
Darstellung und Gliederung	verfasst einen eigenständigen, strukturierten, kohärenten und durchgängig lesbaren Text, der überwiegend den Erfordernissen des Operators *describe* entspricht: • ausführliche Darstellung • keine Zitate oder Verweise

Gesamteindruck	Die inhaltliche Leistung entspricht in vollem Maße den Anforderungen der Aufgabe.

Mögliche inhaltliche Aspekte:

- *a booming city in the making*
- *many international companies moving there*
- *a lot of construction*
- *a city of uncertain future: could turn out to be a terrible place to live but could also develop into a great place*
- *Balram thinks that Bangalore will thrive*

ISBN 978-3-425-73646-4

2. Analysis: Analyse the way in which Balram reflects upon his own past and future in the New Bangalore by considering his use of stylistic devices and syntax.

	Der Schüler/Die Schülerin ...
Umsetzung der Aufgabenstellung	führt die im Sinne der Aufgabenstellung relevanten Informationen weitgehend präzise aus.
Text- und Problemverständnis	durchdringt die Textvorlage weitgehend.
Darstellung und Gliederung	verfasst einen eigenständigen, strukturierten, kohärenten und durchgängig lesbaren Text, der den Erfordernissen des Operators *analyse* überwiegend entspricht: • Untersuchung der sprachlichen Mittel und der Syntax, um Balrams Einschätzungen seiner Vergangenheit und Zukunft zu analysieren • Untermauerung durch sinnvolle und prägnante Beispiele aus dem Romanauszug

Gesamteindruck	Die inhaltliche Leistung entspricht in vollem Maße den Anforderungen der Aufgabe.

Mögliche inhaltliche Aspekte:

Stylistic devices:

- ***imagery:***
  - *"A school full of White Tigers, unleashed an Bangalore" → underlines Balram's aggressiveness and determination in the past and in the future; he sees himself as a predator prepared to educate other predators*
  - *"masked in smoke", "under a veil" → underlines that a lot is hidden and secret in Bangalore, including his past*
- ***contrast:*** *"You see, I am always a man who sees 'tomorrow' when others see 'today' → sets him apart from the others, shows that he sees himself as someone special, a visionary, a man of the future*
- ***alliteration/enumeration:*** *"slums, sewage, shopping malls" → draws attention to possible negative consequences of the city's growth and could reflect aspects of Balram's past that he tries to leave behind*

Syntax:

- ***elliptical sentences:*** *"Piles of mud everywhere. Piles of stone. Piles of brick." → draws attention to the the level of construction going on in Bangalore; also shows that Balram is a close observer of the city*
- ***slogans:*** *"A new Bangalore for a new India" → shows that Balram is taking part in "selling" Bangalore to the world, but that he is also aware that this is what it's all about: selling, making money*
- ***rhetorical questions:*** *"Why not? Am I not a part of all that is changing in this country?" → is a way of convincing the Chinese premier; at the same time it shows that Balram is seeking some sort of validation for his past and future choices*

3. Writing a discussion: Discuss Balram's vision of a New Bangalore against the background of your knowledge of globalization.

	Der Schüler/Die Schülerin ...
Umsetzung der Aufgabenstellung	kann einen selbstständig formulierten und zusammenhängenden Text verfassen, in dem die Vor- und Nachteile des neuen Bangalore diskutiert werden. Dabei wird Hintergrundwissen über die Globalisierung einbezogen.
Text- und Problemverständnis	weist ein weitgehend differenziert umfassendes Textverständnis im Sinne der Aufgabenstellung nach.

	Der Schüler/Die Schülerin ...
Darstellung und Gliederung	erfüllt mit seinen/ihren klaren und logischen Ausführungen überwiegend die Erfordernisse des Operators *discuss*: • ausgewogene Darstellung der Vor- und Nachteile • Verweise auf den Romanauszug • Einbeziehung von Hintergrundwissen • Fazit

Gesamteindruck	Die inhaltliche Leistung entspricht in vollem Maße den Anforderungen der Aufgabe.

Mögliche inhaltliche Aspekte:

Pros:

- *the new Bangalore as envisioned by Balram can be a place of opportunity for every Indian no matter where he comes from and what his social background is ("where humans can live like humans"); globalization can free people from the restrictions of tradition*
- *if you are smart and business-savvy, you can be successful in Bangalore ("If the place has a future as the home of an American, I put down payment on it at once.")*
- *modern and international ("glass-and-steel boxes")*
- *a place where children are going to be educated for success ("an English-language school"); with English as the global language*

Cons:

- *Bangalore will probably look like any other big city in the world with the same companies ("General Electric, Dell, Siemens") and the same kind of buildings; globalization makes every place look indistinctive*
- *the future Bangalore seems entirely business- and money-orientated and to be successful you also have to be prepared to "kill"; globalization can be a cut-throat, reckless force*

ISBN 978-3-425-73646-4

Erwartungshorizont für eine gute sprachliche Leistung

Für die Einschätzung der sprachlichen Leistung schriftlicher Arbeiten kann folgende Tabelle eine Orientierung bieten.

Die Bewertung der sprachlichen Leistung erfolgt auf der Grundlage der in der Tabelle genannten Kriterien ganzheitlich über die in der linken Spalte genannten Teilaspekte hinweg; es werden also keine Einzelnoten zu diesen Teilaspekten gebildet. Die Gewichtung der einzelnen Kriterien innerhalb der Kategorien hängt von den Anforderungen der jeweiligen Aufgabenstellung ab.

	Der Schüler/Die Schülerin ...
Kommunikative Textgestaltung Textaufbau Textsortenspezifik Situationsangemessenheit und Adressatenbezug (Register)	• verfasst einen weitgehend zielgerichteten, strukturierten und kohärenten Text. • setzt die geforderten Textsortenmerkmale weitgehend überzeugend um. • schreibt weitgehend situationsangemessen und mit gelungenem Adressatenbezug.
Ausdrucksvermögen, Verwendung sprachlicher Mittel Eigenständigkeit Wortschatz Idiomatik Satzbau Umgang mit Materialien/ Belegtechnik	• verfasst eine eigenständige Darstellung. • verwendet sowohl allgemeinen als auch themenspezifischen Wortschatz weitgehend treffsicher und variabel. • verwendet weitgehend angemessene idiomatische Strukturen. • formuliert mit weitgehend variablem und funktionalem Satzbau unter Verwendung angemessen komplexer Strukturen. • verwendet Zitate weitgehend funktional und bettet diese weitgehend korrekt in den Textfluss ein. • kennzeichnet Zitate/Textverweise weitgehend korrekt.
Sprachrichtigkeit Lexik Grammatik/Syntax Orthografie Verständlichkeit	• drückt sich lexikalisch, grammatisch, syntaktisch und orthografisch weitgehend korrekt aus. • drückt sich verständlich aus: Sprachliche Verstöße beeinträchtigen die Verständlichkeit nicht.

Gesamteindruck	Die sprachliche Leistung entspricht in vollem Maße den Anforderungen der Aufgabe.

ISBN 978-3-425-73646-4

Lösungen und Erwartungshorizont für eine gute inhaltliche Leistung

Listening 1: Politics through the eyes of Shakespeare Webcode: WES-73646-33

1. how men and women lust for power and use it in the worst way
2. looking at the past to (help) understand the present/(looking at the present to understand the past)
3. a) finding an answer as to why societies fall for catastrophic leaders, b) enablers
4. a) politics becoming factionalized, b) lure of (fraudulent) populism
5. a) assassination of the leader, b) resistance leaders/people (often women) who speak truth to power, c) ordinary politicians who insist on the observing of democratic procedures

Listening/Viewing 2: Why study Shakespeare? Webcode: WES-73646-34 (Ausschnitt: 00:05–02:24)

1. even bother
2. consequential
3. vividly alive
4. human culture
5. a real vital force
6. give the working class
7. intimately involved
8. hymn book
9. off by heart
10. superficial commitment
11. naturally unfolded into
12. political prisoners
13. amazing conjunction
14. struggle for freedom
15. exciting time
16. time of renewal
17. being re-imagined
18. globalized world
19. best thing
20. experience of

Listening/Viewing 3: Shakespeare in virtual reality games Webcode: WES-73646-35

1. *three of these aspects:* actors/screen/avatars/(motion picture) cameras
2. older style of acting/exaggerated gestures
3. a) costume, b) stage, c) play
4. teaching tool/to make Shakespeare more accessible in a digital age
5. focus on the character (Falstaff) rather than on classmates or (on) the teacher
6. they want to understand the language (because it's part of the game)
7. you get a better feel for what's going on/you think about the body language
8. North America/Washington
9. in 1932
10. it will be digitally scanned
11. Shakespeare has been used in all other types of media (book, television, radio, film)

Listening 4: High school students perform *Romeo and Juliet* Webcode: WES-73646-36 (Ausschnitt: 03:41–06:21)

1D, 2F, 3G, 4A, 5C

Mediation 1: Shakespeare in Weimar

You are taking part in an international school project called "Global Shakespeare". Your task is to write a blog post for the project's website. Based on an article you have found, you describe how Shakespeare's work found its way to Germany and the relationship between Weimar and Shakespeare.

ISBN 978-3-425-73646-4

	Der Schüler/Die Schülerin ...
Umsetzung der Aufgabenstellung	erfüllt weitgehend die Erfordernisse einer *Mediation*-Aufgabe: • Verzicht auf wortwörtliche Übersetzungen • Entnahme der nötigen Informationen aus dem deutschen Text (Textsorte: Zeitungsartikel) zum Verfassen eines eigenen Textes (Textsorte: Blogeintrag)
Textsortenspezifik	setzt die textsortenspezifischen Merkmale für *blog post* weitgehend um: • Titel • Einleitung, die auf das Thema hinführt • Gliederung in Absätzen • zusammenfassender Schluss, der die Leserschaft ggfs. aufgefordert, den Eintrag zu kommentieren und Ihre Informationen zu teilen • optional: Name
Situationsangemessenheit und Adressatenbezug	schreibt weitgehend situationsangemessen und adressatenbezogen: • am Thema interessierte Gleichaltrige • Register: informell, sachlich
Kulturspezifik	kann relevante kulturspezifische Aspekte (z. B. Deutsche Klassik, Hoftheater) nachvollziehbar erläutern.
Text- und Problemverständnis	kann das Thema des Artikels ggfs. in größere Zusammenhänge (*Shakespeare's global appeal*) einordnen.
Darstellung und Gliederung	beschreibt die Verbindung Weimars zu Shakespeare überwiegend treffend in Form des Blogeintrags.

Gesamteindruck	Die inhaltliche Leistung entspricht in vollem Maße den Anforderungen der Aufgabe.

Mögliche inhaltliche Aspekte:
- *reception of Shakespeare's work originated in Weimar; Shakespeare unknown in Germany until the latter half of the 18th century*
- *Christian Martin Wieland, one of the founders of the classical period in Germany, was the first to translate Shakespeare into German (between 1762 and 1766)*
- *other admirers of Shakespeare, such as the famous poets Goethe and Herder, were also in Weimar at the time*
- *Shakespeare was played at the court theatre in Weimar*
- *in 1864, the Shakespeare Society was founded in Weimar; it still exists today and is the oldest literary association in Germany*
- *40 years later, in 1904, a Shakespeare monument was erected in the Ilm Park in Weimar; since 1998, the statue has been protected by Unesco (as a World Heritage Site)*

Mediation 2: Shakespeare on German stages

Your English pen pal is working on an essay about Shakespeare's global appeal and asks you whether Shakespeare is played in German theatres. You have found an interesting article explaining why producers in Brandenburg still put on Shakespeare's plays. In an email to your pen pal, outline the reasons each producer gives for staging Shakespeare.

	Der Schüler/Die Schülerin ...
Umsetzung der Aufgabenstellung	erfüllt weitgehend die Erfordernisse einer *Mediation*-Aufgabe: • Verzicht auf wortwörtliche Übersetzungen • Entnahme der nötigen Informationen aus dem deutschen Text (Textsorte: Zitate aus Zeitungsartikel) zum Verfassen eines eigenen Textes (Textsorte: E-Mail)

ISBN 978-3-425-73646-4

	Der Schüler/Die Schülerin ...
Textsortenspezifik	setzt die textsortenspezifischen Merkmale für *email* weitgehend um: • Betreff • Anrede • Einleitung, die in das Thema und die Situation ein-/hinführt (Shakespeare-Aufführungen in deutschen Theatern) • inhaltlich aspektorientierte Strukturierung (Reiz Shakespeares für Theatermacher) • zusammenfassender Schluss, der die Situation (Frage des Freundes/der Freundin) aufgreift • persönliche Schlussgrußformel
Situationsangemessenheit und Adressatenbezug	schreibt weitgehend situationsangemessen und adressatenbezogen: • Freund/Freundin • Register: informell, informativ
Text- und Problemverständnis	kann das Thema des Artikels ggfs. in größere Zusammenhänge (*Shakespeare's timeless appeal*) einordnen.
Darstellung und Gliederung	zeichnet die Meinungen der Theatermacher zu Shakespeare weitgehend treffend nach.

Gesamteindruck	Die inhaltliche Leistung entspricht in vollem Maße den Anforderungen der Aufgabe.

Mögliche inhaltliche Aspekte:

Drama director Mario Holetzeck:
- *although Shakespeare has been dead for 400 years, his plays could not be more current*
- *Shakespeare has a unique portrayal of good and evil characteristics of human nature and something (surprisingly) new can always be found in his work*
- *Shakespeare's plays hold a mirror up to the audience, meaning the audience recognize aspects of themselves within them/the plays/the characters*

Theatre manager Tobias Wellemeyer:
- *Shakespeare was the most influential dramatist and has certainly left his imprint on theatre; without him there would supposedly be no Goethe, Schiller or Brecht – all famous German writers*
- *(Huxley's 'Brave New World' would also never have been written)*
- *poetic, brilliant and complex portrayal of the abyss of human nature; Shakespeare shows a variety of human facets: the rise and fall of tyrants, human squalidness, weak heroes, strong women, dark clowns*
- *compares Shakespeare's legacy to the world famous reputations of German composer Bach and Italian artist Michelangelo*

Theatre manager Reinhard Simon:
- *Shakespeare's words have great poetic and rhetorical power*
- *his plays were written for a broad audience*
- *his tragedies include humorous scenes and his comedies contain tragic moments; therefore his plays offer something for everybody without being simplistic*
- *Shakespeare's secret is to be able to touch the innermost emotions of each and every person in the audience*

Dramatic adviser Igor Holland-Moritz:
- *the vast quantity of Shakespeare's works alone means you cannot avoid him*
- *his works have been translated into more than 100 languages and differently in different eras, yet his portrayal of human nature remains timeless*
- *Romeo and Juliet, for example, is not only one of the most beautiful love stories ever written, with its promise of love being stronger than death, but also stands for the passion of youth which we long for today*

ISBN 978-3-425-73646-4

Writing 1: A sonnet

1. Comprehension: Briefly outline what each quatrain and the couplet are about.

	Der Schüler/Die Schülerin ...
Umsetzung der Aufgabenstellung	kann wesentliche Hauptaussagen eines jeden Vierzeilers und des Zweizeilers in einer strukturierten, kohärenten und präzisen Darstellung zusammenfassen.
Text- und Problemverständnis	durchdringt die Textvorlage weitgehend.
Darstellung und Gliederung	verfasst einen strukturierten und kohärenten Text, der überwiegend den Erfordernissen des Operators *outline* entspricht: • knappe Darstellung • *Zeitform: present tense* • eigene Worte, keine Zitate, keine Verweise • keine Nacherzählung • keine Wertung

Gesamteindruck	Die inhaltliche Leistung entspricht in vollem Maße den Anforderungen der Aufgabe.

Mögliche inhaltliche Aspekte:

- *first quatrain: the speaker addresses his lover and says that he loves her despite her lack of physical beauty*
- *second quatrain: the speaker continues to enumerate senses other than vision, namely hearing, feeling and smelling, and states that none of them are pleased with his lover's attributes*
- *third quatrain: although it does not make any sense, he is emotionally devoted to her, and feels that he is a slave to her proud heart.*
- *couplet: the only thing the speaker has gained from this relationship is pain and suffering, because his lover is too proud to accept his love; nevertheless, he cannot stop loving her*

2. Analysis: Analyse the sonnet with regard to the portrayal of the lover and the contradictory presentation of the relationship between speaker and lover. In doing so, focus on how the structure, imagery and stylistic devices complement the content.

	Der Schüler/Die Schülerin ...
Umsetzung der Aufgabenstellung	kann die Darstellung der Geliebten und die Widersprüchlichkeit der Beziehung, die der Sprecher mit ihr hat, durch zieltreffende Struktur- und Stilanalyse darstellen und so explizit und implizit dargestellte Aussagen aufgabenbezogen analysieren und deuten.
Text- und Problemverständnis	weist ein analytisches Textverständnis durch einen weitgehend hohen Grad der Durchdringung der Textvorlage und dessen strukturellen sowie rhetorisch expliziten und impliziten Aussagen nach.
Darstellung und Gliederung	verfasst einen strukturierten und kohärenten Text, der überwiegend den Erfordernissen des Operators *analyse* entspricht: • Gliederung: Einleitung, Hauptteil, Schluss • Trennung zwischen Form und Funktion der jeweiligen analytischen Aspekte • Aspekte mit relevanten Details ausführen und mit Beispielen konsequent stützen/untermauern • Zitate adäquat integrieren

Gesamteindruck	Die inhaltliche Leistung entspricht in vollem Maße den Anforderungen der Aufgabe.

ISBN 978-3-425-73646-4

Mögliche inhaltliche Aspekte:

- *Shakespearean sonnet structure: 14 lines, three quatrains (ll. 1–4, 5–8, 9–12) and a couplet (ll.13-14); iambic pentameter and ababcdcdefefgg as a rhyme scheme → the structural complexity of this literary work indicates the lover's value to the speaker*
- *the first quatrain presents a* ***paradox****; while the lover has visibly "thousands of errors" (l. 2), the speaker loves her helplessly and uncritically (l. 4).; this* ***contrast*** *is underlined by strong verbs like "despise" (l. 3) and "dote" (l. 4)*
- *the second quatrain further reveals the speaker's spite towards his lover using a* ***parallel structure*** *and* ***enumerating*** *more of his (perceptual) senses (hearing/feeling/smelling, ll. 5–7) that are repelled by her; the first three lines of the second quatrain begin with "Nor…" which is an* ***anaphora*** *that emphasizes that it is not just with his vision, but rather with all of his senses that he has failed to find anything beautiful in his lover's attributes*
- *the third quatrain starts with a* ***turn*** *as introduced by "But" (l. 9) stating that neither the speaker's senses nor his common sense can dissuade him from loving his lover; the paradox from the first quatrain can be seen in the* ***antithesis*** *"foolish heart" (l. 10) versus "proud heart" (l.12), which highlights that the lover has all the power in this relationship, thus intensifying the audience's confusion as to why the speaker remains in this relationship; the* ***exaggerated*** *outcome of being the lover's "slave and vassal wretch" (l. 12) stresses his inexorable devotion, but sounds polemic; this metaphor of the speaker's heart as a slave to the heart of his lover indicates that he is powerless to his feelings despite their contradictory nature, which resolves any earlier confusion by showing that he is not willingly in this relationship*
- *in the couplet the speaker indirectly compares his love to an illness (l. 13), which is an example of using* ***figurative language*** *to make his description more powerful; the claim that this "illness" is nevertheless beneficial ("gain", l. 13, "awards", l. 14) completes the contradictory content of the poem; this positive language is clearly ironic, as pain and suffering are not "gains", and this irony emphasizes the speaker's sense of helplessness and despair, as he is a slave to his feelings*

3. Comment: While browsing the Internet you have come across a blog titled "Shakespeare is dead!" in which students complain about the the difficulties they experienced when dealing with Shakespeare at school. One statement in particular has sparked your interest: "Shakespearean sonnets are not contemporary and should not be taught in schools anymore." Comment on this statement in the comment section of the blog. Refer to materials dealt with in class.

	Der Schüler/Die Schülerin …
Umsetzung der Aufgabenstellung	kann einen selbstständig formulierten, strukturierten und zusammenhängenden Kommentar verfassen, indem sich argumentativ mit unterschiedlichen Positionen bezüglich der Behandlung von Shakespeares Sonetten im Englischunterricht auseinandergesetzt wird.
Textsortenspezifik	setzt die textsortenspezifischen Merkmale für *comment* weitgehend um: • optional: sehr knappe Einleitung mit einem prägnanten Statement • Hauptteil: Zustimmung oder Widerspruch; Gründe/Argumente/Belege • Schluss
Situationsangemessenheit und Adressatenbezug	schreibt situationsangemessen und adressatenbezogen: • interessierte Leserschaft von hauptsächlich Gleichaltrigen • Register: sachlich, nicht zu formell, da Kommentar auf einem Blog
Text- und Problemverständnis	• durchdringt die Textvorlage weitgehend. • kann das Thema des Blogs in größere Zusammenhänge *(why study Shakespeare?)* einordnen und dabei auf im Unterricht besprochenes Material zurückgreifen
Darstellung und Gliederung	verfasst einen klaren und logischen Text, der überwiegend den Erfordernissen des Operators *comment* entspricht: Begründete Darlegung des eigenen Standpunktes

Gesamteindruck	Die inhaltliche Leistung entspricht in vollem Maße den Anforderungen der Aufgabe.

ISBN 978-3-425-73646-4

Mögliche inhaltliche Aspekte:

Agree:
- *the language is old-fashioned and very difficult to understand*
- *sonnets are always about love, beauty, transience, old age, or death, so dealing with them becomes tedious*
- *Shakespeare's plays can be modernized in stage productions but the sonnets are static and cannot be made more relatable*
- *studying Shakespeare's complex sonnets is not going to help improve one's own writing (because the English language has changed so much)*

Disagree:
- *Shakespeare's sonnets are short and therefore faster to read than his plays; this means that you don't need very much time to learn about one of the world's most important writers*
- *the sonnets reflect Shakespeare's universal appeal as their main topics, such as love and beauty, are timeless*
- *Shakespeare had a huge impact on the English language, which is why studying his sonnets can be useful*
- *the sonnets are diverse in terms of content and stylistic devices; dealing with them can increase analytical knowledge or even problem-solving skills*
- *the sonnets are not only a historical but also a cultural product that provide insights into the time of Shakespeare*

Writing 2: Variation on a sonnet

The romantic comedy *10 Things I Hate About You* (1999) is based on William Shakespeare's comedy *The Taming of the Shrew* (1593). Both the names of the protagonists, Katharina (Kat) und Bianca, and major storylines from Shakespeare's comedy were reused and adapted for a modern American high school setting. The film also alludes to various other Shakespearean elements. In the film, Kat confesses her true feelings for Patrick by reciting a homework assignment, which was to rewrite Shakespeare's *Sonnet 141*.

1. Comprehension: Summarize Kat's version of the sonnet.

	Der Schüler/Die Schülerin ...
Umsetzung der Aufgabenstellung	kann aus dem Sonett wesentliche Hauptaussagen in einer kohärenten, präzisen Darstellung unter Beachtung der Textsortenmerkmale für *summary* zusammenfassen.
Textsortenspezifik	setzt die textsortenspezifischen Merkmale für *summary* weitgehend um: • Einleitungssatz (Genre, Titel, Autor/in, Quelle, Jahr) • *present tense* • eigene Worte, keine Zitate, keine Verweise • keine Nacherzählung • keine Wertung • pointierte, straffe, knappe Darstellung
Text- und Problemverständnis	durchdringt die Textvorlage weitgehend.
Darstellung und Gliederung	verfasst einen strukturierten und kohärenten Text, der überwiegend den Erfordernissen des Operators *summarize* entspricht.
Gesamteindruck	Die inhaltliche Leistung entspricht in vollem Maße den Anforderungen der Aufgabe.

Mögliche inhaltliche Aspekte:

- *as the title of Katharina's sonnet, "10 Things I Hate About You", indicates, it is (ostensibly) about reasons why the speaker hates the addressee*
- *the speaker enumerates certain negative aspects about Patrick's outward appearance and actions, and describes her reactions to these, for example, feeling sick*
- *the speaker concludes that what she despises the most is not being able to hate the addressee at all, thus confessing that she actually loves rather than hates him*

ISBN 978-3-425-73646-4

2. Analysis: Critically analyse Kat's version of the sonnet by first examining her sonnet and then contrasting it with the regular Shakespearean sonnet form.

	Der Schüler/Die Schülerin ...
Umsetzung der Aufgabenstellung	kann das Sonnet treffend hinsichtlich Struktur und Stil analysieren und explizit und implizit dargestellte Aussagen aufgabenbezogen deuten sowie dieses mit Shakespeares Sonettform kontrastiv vergleichen.
Text- und Problemverständnis	durchdringt die Textvorlage weitgehend.
Darstellung und Gliederung	verfasst einen strukturierten und kohärenten Text, der überwiegend den Erfordernissen des Operators *analyse* entspricht: • Gliederung: Einleitung – Hauptteil – Schluss • Trennung zwischen Form und Funktion der jeweiligen analytischen Aspekte • Aspekte mit relevanten Details ausführen und mit Beispielen konsequent stützen/untermauern • Zitate adäquat integrieren • den Unterschied zu der Sonettform Shakespeares kontrastiv herausarbeiten
Gesamteindruck	Die inhaltliche Leistung entspricht in vollem Maße den Anforderungen der Aufgabe.

Mögliche inhaltliche Aspekte:

Analysis:

- *structure: 14 lines, rhyme scheme (abcb/defe/ghih/jj), masculine verse endings but imperfect rhymes; the poem is mostly iambic, but the metre is not pentameter; three quatrains and one couplet: in the first quatrain, short stanzas enumerate things the speaker hates about the addressee; the second quatrain has longer stanzas and explains how the speaker's hatred for the addressee affects her; the third quatrain then starts to indirectly acknowledge positive aspects, and reveals that the speaker's anger comes from the way the addressee has treated her; the message is finally resolved in the couplet, where the speaker admits they do not hate the addressee at all*
- *"I hate" is repeated ten times in a **parallel, anaphoric** manner, which emphasizes the speaker's deep disappointment/hate*
- *the **alliteration** "big dumb combat boots" (l. 5) not only evokes rhythm, but stresses that this item of clothing completely contrasts with the speaker's own fashion taste, highlighting that the pair are complete opposites*
- *the intensity of the feeling of hate progressively increases from the first ("I hate you…" l. 1) through the second ("I hate you so much…"l. 7) to the third quatrain ("Even worse when …" l. 12), building up to a **climax** of emotion in the line "you make me cry" (l. 12); as the objects of hate have gone from trivial, material things like "hair" (l. 2), a "car" (l. 3) and "boots" (l. 5) to deep emotion ("cry" l. 12), this suggests that beneath the anger, the speaker has actually been really hurt by the addressee, and so this treatment is the true focus of her hate; this climactic moment also evokes tension and curiosity about the sonnet's outcome.*
- *the turn is introduced within the couplet but only in the sonnet's last line, which starts with "But" (l. 14); the last stanza explicitly underlines the true meaning of the sonnet using the **paradox/juxtaposition** "I hate the way I don't hate you" which is both contradictory to the previous quatrains and (also) self-contradictory; yet this contradictory statement illuminates the truth that the speaker actually loves the addressee, which makes him and the audience re-examine the sonnet and its real message; additionally, the repetition of "not even" within an enumeration of the decreasing degree of hate ("close" – "a little" – "at all") exemplifies the real affection the speaker has for the addressee, despite certain flaws and the addressee's treatment of her*

Contrast:

- ***structure:** the same (three quatrains and a couplet); but different **rhyme schemes** and different **metres***
- ***turn**: the turn usually comes at the beginning of the couplet (l. 13); in Kat's version the turn comes in the very last line (l. 14)*
- ***language**: modern, easy to understand English vs. old-fashioned, Elizabethan English*
- ***style**: stylistically rather simple vs. stylistically rather complex*
- *the same **topic** but for opposite sexes – both speakers state that they hate the addressee, but actually love him/her*

ISBN 978-3-425-73646-4

3. Comment: This is how Kat's teacher introduces the homework assignment:
"Let's open our books to page 73, *Sonnet 141* and listen up: [he freely recites the first quatrain of the Shakespearean sonnet in a modern rap version sticking to the original lines]

In faith, I do not love thee with mine eyes,
For they in thee a thousand errors note;
But 'tis my heart that loves what they despise,
Who in despite of view is pleased to dote;

Now, I know Shakespeare's a dead white guy but, he knows his shit, so we can overlook that. I want you all to write your own version of this sonnet."

You have come across a blog called "How to teach Shakespeare" and decide to contribute to the discussion with a comment piece which evaluates the approach Kat's teacher uses in the film *10 Things I Hate About You*. You may also refer to materials dealt with in class and your own experiences as a student.

	Der Schüler/Die Schülerin ...
Umsetzung der Aufgabenstellung	kann einen selbstständig formulierten, strukturierten und zusammenhängenden Kommentar zu einem Blog verfassen, in dem sich ausgewogen mit der Unterrichtsart von Kats Lehrer auseinandergesetzt wird.
Textsortenspezifik	setzt die textsortenspezifischen Merkmale für *comment on a blog* weitgehend um: • Einleitung, die den situativen Kontext aufgreift • Hauptteil mit pro/contra-Positionen bezüglich der Art und Weise wie Kats Lehrer versucht, seinen Schülern Shakespeares Sonette nahe zu bringen • zusammenfassender, resümierender Schluss
Situationsangemessenheit und Adressatenbezug	schreibt situationsangemessen und adressatenbezogen: • interessierte Leserschaft • Register: sachlich, nicht zu formell, da Kommentar auf einem Blog
Text- und Problemverständnis	• durchdringt die Textvorlage weitgehend. • kann das Thema des Blogs in größere Zusammenhänge (*why study Shakespeare?*) einordnen und dabei auf im Unterricht besprochenes Material und eigene Erfahrungen zurückgreifen
Darstellung und Gliederung	verfasst einen klaren und logischen Text, der überwiegend den Erfordernissen des Operators *evaluate* entspricht: • differenzierte Abwägung • fundiertes Fazit

Gesamteindruck	Die inhaltliche Leistung entspricht in vollem Maße den Anforderungen der Aufgabe.

Mögliche inhaltliche Aspekte:

Pros:
- *rapping Shakespeare's sonnet might capture the class' attention, as they are likely to be more familiar with rap music than with Elizabethan English*
- *offering a challenging and creative homework assignment might motivate the students*
- *the use of a rap style might make it more accessible to the students, as if they realize that rap uses similar techniques and rhythms to those used by Shakespeare, they are more likely to want to analyse these techniques*

Cons:
- *as the teacher requires the students to write their own versions of* Sonnet 141*, it should have been entirely recited and discussed in terms of form and content first – students may struggle to cope with this assignment if they did not fully understand the sonnet's content and its complex structure*
- *the statement "Shakespeare's a dead white guy, but he knows his shit" is rather disrespectful – Shakespeare deserves more serious academic study*
- *his decision to rap the poem to the students may be seen as patrionizing; it suggests that the students cannot understand any language or texts outside of popular culture*

ISBN 978-3-425-73646-4

Erwartungshorizont für eine gute sprachliche Leistung

Für die Einschätzung der sprachlichen Leistung schriftlicher Arbeiten kann folgende Tabelle eine Orientierung bieten.

Die Bewertung der sprachlichen Leistung erfolgt auf der Grundlage der in der Tabelle genannten Kriterien ganzheitlich über die in der linken Spalte genannten Teilaspekte hinweg; es werden also keine Einzelnoten zu diesen Teilaspekten gebildet. Die Gewichtung der einzelnen Kriterien innerhalb der Kategorien hängt von den Anforderungen der jeweiligen Aufgabenstellung ab.

	Der Schüler/Die Schülerin …
Kommunikative Textgestaltung Textaufbau Textsortenspezifik Situationsangemessenheit und Adressatenbezug (Register)	• verfasst einen weitgehend zielgerichteten, strukturierten und kohärenten Text. • setzt die geforderten Textsortenmerkmale weitgehend überzeugend um. • schreibt weitgehend situationsangemessen und mit gelungenem Adressatenbezug.
Ausdrucksvermögen, Verwendung sprachlicher Mittel Eigenständigkeit Wortschatz Idiomatik Satzbau Umgang mit Materialien/ Belegtechnik	• verfasst eine eigenständige Darstellung. • verwendet sowohl allgemeinen als auch themenspezifischen Wortschatz weitgehend treffsicher und variabel. • verwendet weitgehend angemessene idiomatische Strukturen. • formuliert mit weitgehend variablem und funktionalem Satzbau unter Verwendung angemessen komplexer Strukturen. • verwendet Zitate weitgehend funktional und bettet diese weitgehend korrekt in den Textfluss ein. • kennzeichnet Zitate/Textverweise weitgehend korrekt.
Sprachrichtigkeit Lexik Grammatik/Syntax Orthografie Verständlichkeit	• drückt sich lexikalisch, grammatisch, syntaktisch und orthografisch weitgehend korrekt aus. • drückt sich verständlich aus: Sprachliche Verstöße beeinträchtigen die Verständlichkeit nicht.

Gesamteindruck	Die sprachliche Leistung entspricht in vollem Maße den Anforderungen der Aufgabe.

ISBN 978-3-425-73646-4

Bildquellen

|Cagle Cartoons, Santa Barbara, CA: Granlund, Dave 61. |Cartoonist Group, Santa Fe, NM: Danziger, Jeff 37. |CartoonStock.com, Bath: 18, 55, 55. |iStockphoto.com, Calgary: ranckreporter Titel; vikialis 8. |Jones, Clay, Fredericksburg, Virginia: 61. |Shutterstock.com, New York: 49; marako85 75; Popov, Andrey 44; Sarkisian, Nadezhda 22.

Textquellen

S. 6 "Thousands Of Haitians Enter Canada Amid Fears Of Deportation From U.S.", 31 August 2017 © North Country Public Radio.
S. 8 "Kanada: Die 5 Schattenseiten über das Auswandern" by Irene Giesbrecht, *The Black Hoodie Blog*, 22 November 2015, www.theblackhoodieblog.com.
S. 9 "Canada's multiculturalism is our identity" by Erna Paris, in *The Globe and Mail*, 27 April 2018.
S. 12 Naomi O'Leary und Tim Mc Inerney, The Irish Passport, season 1, episode 3: The Irish Language https://theirishpassport.com/.
S. 13 SPIEGEL ONLINE, Valerie Höhne, 12.03.2018 http://www.spiegel.de/politik/deutschland/paragraf-218-wir-muessen-wieder-ueber-abtreibung-reden-a-1243580.html
S. 14 "'Young people of Ireland' have mixed views on church" by Jackie Fox, in *RTE News*, 23 August 2018.
S. 16 This real-life cyborg has an antenna implanted into his skull, Business Insider Tech © Wright's Media.
S. 17 "Künstliche Kunst" by Michael Moorstedt, in *Süddeutsche Zeitung online*, 10 March 2019.
S. 18 "Can the UK's first 'automated shop' vending machine keep customers satisfied?" by Chris Green, *The Independent*, 21 March 2014.
S. 21 "Genmanipulierte Babys in China: Empörung über 'Designerbabys'" by Stephan Cezanne, 29 November 2018. Copyright epd kfr/lnb/cez mih.
S. 22 *The forever kitten* by Peter F. Hamilton, *Nature* 436, 602 (2005).
S. 26 "Ein Fall für die Lehrbücher" by Holger Stark, in *Zeit Online*, 21 December 2018.
S. 27 *The Organized Mind* by Daniel Levitin, Penguin Books 2015.
S. 28 "Why people are still trying to 'lose' their accents", Patrick Cox / PRI®.
S. 30 "Was will ich im Ausland" by Marie Gamillscheg, in *Zeit Campus*, 5 April 2016.
S. 31 "Behemoth, bully, thief: how the English language is taking over the planet" by Jacob Mikanowski, in *The Guardian*, 27 July 2018. Copyright Guardian News & Media Ltd 2019.
S. 35 "The Future of Work: What Do We Do?" by Stijn Broecke , 4 September 2018, with permission of the School of Policy Studies, Queen's University, Kingston, Ontario, Canada.
S. 36 "Verführerische Isolation" by Mark Schieritz, in *Zeit Online*, 26 December 2018.
S. 37 "How your flip-flops reveal the dark side of globalization" by Caroline Knowles, 9 July 2018, www.theconversation.com.
S. 38 "Globalisation: the rise and fall of an idea that swept the world – podcast" by Nikil Saval. Copyright Guardian News & Media Ltd 2019.
S. 40 "Diese sechs Jobs sind in zehn Jahren gefragt" by Lars-Thorben Niggehoff, in *Welt online*, 22 February 2019.
S. 41 *Exit West* by Mohsin Hamid, Penguin Books 2018.
S. 44 "Auf der Suche nach dem Wirgefühl" by Ulrike Scheffer, in *Der Tagesspiegel online*, 17 September 2017.
S. 45 *We're British and We Know It* by Josie Whitehead, www.josiespoems.webeden.co.uk.
S. 45 *The How To Be British Collection* by Martyn Ford and Peter Legon, Lee Gone Publications 2003.
S. 48 "Engländer in Hamburg: Keinen Bock auf Brexit" by Bert Beyers, in *NDR*, 23 March 2019.
S. 49 "Writing Divided: can you tell a Scottish novelist from an English one?" in *The Scotsman*, 7 July 2011. This is copyright of The Scotsman Publications and is being used with their kind permission for this purpose.
S. 53 "Dirk Roßmann besucht seine alte Schule" by Saskia Döhner, in *Hannoversche Allgemeine*, 2 May 2019.
S. 54 "New Research Debunks the Upward Mobility Myth" by Tom Jacobs, in *Pacific Standard*, 6 September 2018. Reprinted by permission of Pacific Standard © 2018.
S. 58 "Anstand reicht nicht", interview by Vanessa Vu, in *Zeit Online*, 24 June 2017.
S. 60 "Oprah Winfrey: from poverty to America's first black billionaire ... to #Oprah2020?" by Emine Saner, in *The Guardian*, 12 January 2018. Copyright Guardian News & Media Ltd 2019.
S. 64 "Nigeria" by Maximilian Brommer, *Mr. Frizzante*, 12 January 2019, www.mrfrizzante.de.
S. 65 *The Other Hand* by Chris Cleave, Sceptre 2008.
S. 69 "Mumbai" by Sonja Ernst, *Bundeszentrale für politische Bildung*, 19 October 2006, www.bpb.de.
S. 70 *The White Tiger* by Aravind Adiga, Atlantic Books 2008.
S. 75 "Wie Shakespeares Denkmal in den Weimarer Ilmpark kam" by Wolfgang Hirsch, in *Thüringer Allgemeine*, 24 April 2016.
S. 76 "Darum spielen wir Shakespeare" by Karim Saab, in *Märkische Allgemeine*, 23 April 2016.
S. 78 "10 Things I Hate About You" from the film *10 Things I Hate About You* by Gil Junger, Karen McCullah Lutz, Kirsten Smith, 1999.

ISBN 978-3-425-73646-4